THE ORIGINS OF THE SECOND WORLD WAR IN ASIA AND THE PACIFIC

ORIGINS OF MODERN WARS
General editor: *Harry Hearder*

THE ORIGINS OF THE SECOND WORLD WAR IN ASIA AND THE PACIFIC

Akira Iriye

LONDON AND NEW YORK

First published 1987 by Pearson Education Limited

Published 2013 by Routledge
2 Park Square, Milton Park, Abingdon, Oxon OX14 4RN
711 Third Avenue, New York, NY 10017, USA

*Routledge is an imprint of the Taylor & Francis Group,
an informa business*

ISBN 13: 978-0-582-49349-0 (pbk)

British Library Cataloguing In Publication Data
Iriye, Akira.
   The origins of the Second World War in
   Asia and the Pacific.
   — (Origins of modern wars)
   1. World War, 1939–1945 — Causes
   2. World War, 1939–1945 — Japan
I. Title   II. Series
940.53'11   D742.J3

Library Of Congress Cataloging-In-Publication Data
Iriye, Akira.
   The origins of the Second World War in Asia and
   the Pacific.

   (Origins of modern wars)
   Bibliography: p.
   Includes index.
      1. World War, 1939–1945 — Causes. 2. Japan — Foreign
relations — 1912–1945. 3. World War, 1939–1945 —
Diplomatic history. 4. World War, 1939–1945 — Pacific
Area. 5. World War, 1939–1945 — Asia. I. Title.
II. Series.
D742.J3175 1987   940.53'112   86-2763

CONTENTS

LIST OF MAPS

EDITOR'S FOREWORD

Professor Akira Iriye's contribution to the *Origins of Modern Wars* series deals with the Second World War in Asia and the Pacific, and so complements Mr Philip Bell's volume on the Second World War in Europe. Professor Iriye's study casts a brilliant shaft of light on the Japanese and American policies which led to the fatal denouement at Pearl Harbor. If the motives of all Japanese ministers were basically the same – to secure economic independence and a greater degree of authority for Japan in Asia and the Pacific, their theories on how those aims could be achieved varied profoundly. A special value of this book is the author's familiarity with the domestic political struggles in Tokyo, and his profound understanding of the complexities in a situation which at first sight appears a simple one. He shows how policies with basic flaws could seem to have an unanswerable logic of their own, and how nuances of difference in strategic hypotheses could come to have a catastrophic significance.

From the early 1930s onwards there were some Japanese ministers whose recommendations, if accepted, would have led away from war, and others whose recommendations would lead, often unwittingly, towards war. Once again, as so often in this series, it is made apparent that the ideas of individual ministers, officials or diplomats influence events, sometimes in a fundamental sense. They are by no means always at the mercy of forces beyond their control. Akira Iriye demonstrates that Japanese ministers would have preferred to avoid war with the USA and Britain, but were prepared – in degrees which varied from one minister to another – to face war if it became, by their judgement, unavoidable. The emperor remained throughout more doubtful about the wisdom of going to war with the USA than were his ministers. The army leaders were more eager for war than the civilians. It would be tempting to argue that such is always the case, but Dr Peter Lowe has shown that American military leaders before the Korean War (apart from General MacArthur, about whom most generalizations would be misleading) were more cautious than were Truman and the civilians in Washington. While it is reasonable to assume that generals are more belligerent than civilian ministers simply because war is the *raison d'être* of generals, it is also true that generals are often more aware than their civilian colleagues of the unpreparedness of their armies.

The miscalculations, or failures of imagination, by political leaders as causes of wars are becoming familiar features of this series. They were present in James Joll's *Origins of the First World War*, Ian Nish's *Origins of the Russo-Japanese War* of 1904 and T. C. W. Blanning's *Origins of the French Revolutionary Wars*. In the present work by Akira Iriye misconceptions and miscalculations play a subtle role. When Japan went to war with China in 1937 the Japanese had probably assessed the relative military strengths of the two nations correctly. But they failed to appreciate the complexity and fluid nature of the diplomatic situation in the world as a whole. That complexity is illustrated by the fact that Nazi Germany had military advisers in China, and Soviet Russia was sending arms to Chiang Kai-shek's government in spite of the presence in China of Communists hostile to Chiang's regime. Professor Iriye will probably surprise many readers by his account of how Hitler's government was called upon to mediate between China and Japan, and might possibly have succeeded in doing so if Chiang had been prepared to compromise, though his refusal to do so was understandable enough. Not until 1938 did Hitler finally decide to side with Japan against China.

If Japanese ministers were reluctant to face diplomatic complexities in 1937 they were more prepared to do so after the war had started in Europe, although the complexities had become even more confusing. The Japanese assumption that Russia would always ultimately be the enemy had been shaken by Hitler's pact with Stalin in 1939. It then became possible that Russia could, at least temporarily, become an ally of Japan against the Anglo-Saxon powers. But when Hitler in 1941 invaded Russia without giving his Japanese ally any forewarning of his intentions, even the most imaginative diplomat in Tokyo could have been excused for feeling that his task was becoming an impossible one. Yet successive Japanese ministers analysed the position with some thoroughness. To ask whether the Japanese government then decided on war with the USA in the mistaken belief that they were bound to win is grossly to over-simplify the question. Sometimes countries have gone to war in the assumption that they will win easily, and have proceeded to do so. Dr Ritchie Ovendale's account of Israel going to war in 1956 is perhaps as good an example as any of such a development. More often, confidence in a quick victory has proved to be a delusion. The Japanese in 1941 do not fit into either category. Their military and naval leaders believed in a quick initial victory, and this they secured. They had also convinced the government that if they did not go to war at that moment their position would deteriorate and they would fall slowly but irretrievably under the economic control of America. A gamble was therefore worth taking. In Professor Iriye's words: 'As Nagano explained to the emperor, Japan had the choice of doing nothing, which would lead to its collapse within a few years, or going to war while there was at least a 70 or 80 per cent chance of initial victory.' 'Initial' was still the operative word, and it was therein that the flaw in the argument lay.

Britain did not adopt a policy of appeasement towards Japan from 1937 to 1941 in the same way that she did towards Germany from 1936 to 1938. Instead she followed the USA in an attempt to deter Japan from aggression. Professor Iriye shows that the concept of 'deterrence' in a fully fledged form was put across by Roosevelt towards Japan during the 'phoney' war in Europe in the winter of 1939–40. 'Deterrence' is not, of course, a form of defence, although in the 1980s its day-to-day administration is sometimes left in the hands of so-called ministers of 'defence'. Deterrence is an alternative to defence. Anthony Eden backed up Roosevelt's policy of deterrence of Japan in 1940 and 1941, saying that a 'display of firmness is more likely to deter Japan from war than to provoke her to it'. The policy of deterrence failed miserably. It was not only the Japanese who miscalculated in 1941.

HARRY HEARDER

PREFACE

In this book I have tried to examine the origins of the 1941–1945 war in Asia and the Pacific in what may be termed a systemic perspective; the focus is on changing international frameworks that provided the setting for the foreign policies of the principal actors. That, obviously, is only one of many perspectives, and other historians have presented them with skill. I have thought it useful to adopt the systemic approach since the Asian-Pacific war was a multinational conflict, a chapter in modern international history. What follows, then, is an international history of the prewar period.

Professor Hearder, editor of the series of which this book is a volume, first approached me in 1978 with the suggestion that I attempt such a book. Since then, he has been patient and thoughtful as he has kept in touch with me at every stage of my writing. I am grateful for his support, and for the help of the editors at Longman for their efficient assistance. My indebtedness to co-workers in international history is too heavy and extensive to enumerate, but I would like to express my special thanks to nine historians with whom I have met regularly to exchange ideas, and who have helped me enormously in clarifying my ideas: Sherman Cochran, Warren Cohen, Waldo Heinrichs, Gary Hess, Chihiro Hosoya, Luo Rong-qu, Robert Messer, Katsumi Usui, and Wang Xi. To Marnie Veghte who edited and typed the manuscript, Masumi Iriye who proofread it, and my wife who did everything else to help me complete it, I remain grateful.

AKIRA IRIYE
Chicago, April 1986

Chapter 1

INTRODUCTION

On 18 September 1931, a small number of Japanese and Chinese soldiers clashed outside of Fengtien (Mukden) in southern Manchuria – an event which soon developed into what was to be a long, drawn-out, intermittent war between China and Japan. Over ten years later, on 7 December 1941, Japanese air, naval, and land forces attacked American, British, and Dutch possessions throughout Asia and the Pacific. It marked the beginning of Japan's war against the combined forces of China, America, Britain, the Netherlands and, ultimately, France and the Soviet Union.

How did a war between two Asian countries develop into one in which a single nation was pitted against a multinational coalition? Clearly, from Japan's perspective the development signalled a failure to prevent the formation of such a coalition; on the other hand, for China it was a culmination of its efforts to create an international force to isolate and punish Japan. Why did the Western powers, which stood by while Japanese forces overran Manchuria in 1931, end up by coming to China's assistance ten years later even at the risk of war with Japan?

These are among the central questions as one considers the origins of the Second World War in the Asian-Pacific region. The Second World War actually consisted of two wars, one in Europe and the Atlantic, and the other in Asia and the Pacific. The two theatres were, for the most part, distinct; battles fought and bombings carried out in one were little linked to those in the other. However, while it is quite possible to discuss the origins of the European war without paying much attention to Asian factors, the obverse is not the case. European powers were deeply involved in the Asian-Pacific region and played an important role in transforming the Chinese–Japanese conflict into a multinational one. Moreover, the United States, which too was of little relevance to the immediate causes of the European war, steadily developed into a major Asian-Pacific power so that its position would have a direct bearing on the course of the Chinese–Japanese War. The Asian-Pacific region, then, was an arena of more extensive global rivalry than Europe, and this fact should always be kept in mind as one discusses the origins of the Pacific war. Still, in 1931 it might have seemed that the region was isolated from the rest of the world, and that Japan could engage in its acts of aggression without fearing a collective reprisal. Why it was able to do so at the beginning of the decade, whereas ten years later it would be confronted by a multinational coalition, provides the framework for this book.

JAPAN'S CHALLENGE TO THE WASHINGTON CONFERENCE SYSTEM

Japan had not always been an international loner. On the contrary, the country's leadership and national opinion had emphasized the cardinal importance of establishing Japan as a respected member of the community of advanced powers. And in the 1920s it had enjoyed such a status. The treaties it signed during the Washington Conference (1921–22) symbolized it. In one – the naval disarmament treaty – Japan was recognized as one of the three foremost powers; together with the United States and Britain, the nation would seek to maintain an arms equilibrium in the world and contribute to stabilizing the Asian-Pacific region. Another treaty, signed by these three plus France, provided for a mechanism whereby they would consult with one another whenever the stability was threatened. Most important, the nine-power treaty (signed by Japan, the United States, Britain, France, Italy, Belgium, the Netherlands, Portugal, and China) established the principle of international co-operation in China. Eight signatories were to co-operate with respect to the ninth, China, to uphold the latter's independence and integrity, maintain the principle of equal opportunity, and to provide an environment for the development of a stable government. Japan was a full-fledged member of the new treaty regime, which historians have called the Washington Conference system.[1] Since much of the story of the 1930s revolves around Japan's challenge to these treaties, it is well at the outset to examine what was involved in the regime.

The term 'the Washington Conference system', or 'the Washington system' for short, was not in current use in the 1920s, nor was it subsequently recognized as a well-defined legal concept. None the less, immediately after the conference there was much talk of 'the spirit of the Washington Conference', and a country's behaviour in Asia tended to be judged in terms of whether it furthered or undermined that spirit. As such it connoted more a state of mind than an explicit mechanism; it expressed the powers' willingness to co-operate with one another in maintaining stability in the region and assisting China's gradual transformation as a modern state. It was viewed as an alternative to their unilateral policies or exclusive alliances and *ententes* aimed at particularistic objectives. Instead, the Washington system indicated a concept of multinational consultation and co-operation in the interest of regional stability. By the same token, this spirit was essentially gradualist and reformist, not radical or revolutionary. It was opposed to a rapid and wholesale transformation of Asian international relations, such as was being advocated by the Communist International and by an increasing number of Chinese nationalists. Rather, the Washington powers would stress an evolutionary process of change so as to ensure peace, order, and stability.

In that sense, there *was* a system of international affairs defined by the Washington treaties, for a system implies some status quo, a mechanism for maintaining stability against radical change. The status quo was envisaged by the Washington powers not as a freeze but as a regime of co-operation among them in the interest of gradualism. As such, it was part of the postwar framework of international affairs that had been formulated in the Covenant of the League of Nations and reaffirmed through such other arrangements as the Locarno treaty of 1925 and the pact of Paris of 1928. The former stabilized relations among Britain, France, and Germany, while the latter, signed by most countries, enunciated the principle that they should not resort to force for settling international disputes. The Washington treaties were thus part of an evolving structure that embraced the entire world.

Moreover, there was an economic system that underlay the structure. All the Washington signatories were linked to one another through their acceptance of the gold standard. More precisely called 'the gold exchange standard', the mechanism called upon nations to accept gold as the medium of international economic transactions, to link their currencies to gold, and to maintain the principle of currency convertibility. Through such devices, it was believed that commercial activities across national boundaries would be carried out smoothly for the benefit of all. The gold-currency nations accounted for the bulk of the world's trade and investment, so that the Washington system was synonymous with and sustained by the gold regime. Since the majority of these countries were advanced capitalist economies, it is possible to characterize the Washington Conference system as capitalist inter-nationalism, or even as a new form of imperialism.

Certainly, the Washington Conference did not eliminate empires. Most of the treaty signatories continued to maintain colonies, and some of them had even added new ones after the First World War. At the same time, however, they pledged themselves not to undertake further expansion at the expense of China. Instead, they would co-operate to restore to it a measure of independence so that in time it would emerge as a stabilizing factor in its own right. For this reason, China was a key to the successful functioning of the new system. Unlike the old imperialism, it would call upon the advanced colonial powers to work together to encourage an evolutionary transformation of that country.

At the same time, China must also co-operate in the task so that it would become a full-fledged member of the community of Washington powers.

Till the late 1920s, the system worked by and large to bring order and stability to the Asian-Pacific region. There were few overtly unilateral acts by a Washington signatory, and the powers continued their mutual consultation as they sought to revise the old treaties with China. The latter, on its part, had come steadily to seek to realize its aspirations in co-operation with, rather than defiance of, the Washington powers. To be sure, Chinese Nationalists were initially adamantly opposed to the Washington Conference treaties, viewing them as a device for perpetuating foreign control. However, with their military and political successes, they emerged as the new leaders of the country, and with them there came a willingness to modify some of the radical rhetoric. After 1928, when they established a central government in Nanking under Chiang Kai-shek, they had to concentrate on domestic unification and economic development, tasks which necessitated foreign capital and technology, as well as a respite in international crises that would drain resources away from much-needed projects at home. Between 1928 and 1931, they achieved some significant gains. Nanking's political control was more extended than at any time since the end of the Manchu dynasty in 1912. The country's infrastructure – roads, bridges, telephone and telegraph networks – was being constructed through imported capital, mostly American. A modern system of education was producing the next generation's élites. The volume of China's foreign trade increased steadily, as did customs receipts. Reforms of internal tax and currency systems, again with the aid of foreign experts, were gradually putting an end to the fiscal chaos that had plagued the country for decades.[2]

The Chinese leadership at this time was thus not seeking to do away with the existing international order, but to integrate their country into it as a full-fledged member. China would persist in its efforts to regain its sovereign rights and to develop itself as a modern state, but these objectives were not incompatible with the co-operative framework of the Washington treaties. In fact, it could be argued that the Washington system was serving as an effective instrument for obtaining foreign support for Chinese development. The United States, Britain, Japan and others one by one recognized the Nanking regime, signed new treaties for tariff revision, and began negotiations for an ultimate abrogation of extra-territoriality, the traditional symbol of China's second-class status. Although these negotiations dragged on, by 1931 differences between China and the powers had narrowed considerably, so that a full restoration of jurisdictional authority to Chinese courts seemed to be a matter of time. It was at that juncture that the Japanese army struck, not only to oppose further concessions to Chinese nationalism, but ultimately to redefine the international system itself.

The revolt against the Washington Conference system may, paradoxically, be viewed as evidence that the system had steadily become strengthened; those opposed to it would have to resort to drastic measures to undermine it. Within the framework of the Washington treaties, the powers had by and large succeeded in stabilizing their mutual relations, putting a premium on economic rather than military issues as they dealt with one another, and co-opting Chinese nationalism by integrating the country step by step into a global economic order. This very success drove some forces in Japan – army and navy officers, right-wing organizations, nativist intellectuals – to desperation. They saw nothing but disaster in an international system that was steadily making concessions to China and in a global economic order that linked the nation's well-being so intimately to fluctuations in trade balances and rates of exchange. They accused the Japanese leadership of having created a situation where the nation's destiny appeared to depend more and more on the goodwill of the powers and of China. Unless something were done, Japan would soon be completely at the mercy of these outside forces. Japan's anti-internationalists saw only one solution: to reverse the trend in national policy by forcefully removing the country's leadership committed to internationalism, and to act in China in defiance of the Washington treaties. They judged that the early 1930s was the time to carry out such tasks, perhaps the last possible chance to do so.

The precise timing for action was a matter of some deliberation. But in many ways the year 1931 appeared the right moment.[3] For one thing, the government's commitment to the existing international order had begun to encounter widespread domestic opposition. In 1930 Japan under the cabinet of Hamaguchi Osachi had signed a new naval disarmament treaty in London. The treaty covered 'auxiliary craft' such as light cruisers and submarines which had been excluded from the provisions of the Washington naval treaty, and limited the total sizes of these ships that Japan, Britain, and the United States were allowed to possess. The new treaty established the allowable tonnages in the ratio of 6.975 for Japan and 10 for the other two. This was a higher ratio for Japan than the 6 to 10 formula for capital ships adopted by the Washington treaty, but it split the Japanese navy. Those who supported the government's acceptance of the new ratio (the 'treaty faction') confronted the adamant opposition of the 'fleet faction', determined to wage a public campaign against the treaty. The latter made it a constitutional issue, accusing the civilian government of having violated the emperor's 'right of supreme command', according to which the military presumably had direct access to the emperor as his advisers on command problems. Although no such case had been made after the Washington Conference, now the naval activists believed the public would be more receptive to this type of argument.

They judged the public mood and political climate of the country quite accurately. In 1925 Japan had instituted a universal manhood suffrage, and the political parties had become sensitive to changing moods and diverse interests of the population. Although the bulk of the newly enfranchised public may have understood or cared little for international affairs, it appears that it paid attention to and was fascinated by the kind of argument put forth by the navy's anti-government minority and its sympathizers. This receptivity reflected the economic situation, for the coming of the age of mass politics coincided with the world economic crisis that began with the Wall Street crash of October 1929.[4] Although its effects in Japan were not as severe as those in the United States or Germany, in 1930 Japanese unemployment reached 1 million, while farm prices (particularly rice and silks) fell to the lowest point in years. Tenant farmers, unable to make their rent payments, sold their daughters into prostitution, and their sons were encouraged to move to Korea or Manchuria. Particularly hard-hit was Japan's export trade, of which more than 30 per cent consisted of silks. The worldwide recession drastically reduced silk exports and created huge balance of trade deficits.

Like most other countries at this time, the Japanese government sought to cope with the situation through monetary measures. In those pre-Keynesian days, monetarism provided orthodoxy. What determined prices, it was argued, was the amount of liquidity, which in turn depended on the gold reserve in a country's possession. As trade declined and exports fell, the gold reserve would dwindle, necessitating a tight money policy, presumably because such a policy would serve to reduce demand and ultimately balance trade. But it inevitably involved declining purchasing power and consequent unemployment. Whereas the monetarists believed these were temporary phenomena, those who suffered from the economic crisis thought otherwise, and demanded that something be done by their leaders to alleviate the situation. It is most likely that the Japanese public, even without understanding the niceties of economic theory, was now more receptive to anti-governmental propaganda and agitation because of the crisis. When the Hamaguchi cabinet decided, at the late hour of November 1929, to go back on the gold standard at an artificially high rate of exchange, it immediately condemned itself as a government of élites insensitive to popular suffering.

Japanese politics was thus at a point where anti-governmental agitation could go a long way, threatening the existing domestic order and the foreign policy built on it. A clear indication of this was the assassination of Prime Minister Hamaguchi by a right-wing terrorist in November 1930, barely a month after the ratification of the London disarmament treaty. The assassin was given sympathetic treatment in the press and in supportive mass rallies as a true patriot, selflessly trying to purge the country of a politician committed to unworkable solutions. The incident encouraged similar acts, so that between 1930 and 1936 several other leaders, those identified with the internationalism of the

1920s, would be murdered. Even more serious, the passivity of the political and business élites in the face of such terrorism abetted the movement of military officers and right-wing intellectuals to 'restructure the nation'. The movement became more than a matter of ideology when a group of army officers organized a secret society (the Cherry Blossom Society) in 1930, dedicated to 'the restructuring of the nation even through the use of force'. The conspiracy was aimed at reorienting the country away from its infatuation with Western liberalism and capitalism, towards an embracement of the unique qualities of the country. In particular, the conspirators were determined to put an end to the élite's internationalist diplomacy which they believed had subordinated the country to the dictates of capitalist powers. What they visualized was a break with this pro-Western phase of the nation's history and the establishment of a military dictatorship more attuned to its traditional spirit.[5]

The Cherry Blossom Society planned to stage a *coup d'état* in March 1931, but the plot was nipped in the bud as some army leaders refused to go along at this time. Nevertheless, the incident indicated how far some radicals were willing to go to put an end to the existing world, both domestic and external.

Such background explains the timing of 1931, why that year must have seemed particularly auspicious for those who had chafed under what they considered undue constraints of foreign policy and domestic politics over a legitimate assertion of national rights. A group of Kwantung Army officers, led by Ishiwara Kanji and Itagaki Seishirō, judged that the moment was ripe for bold action. Unless it were taken, they feared that the powers would continue to give in to China's demands, and Japan's position become more and more untenable. The thing to do, they reasoned, was not to seek to preserve Japanese interests within the existing system of co-operation with the Western powers, but to act unilaterally and entrench Japanese power once and for all in Manchuria. Since such action would be opposed by Tokyo's civilian regime, the latter too would have to be eliminated if necessary. Actually, the conspirators may have felt they could count on enough support at home, for throughout 1931 public opinion and party politics were turning against the cabinet of Wakatsuki Reijirō - who had succeeded Hamaguchi after the latter's assassination - for its reliance on international co-operation to limit the demands of Chinese nationalism. The Seiyūkai, the major opposition party, intensified its attacks on the Minseitō cabinet, denouncing the latter's 'weak-kneed' diplomacy and calling for a fundamental solution of the 'Manchurian–Mongolian problem', a euphemism for use of force. To add fuel to the agitation, representatives of the Manchurian Youth League returned to Japan and held a series of public meetings to call for a determined effort to cope with the Chinese assault on Japanese rights.[6]

Judging that they would succeed if they acted boldly, the conspirators carried out their plan in September. It involved an attack on South Manchuria Railway tracks some 5 miles north of Mukden. It took place on the night of 18 September. The perpetrators of the attack were officers and troops of the Kwantung Army, acting under orders from Ishiwara and Itagaki. As they used explosives to destroy 2 to 3 feet of rail, the action ignited a much larger-scale assault on Chinese forces, also stationed in Mukden. Under the pretext that Chinese had attacked the South Manchuria Railway, a company of Japanese troops marched in and opened fire at Chinese forces. War was on. It was only after these initial moves that the commander-in-chief of the Kwantung Army, Honjō Shigeru, was notified of what was happening. General Honjō, on his own, approved the conspirators' moves and ordered military action against Chinese troops and garrisons, not just in Mukden but elsewhere in Manchuria. As he telegraphed the supreme command in Tokyo, the time was ripe for the Kwantung Army 'to act boldly and assume responsibility for law and order throughout Manchuria'.[7] Within a day, both Mukden and Changchun (the northern terminus of the South Manchuria Railway) had been seized by Japanese troops.

In retrospect, it is entirely clear that the Mukden incident was the first serious challenge to the postwar international system in the Asian-Pacific region as exemplified by the Washington Conference treaties. An act of defiance on the part of a determined minority challenged that system and the domestic leadership that sustained it, and ultimately brought about the demise of both. In 1931 few understood the issues clearly, but there was general recognition that the future stability of the region depended on the degree to which the Washington system survived the challenge. If Japanese and Chinese forces could restore the status quo of 18 September, or if the two governments as well as others could somehow accommodate the new developments into the existing treaty framework, then the challenge might possibly be contained. If not, the conspirators' determination to establish an alternative regime of international affairs might succeed.

Cabinet meetings in Tokyo immediately following the crisis revealed that the restoration of the status quo was unobtainable. Although, at a meeting held on 19 September, the principle of 'non-extension' of hostilities was agreed to, this was a vague formula, and the army virtually ignored it. High officials of the General Staff, some of whom had been privy to the conspiracy, were determined to seize the opportunity for 'the achievement of our ultimate purpose'. The 'ultimate purpose' here may not have meant control over the whole of Manchuria, but it certainly implied the assertion of Japanese rights in the area. From the military's point of view, it would be out of the question to go back to the status quo before 18 September. If the cabinet should insist on such a policy, army leaders agreed, then they would withdraw their support from it and 'would be totally unconcerned even if the government should be overthrown as a result'.[8]

How could civilian supremacy still have been preserved? It would have taken determined efforts by individuals and groups committed to the existing framework of domestic politics and foreign policy. Unfortunately, there were not enough of them. One could cite several obvious examples: the emperor and court circles, civilian diplomats and bureaucrats, some party leaders, business executives, and intellectuals. They were not, however, unified in opposition to the military, and only a few of them were convinced of the need to preserve the status quo at home and abroad.

The emperor apparently conveyed his preference for a non-extension of hostilities to Prime Minister Wakatsuki on 23 September, but by that time the cabinet had already given *ex post facto* approval to the crossing of the Yalu by a detachment of Japanese forces in Korea to reinforce the Kwantung Army. Japanese diplomats in China were extremely annoyed at such a course of events, and they appealed to their chief, Foreign Minister Shidehara Kijūrō, to put an end to military unilateralism. Shidehara, unfortunately, found himself more and more isolated. Few of his civilian colleagues in the cabinet would come to his rescue as he fought a losing battle for putting an end to the crisis. This was both because the bureaucrats had been trained not to meddle in strategic decisions, and also because not a few of them welcomed the military's bold strike to cut the Gordian knot in Manchuria. Undoubtedly they were affected by the prevailing climate of Japanese politics in which foreign policy had become a partisan issue. The opposition party, Seiyūkai, early declared its support for the Kwantung Army and was calling on the government to back up the latter's attempt to deal sternly with Chinese infringements on the nation's rights.

The situation was abetted by mass journalism. Newspapers and radio stations immediately grasped the potential of the Manchurian incident for reaching out to the mass public and expanding their readership/audience. From the very beginning, special bulletins were printed and broadcast, describing in colourful fashion how brave Japanese soldiers had meted out justice to Chinese 'aggressors'. (The Kwantung Army conspiracy was known only to a handful, and all official announcements accused the Chinese of having blown up the railway.) Newsreels were coming into existence, and already on 21 September the Asahi news showed a film about the occupation of the city of Mukden by Japanese soldiers. Sensationalist headlines inflamed public opinion.[9] Reading such accounts, and seeing propaganda films, the Japanese would certainly have formed an extremely simplistic idea of what was happening, a fact that the government could not ignore. But the sensationalist nature of the press coverage also indicates the readiness on the part of Japanese journalists to take official propaganda at its face value and willingly endorse a unilateral use of force. This in turn may be linked to the intellectual climate of the time. Some of the country's leading intellectuals had sensed a crisis of Japanese politics even before

1931. They believed that neither Western-style parliamentary democracy nor capitalist internationalism had helped create a stable, prosperous nation. The masses, they argued, were as impoverished and alienated as ever, and there was a prevailing atmosphere of malaise. Several leading intellectuals responded to this perceived crisis by turning to communism, socialism, or to fascism and right-wing dictatorship.[10] Although as yet a minority view, such thinking undoubtedly contributed to a favourable reception for bold military action like the Mukden takeover.

Even the most enthusiastic supporters of the Kwantung Army, however, were not necessarily advocating a revolutionary diplomacy, aimed at completely uprooting the existing framework of international affairs. Although this was what worried Foreign Minister Shidehara and his colleagues, at first only a few called for such action. In fact, the press, politicians, and intellectuals justified military action in Manchuria as a 'punishment' of Chinese intransigence, implying that they did not view the incident as undermining the Washington system; on the contrary, they argued that Japan was contributing to its strengthening by dealing decisively with Chinese lawlessness and irresponsible attacks on treaty rights. The civilian government, too, chose to present the Manchurian affair in such a framework, assuring the powers that what was involved was essentially police action in support, rather than violation, of the nine-power treaty and other provisions.[11]

Such a stance was extremely difficult to maintain in view of the widening of Japanese military operations; and it did not take long before Japan would be accused of having violated the nine-power treaty. Moreover, Japanese diplomacy at the outset was ineffectual; if its aim were to convince the powers that the nation was acting on behalf of the Washington system, Japan should have taken the initiative to communicate with the treaty signatories to appeal for their support and understanding. Instead, Tokyo at first decided to insist on a bilateral settlement of the dispute with China. The cabinet early instructed the Foreign Ministry to commence talks with the Chinese government with a view to terminating the hostilities. From Japan's standpoint, of course, no settlement would be acceptable that did not guarantee the rights of Japanese residents in Manchuria to engage in business. It was assumed that the Kwantung Army would continue to occupy cities to ensure this end. Somehow it was believed that the Chinese would accept these terms and that a quick settlement between the two countries along these lines would prevent the incident from developing into an international crisis. The powers, in the meantime, would endorse such a settlement as being for the benefit of all foreigners in Manchuria.[12]

Here was the first of a series of miscalculations by Japan that were to bring about its steady isolation in world affairs. By choosing to deal directly with China instead of putting the affair in the framework of multinational co-operation, Japan was belying its own professions of internationalism. China, on the other hand, seized the opportunity to present itself as a responsible member of the international community that had been wronged. From the very beginning, China's leaders presented the Mukden incident as Japan's assault on peace, civilization, and international morality. As Chiang Kai-shek noted in a speech to Kuomintang officials on 22 September, Japan had violated 'international morality, the League Covenant, and the [1928] treaty outlawing war'. General Jung Ch'in, chief of the General Staff, insisted in his report on the Manchurian collision that China was defending international order against Japan's lawless act; it was against international law to seize another country's territory just because a nation lacked natural resources, or to call a neighbouring land a 'line of national defence', as the Japanese were terming Manchuria. Such being the case, the Chinese were confident that 'world public opinion' would condemn Japan's barbarism and censure its violation of 'international public justice'.[13] They would never consent to dealing bilaterally with Japan, for that would play into the latter's hands and be tantamount to accepting the Japanese contention that the incident was a minor affair involving their treaty rights.

Thus from the very beginning China identified itself with international law and order and sought its salvation through the support of other nations and of world public opinion. A country which, throughout most of the 1920s, had been divided, unstable, and revolutionary, challenging the existing order of international affairs, was almost overnight transforming itself into a champion of peace and order, pitting itself against another which hitherto had been solidly incorporated into the established system but which could now be accused of having defied it. This way of presenting the crisis was not only brilliant propaganda; it also reflected the Kuomintang leadership's conscious decision to work with and through other powers to compel Japan to give up its aggression. Although Chiang Kai-shek recognized that ultimately – perhaps in ten years' time – the Chinese might have to fight, for the time being it was best to trust in world pressures, especially the League of Nations, to restrain Japan. China was far from being unified; in fact, the Nationalists were in the middle of a campaign against Communists, and, moreover, there had been devastating floods in the northern provinces, resulting in acute food shortages. Under the circumstances, Chiang declared in October, the best way to save the nation was through 'peaceful unification' of the country. The Chinese should first concentrate on political unity and economic development, and then take on Japan, relying in the meantime on the world at large to punish Japan.[14] Specifically, Chinese diplomats abroad were instructed to apprise their host governments of the Japanese aggression, and the League of Nations was asked to convene an emergency meeting of the Council. (China had just been elected to the Council as one of the non-permanent members; Japan was a permanent member.)

Unfortunately for China, the international system with which it so strongly identified and to which it turned for help, was itself going through a major crisis of another sort: the beginning of the world depression. Those powers that had constructed and preserved the international system – advanced industrial economies – were in the midst of a severe crisis. Between 1929 and 1931 industrial production, employment, commodity prices, purchasing power – all such indices of economic health, had plummeted, with national incomes cut to nearly one-half in the United States, Germany, and elsewhere. The situation severely affected their economic interactions, and thus the world economy as a whole. Domestic crises led these countries to institute protectionist measures to reduce imports, restrict shipments of gold, and control foreign exchange transactions, all such measures tending to undermine the gold standard and the principle of convertibility on which world trade and investment activities had been based. By the autumn of 1931, only France and the United States, among the major powers, still maintained the gold standard, but they were practising trade protectionism and were unwilling to help more severely affected countries. At such a time, only a concerted effort by capitalist countries would have brought about the restoration of confidence and led to restabilization, but international co-operation was extremely hard to achieve when it was seen by domestic constituents – labourers, farmers, the unemployed – as detrimental to their own interests. Governments would have to cater to their demands before undertaking serious negotiation for restoration of a world economic framework.

International co-operation, in other words, had already begun to break down when the Manchurian incident broke out. In retrospect, it is clear that the latter did in the political arena what the Depression accomplished in the economic, namely, to discredit internationalism – particularly of the kind that had prevailed during the 1920s. Nations that assembled at Geneva to consider the Chinese protests were participants in this drama. It was ironic that just at the time when China became a more self-conscious participant in the world order, the whole framework was collapsing.

It was collapsing, but was not yet dead. In fact, the Manchurian crisis and China's urgent appeals to world public opinion catapulted the powers to serious action, to see if they could somehow preserve the system. If they could help restore the peace in Manchuria, they would not only succeed in reconciling two Asian nations but would contribute to strengthening the peace mechanism. Confidence in internationalism would be renewed, and China would emerge as a conservative force in Asian affairs, while Japan would remain in the community of nations. Thus the stakes were extremely high.

Both the United States and Britain showed a strong interest in exploring such a possibility. Although the former was not a member of the League of Nations, it kept in close touch with the nations represented at the Council, which held several meetings following the Mukden incident in response to China's request. To the latter's disappointment, however, the Council at first failed to adopt any drastic measures to sanction Japan, instead adjourning on 30 September after exhorting the two countries not to worsen the situation in Manchuria. The lack of strong action in support of China reflected the views of officials in Washington and London that it would be best to let the Japanese settle the incident with a minimum of outside interference, to see if this really was a case involving a minor dispute over treaty rights. In other words, Tokyo's civilian government, which was insisting on such a construction, should be given a chance to act on that basis. For this reason, neither Secretary of State Henry L. Stimson nor Foreign Secretary John Simon was willing at that time to condemn Japan's military action as a violation of the pact of Paris. To do so would be to accept China's contentions and to take the latter's side. Before October, the United States and Britain were reluctant to take that step, but hoped that the civilian leaders in Tokyo would adopt measures to restore the status quo so as to confirm Japan's commitment to the existing system of international affairs.[15]

Initially, the Soviet Union may have been the only outside power seriously concerned with the implications of the Manchurian incident for Asian international order. To be sure, it had never been party to the Washington system, and had in fact sought to undermine it by encouraging China's radical nationalism. By the early 1930s, however, Soviet foreign policy had become more open to participation in international affairs as carried on by capitalist countries. In 1928 Moscow had signed the pact outlawing war, and with the first five-year plan under way, Joseph Stalin and his advisers had begun stressing the need for global stability. Their view of the League of Nations, which they had denounced as a tool of bourgeois imperialism, was changing, and they were particularly interested in improving relations with the United States. In the meantime, relations with China had deteriorated after 1929, when the Chinese had sought to take over the Soviet-operated Chinese Eastern Railway. Diplomatic ties between the two countries had been severed. Under the circumstances, Soviet policy needed to be reoriented, away from an identification with revolutionary forces in Asia to an emphasis on safeguarding the country's security and position in the region. How this was to be done was not yet clear, but from the very beginning Soviet officials expressed concern over the possible spread of Japanese military operations to northern Manchuria, affecting the safety of the railway and Soviet nationals. During the first few weeks, however, the Soviet government was satisfied with Tokyo's assurances that no extension of hostilities was being contemplated.[16]

At that time, therefore, there was a chance that the Manchurian incident could be limited to small-scale fighting between Japanese and Chinese forces, without the involvement of outside powers. To that extent, Japan's military conspirators had chosen the correct timing; both the civilian officials and outside governments were willing to view the event as manageable within the existing treaty framework. They would condone military action as an unfortunate but understandable aberration, which might even lead to the strengthening of the Washington system by clarifying the nature of Japanese rights and Chinese obligations in Manchuria.

Developments in October, however, soon belied such expectations. The Kwantung Army had been encouraged by the failure of the League and the Western powers to respond more positively to China's pleas for support, and judged the opportunity was ripe for acting further to separate Manchuria from the rest of China. Not being satisfied with merely protecting Japan's treaty rights, the military decided to enlarge spheres of action, to turn the whole of Manchuria and even Inner Mongolia into a war zone so as to establish their control and expel Chinese forces. As a step in that direction, several airplanes took off from Mukden on 8 October to bomb the city of Chinchow, at the south-western corner of Manchuria bordering on China proper. From then on, there was no containing the war; the Chinchow bombing was followed by other operations throughout Manchuria, clearly aimed at detaching the 'north-eastern provinces' from China.

It was then that the League and the powers finally invoked the 1928 pact to denounce Japan's violation of its spirit. When the League Council resumed its meeting on 14 October, the atmosphere had changed drastically. China was now clearly a victim of lawlessness, and by the same token a champion of international law and order, whereas Japan was put in the position of having to defend aggressive military action. For the first time, the United States became actively involved by sending Consul-General Prentis Gilbert to attend the Council meetings. It was symbolic that America was thus identifying itself with the League and what it stood for, thus explicitly joining China's new cause. The result was a Council resolution, with Japan alone opposing, to call on the Japanese army to return to the position it had held prior to 18 September. This resolution, voted on in late October, marked a clear beginning of Japan's ostracization in the world community. It is surprising how fast Japan's international position was collapsing. Already in early November, high officials in Washington were considering sanctions. Although nothing came of this, the willingness of President Herbert Hoover, Secretary of State Stimson, Secretary of War Patrick J. Hurley, and others even to contemplate sanctions against Japan indicates that in their view the latter was clearly undermining the postwar framework of international affairs. As Stimson told the Japanese ambassador in Washington, Japan was in violation of both the nine-power treaty and the pact of Paris, a position that would be maintained by the United States throughout the decade.[17] Since these two treaties had symbolized the regime of international co-operation in the 1920s, to consider Japan as defecting from it was a serious matter. Stimson was still hopeful that Tokyo's civilian leaders would recognize the gravity of the situation and finally succeed in reining in the military. International pressure on Japan, he felt, should prevent it from further wrecking the system. He was encouraged, therefore, when the Japanese government proposed the establishment of a League commission of inquiry to be dispatched to Manchuria. Such a proposal seemed to indicate Japanese sensitivity about world opinion and interest in staying in the League framework.[18] The United States encouraged China to agree to such a scheme, and thus, in early December, the League Council resolved to send a commission of inquiry to investigate the causes of the war and to recommend a settlement. Japan and China both supported this solution, thus enabling the Council to achieve unanimity for the first time since September. The commission of inquiry was to be headed by Lord Lytton of Britain, and to consist of representatives from four other countries (the United States, France, Germany, and Italy). A show of support for the League, the agreement was the last occasion for such unanimity. The Japanese expected the commission to look into Chinese attacks on the treaty rights, whereas the Chinese hoped it would condemn Japanese acts. In either case, there was some hope that it would provide just the sort of compromise that all powers desperately wanted in order to preserve international order.

But that was not to be. Within days of the establishment of the commission of inquiry, the Wakatsuki cabinet fell, and Inukai Tsuyoshi became prime minister. Shidehara left his post as foreign minister, never to return to public life until after the Second World War. It is interesting to note that towards the end of his tenure in office, Shidehara had begun to realize that a return to the status quo in Manchuria was untenable. Domestic forces were applauding Kwantung Army action, and to punish the latter would merely fuel the former and create a grave crisis. As he told Japanese emissaries overseas in November, 'to suppress unnecessarily radical national opinion could play into the hands of the extremists, and bring about an explosion of anti-Chinese sentiment at home, inviting a dangerous situation'.[19] Realizing this, Shidehara sought to save domestic stability by prevailing upon the powers to agree at least to some *faits accomplis* in Manchuria. Even such an effort, however, was doomed to failure, since the establishment of an independent Manchuria, on which the army was working, went far beyond acceptable bounds.

The separation of China's north-eastern provinces as an independent entity under Japanese control was a goal that Kwantung Army activists, Japanese nationalistic groups in Manchuria, and their supporters at home had long advocated. The movement had been contained successfully before 1931, but once the Kwantung Army resorted to military action with impunity, it was a foregone conclusion that the next goal would be to establish a pro-Japanese regime in the region. As the conspirators, in particular Ishiwara, envisaged it, Manchuria would be a self-sufficient haven of stability and prosperity, free from national egoisms and from radicalism. For some it would even be a region where all people – at least all those who inhabited it – could work together in peace. The implication here was that Japan would undertake an act of self-aggrandizement for a new definition of stability.

That definition, of course, was quite destabilizing in the context of post-1919 internationalism. The goal of self-sufficiency would imply an interest in creating an autarkic empire in the area, less linked to the rest of the world than earlier. In the long run, the search for self-sufficiency was as great a challenge to the international system as the use of force in Manchuria, but in that regard Japanese action was not unique. Other countries, too, were undermining the regime of economic internationalism through unilateral measures to protect domestic markets and enhance competitive advantages. Economic autonomy was also being practised; Germany and Austria, for instance, were just then seeking to establish a customs league, while Britain was going ahead with a scheme for imperial preferences in tariff matters. What was unique about Japanese behaviour at this time was that it coupled its military unilateralism with aspirations for economic regionalism so that East Asia would be effectively separated from the rest of the world.

Even so, it is interesting to note that the Japanese government steadfastly refused to denounce the Washington Conference system explicitly. Despite all the obvious acts of aggression in Manchuria and infringement on Chinese sovereignty, Tokyo chose to profess its adherence to the nine-power treaty. This became clear when Secretary of State Stimson issued a statement in January 1932 that the United States government 'did not intend to recognize' any treaty or agreement that Japan might impose on China which 'may be brought about by means contrary to the covenants and obligations of the Pact of Paris' and which affected Chinese sovereignty or the principle of the Open Door. The statement was sent to all co-signatories of the nine-power treaty, indicating an interest on America's part to do its share in upholding the Washington system by branding Japan a violator. The Japanese government, however, responded by denying that any violation of the treaties had occurred. The nation still adhered to the Open Door and other principles of the Washington agreements. However, it insisted, China was now even more divided and unstable than it had been in 1921–22, so that in implementing the treaty provisions, Japan would have to take these changed circumstances into consideration. In other words, the military action in Manchuria did not affect the country's adherence to the existing framework of international affairs.[20]

China, of course, denounced such an assertion, its Foreign Office spokesman sarcastically pointing out that it was Japan that was divided and unstable; its government had utterly failed to control the military.[21] Still, initially the other signatories of the nine-power treaty were reluctant to go as far as the United States in condemning Japan. Britain merely expressed its satisfaction at Japanese professions of treaty observation, as did other countries such as France, Italy, and Belgium. They were not ready to confront Japan as a group. Their governments were preoccupied by more urgent issues closer to home and chose to accept the Japanese contention that the basic structure of Asian international affairs remained intact.

The situation became much more alarming from the powers' point of view when Japanese and Chinese forces fought skirmishes in Shanghai in late January and early February 1932. The so-called Shanghai incident was an extension of the Manchurian crisis in that it pitted Japanese residents and military in coastal China, eager for more action to follow up the successes in Manchuria, against Chinese politicians, students, and radicals who were engaged in an organized movement to protest against Japanese aggression. Here, however, Japan was much more sensitive to international opinion and took care to consult with the powers, in particular the United States, Britain, and France, to ensure the protection of their nationals in Shanghai. The powers, on their part, were eager to keep in touch with one another so as to bring the incident to a speedy conclusion. China, as expected, appealed to the League of Nations. Satō Naotake, the chief Japanese delegate, argued that China was not 'an organized state' and therefore that Japan was trying to restore law and order there so that the powers could enjoy their rights. But the other nations' representatives were not very sympathetic, and Satō sensed Japan's 'complete isolation in world public opinion'.[22]

This was a self-inflicted wound, which became even more damaging when, on 1 March, the new government of Manchukuo was established. A product of Kwantung Army initiatives, it was presented to the world as an expression of the local population's right of self-determination. That way, even such an egregious violation of China's territorial and administrative integrity could, Tokyo reasoned, be made compatible with the Washington treaties. But Japanese officials themselves betrayed the spirit of those treaties when they refused to refer the question of Manchukuo's status to international arbitration or consultation, instead taking unilateral steps to recognize the new puppet regime, which came on 15 September. That fatal decision was made a week before the Lytton commission returned to Geneva and submitted its report to the League of Nations. The report condemned Japanese military action as unjustifiable but also called on China to respect Japanese and other foreign rights. The recommendations were approved by all members of the League Council except Japan.

By then, Japanese politics had entered a new phase. The assassination of Prime Minister Inukai on 15 May, 1932 by a group of terrorist officers, had brought down party government in Japan; it had been preceded by the murder of two financial leaders who had been closely identified with the economic internationalism of the 1920s. These terrorist acts were designed to establish a domestic order commensurate with a new foreign policy in which Japan's control over Manchuria would occupy a central position. In such circumstances, it was not surprising that the Japanese government would become decidedly less interested in trying to retain the goodwill of the Western powers. Nevertheless, Tokyo did not choose to repudiate the existing treaties. It still continued to insist that the independence of Manchukuo and Japan's recognition of it did not violate the nine-power treaty, since the nation had merely exercised the right of self-defence to protect its interests in a country which had no responsible government, and responded favourably to an expression of the indigenous population's movement for self-determination. By using such an argument, Japan was hopeful of gaining the sympathy, if not the support, of the Washington powers.[23]

The unanimous vote at the League Council accepting the Lytton commission's report belied such expectations. For by the autumn of 1932 the Western powers had stiffened their attitude, having been exasperated by Japan's long series of unilateral acts. Not only the United States, which continued to reiterate the non-recognition doctrine, but Britain, France, and others were more critical of Japan and more willing to take the latter to task for its violation of the nine-power treaty. It was, therefore, a foregone conclusion that they would endorse the findings and recommendations of the Lytton commission, which in turn implied ostracization of Japan. As it became clear that its assurances that it had never violated the treaties would not be taken seriously, Japan chose to withdraw from the League of Nations. The fiction that despite the events in Manchuria and Shanghai Japan was still an upholder of the postwar framework of international affairs no longer worked, and the time had come to recognize frankly that no power accepted such an explanation. To remain in the League meant giving up an independent Manchuria, and the leaders in Tokyo judged that the latter objective was worth the price of forfeiting the former.

This did not mean, however, that there was an anti-Japanese coalition forming in the world that would support China's struggle against Japan. This remained the goal of Chinese leaders. The Nationalist government, it is true, faced serious domestic opposition to its policy of turning to the League and world opinion for help. Nationalistic groups wanted more positive action and sought to mobilize the country for anti-Japanese boycotts and other movements. Under pressure from them, Chiang Kai-shek had to resign and leave the government temporarily, between December 1931 and January 1932. The Communists, on their part, endorsed radical nationalism, and from their stronghold in Juichin, Kiangsi Province, declared war on Japan in April. This was a challenge to Chiang's restored leadership, and he mobilized 500,000 troops to try to encircle and crush the Communists. In the meantime, he was hopeful that the powers would stop Japan's wanton assault on the Washington system. It is interesting to note that by 1932 'the spirit of the Washington Conference' had become a Chinese way of reminding the powers of their obligation to punish Japan; as a Kuomintang declaration noted in March, China was fighting for the principle that treaties must be observed, for otherwise there would be no peace in the world. A meeting of concerned citizens issued a statement in April that the Washington Conference had established peace in the Asian-Pacific region which, however, was again being threatened, and there was a danger that the crisis could lead to a second world war. The most important thing now was to coalesce nations which 'preserve justice and treat China equally'.[24]

Despite such hopes, the powers would not go beyond criticizing Japan and endorsing the recommendations of the Lytton commission. Both Washington and London were satisfied with these steps, somehow hoping that ultimately the Japanese would see the light and mend their ways. In the meantime, neither the United States nor Britain was prepared to employ anti-Japanese sanctions to help China. The year 1932 was one of transition in American politics, with public attention focused on the competition for votes between President Hoover and the Democratic Party's candidate, Franklin D. Roosevelt. They did not disagree on policy towards Japan; actually, during the campaign they said little about the Asian crisis. Far more pressing, to them and to their supporters, were domestic recovery measures and, as far as foreign affairs were concerned, the questions of European debts and disarmament. For the European powers were just then holding a disarmament conference to see if they could preserve the Locarno framework of a stable relationship among Britain, France, and Germany. Much depended on the willingness of the United States to help uphold the status quo, which in turn would necessitate a satisfactory settlement of the debt and reparations question. With opposition parties and even the government in Germany calling for revision of the Versailles treaty that had stipulated the payment of reparations and restricted German armament, the future of the Locarno regime was increasingly uncertain. It had not yet broken down, nor was there a strong sentiment that the whole structure of the postwar peace settlement was in jeopardy. But there no longer was confidence that there would be sufficient co-operativeness among the Western powers to maintain the system. In such a situation, they could not bring themselves to agree on a collective approach to strengthen the League efforts to punish Japan.

Neither would the Soviet Union, which stood outside both the League and the Washington treaty structure, act alone to restrain Japan. Moscow did not discourage the Chinese Communists – or Japanese Communists for that matter – from launching a mass movement opposed to Japanese imperialism. The Comintern's May 1932 thesis defined the Manchurian incident as Japan's war of aggression against

China which heightened contradictions among imperialists and increased chances of another world war.[25] But the thesis stressed the importance of Japan's internal transformation, to bring about a bourgeois revolution which would lead to a socialist revolution and eliminate the reactionary emperor system, rather than the formation of an international coalition against Japanese imperialism. Moscow's leaders apparently judged that the West was unlikely to develop such a coalition, and probably feared that the latter might even acquiesce in the Japanese conquest of Manchuria as a desirable step towards weakening the Soviet Union. Deciding that their country was in no position to take on Japan single-handed, they chose to concentrate on avoiding trouble. Specifically, Soviet authorities allowed Japanese troops to use the Chinese Eastern Railway and intimated their willingness to sell the railway to Japan. The Soviet government even suggested the conclusion of a non-aggression treaty between the two countries. (At one point it indicated a readiness to conclude a similar agreement with the state of Manchukuo, which of course would have meant recognizing the puppet government.) Thus at a time when other countries, above all China, were eschewing the bilateral approach, the Soviet Union was willing to try it, if only as a temporary expedient, so as not to precipitate a crisis which might play into the hands of the imperialists.[26]

In some such fashion, Japan was getting away with its unilateral aggression without inviting a hostile coalition other than the League's censure. As Chinese spokesmen lamented frequently, the Japanese had chosen the right moment when Western countries were in disarray because of the economic crisis, and when China itself suffered from internal rebellions and natural disasters. Nevertheless, Japan's acts impressed the other governments as the first open defiance of the Washington system, and that reaction would define their responses to subsequent developments in the Asian-Pacific region. It was far from clear in 1932, however, how far the structure of international affairs established after the First World War had crumbled, or whether somehow the Manchurian incident could be accommodated into it as a minor but not a fatal infringement. Much would depend on the next set of decisions the Japanese would make, and on the powers' interpretations of them. Most fundamental would be the question of the degree to which Japan and the powers, despite what had happened in China, would work together in the area. If they did so, that would befuddle the thinking of Chinese and Russians who confidently spoke of an eventual world war; if not, such an eventuality would come much closer.

A NEW WASHINGTON SYSTEM?

A key question of Asian-Pacific affairs during the years following

Japan's withdrawal from the League of Nations, which became official in March 1933, was the extent to which the Japanese would still continue to act unilaterally or, on the contrary, show some willingness to return to a policy of co-operation with the Washington powers. This was a question as much of Japan's external relations as of internal affairs, for party politics had succumbed to an increasing role of the military in decision-making, so that there was always the risk of 'dual diplomacy', civilian officials pursuing one set of policies and being contradicted by military actions.

For a while after 1933, however, both civilians and military were interested in consolidating the gains in Manchuria and avoiding further complications with other countries. The Japanese military had absorbed an enormous chunk of Chinese territory, and in the process forced a redefinition of domestic politics in Japan. These were enough victories for the time being, and they wanted to digest and enjoy what they had obtained. The first step in this direction was the Tangku truce of May 1933, signed between the Kwantung Army and Chinese Nationalist commanders. It provided for the two sides to cease the use of force and to honour the status quo, defined in terms of the existing lines of battle. The lines were drawn roughly along the Great Wall, separating Manchukuo from the rest of China. Moreover, south of the wall, there was to be created a demilitarized zone, an area of neutrality that would ensure that Chinese forces would not threaten Japan's new position in Inner Mongolia and the three north-eastern provinces which comprised Manchukuo. Thus the truce was tantamount to a semi-permanent detachment of the area north of China proper, and to the Nationalists' tacit recognition of Japanese presence in Manchuria.

The Nationalists chose to accept such humiliating terms rather than continue their resistance, reasoning that the Tangku truce was purely a military agreement, not a diplomatic document which recognized the puppet regime of Manchukuo. That was absolutely unacceptable, but given military inadequacies along the Great Wall, the need to forestall the establishment of Japanese-supported separatist regimes in north China, and the ongoing campaign against Communist forces, the Nationalist leaders reluctantly approved the truce. Moreover, as one of them, Huang Fu, told Chiang Kai-shek, it was all very well to talk of international support, but the powers were not helping China; 'our national disaster is due to our mistaken faith in obtaining international assistance'. The Chinese were still counting on such support; as will be noted, a high official had been dispatched to Washington and London to seek financial aid. Nevertheless, unless Japanese forces overran the Peking–Tientsin region and assaulted foreign interests, which appeared unlikely, the powers could not be expected to intervene. Therefore, if the Japanese were willing to sign a cease-fire and withdraw their forces to areas north of the Great Wall, this would enable China to 'stabilize north China, have some rest, and solidify the foundations of the nation and the party', as General Ho Ying-ch'in stated.[27]

The cessation of military hostilities gave the civilian government in Tokyo an opportunity to take stock of what had happened since 1931 and redefine the country's foreign policy. The task fell primarily to Hirota Kōki, the diplomat who had served as ambassador to the Soviet Union till he was named foreign minister in September 1933. He clearly recognized the need to put an end to the military's unilateral initiatives, and to assure the powers that no further extension of the war was contemplated. Diplomacy, rather than military action, would henceforth take precedence. But that did not mean a return to the pre-1931 situation. Hirota and his cabinet colleagues accepted the *faits accomplis*, especially the independence of Manchukuo, and sought to stabilize Japan's foreign affairs on that basis. This, they reasoned, could be done without rejecting the Washington treaties outright. In other words, they were interested in re-establishing the framework of international co-operation, outside the League to be sure, but through a modified Washington system.

A good idea of what the Japanese government envisaged can be seen in a series of statements issued by the Foreign Ministry in the spring of 1934. Amō Eijirō, its spokesman, first stated at a press conference in April that Japan expected the Western powers to accept the changed circumstances of Asian affairs, and that henceforth the nation would not look favourably upon Western political and economic activities in China. It was, Amō continued, Japan's 'mission' to maintain the peace and order in East Asia. He was paraphrasing one of Foreign Minister Hirota's instructions to the Japanese minister in Nanking, and Vice Foreign Minister Shigemitsu Mamoru had also expressed similar ideas.[28] As the latter wrote, Japan could not tolerate China's turning to Western countries for help against the new status quo; the nation would be prepared to reject such interference. The Amō statement, then, was inherently a serious challenge to the Washington system which had been built on the principle of multinational co-operation in China. For that reason it was dubbed an Asian Monroe Doctrine by its critics and supporters alike. At that time, however, neither the Foreign Ministry nor the Japanese military were willing to risk alienating the powers by acting in accordance with such a doctrine. Hirota's idea was primarily that Japan should make China and the Western powers recognize the nation's enhanced position in Asia without openly calling into question the validity of the existing treaties. Thus when the United States and Britain expressed misgivings about the gist of the Amō statement, Tokyo quickly assured them that it had no intention of infringing on the rights of Western nations in China. Still, Japanese officials were hopeful that they would consider Japan as the power with the primary responsibility for the protection of their rights in China.

Thus instead of the kind of international co-operation envisaged at the Washington Conference, the Japanese were asserting their position as the most influential in Chinese affairs and trying to have other countries accept that primacy. There would be 'co-operation' on that basis. But they would refuse to co-operate with other countries or with the League in helping China undertake economic recovery and fiscal reforms. As will be noted, several such schemes were being put forth, but Japan would not take part because that would imply its acceptance of the older idea of co-operation. For that very reason, the Chinese would be eager to involve as many countries as possible in their national affairs.

In the meantime, Japan tried to extend the new diplomacy to Pacific and naval affairs. In the belief that the United States might accept a new equilibrium in the Pacific reflective of Japan's enhanced position in East Asia, Hirota proposed a two-power agreement to redefine the status quo in the ocean. The two nations, he declared, would never risk a violent clash so long as the boundaries of their respective spheres of influence were clearly drawn. Since Japan was preponderant in the western Pacific and America in the eastern, it made sense for them to recognize the fact and pledge not to infringe on each other's area of predominance. Nothing came of the proposal as the United States was adamantly opposed to such a bilateral arrangement, viewing it as yet another assault on the Washington system. But the idea would not die; its echoes were to be heard throughout the 1930s, all the way up to the eve of the war. It indicated the growing popularity of the view in Japan that it should be possible to preserve the peace in the Pacific if only the United States recognized the new status quo in Asia. By the same token, the latter would refuse such a blatant departure from the multinational agreements that had defined the peace since the 1920s.

The same thinking was behind Japan's insistence on 'parity' among the navies of Japan, the United States, and Britain. For Tokyo's naval leaders who were adamant on this issue, parity was a symbol; they had welcomed the army's victories in Manchuria and asserted that in order to protect the newly won position on the continent, it was essential for the country to have a navy that was at least equal to that of the United States. As the navy minister remarked in October 1933, in order to 'reject resolutely' American interference in East Asia, it would be necessary to build up naval strength beyond the limits imposed by the disarmament treaties.[29] The Japanese cabinet, on the other hand, did not initially want an outright denunciation of the treaties. Prime Minister Okada Keisuke – appointed in July 1934 – was a retired admiral who had accepted the Washington system and had the support of most of his cabinet colleagues. They pinned their hopes on the preliminary naval talks that were carried on in London throughout 1934 for a new naval agreement. If a new treaty could be negotiated, the framework of co-operation among the powers could be preserved. But the navy was adamant on parity, and the United States was equally insistent on retention of the existing naval ratios. The result was Tokyo's decision, in December 1934, to abrogate the Washington naval treaty. Nevertheless, at that time only a handful of officials in Tokyo were calling for an outright rejection of the whole Washington system and for a definition of an entirely new framework of national policy.

At least until 1936, no such departure seemed justified. That was in part because other countries, too, were on the whole reluctant to pursue a new approach to Asian-Pacific affairs to check Japan. The Chinese, for one thing, showed some readiness to stabilize the bilateral relationship with Japan on the basis of the Tangku truce. Not that there was no disagreement among Chinese leaders and public opinion; they were divided between those who were anxious to have a respite in the struggle against Japanese imperialism, and those who were determined to continue it. The Nanking regime under Chiang Kai-shek was built on a subtle balance between the two, the first group represented by Wang Ching-wei and the second by T. V. Soong. The latter, Chiang's brother-in-law and finance minister, sought to bolster up China's position *vis-à-vis* Japan's by obtaining the support of the West and the League of Nations. He visited America and Europe in 1933 to seek loans, technical assistance, and, most important, an international corporation consisting of the major powers except Japan, to provide China with funds for economic development.[30] He was only partially successful, however, as the powers were unwilling to punish Japan further by aligning themselves so explicitly with China. Soong's loss of influence was revealed when he was dismissed as finance minister in October. Most of Chiang's aides urged more cautious dealings with Japan at that time, arguing that too strenuous a concentration on the anti-Japanese struggle would drain resources away from domestic needs, particularly the pacification of the country through eliminating the Communist threat. Chiang and his supporters tended to view anti-Japanese forces as radicals interested in challenging the authority of the Nanking government. Arguing that the Chinese had sufficiently demonstrated their self-respect during 1931–33, and in view of the apparent unwillingness of the West to unite in support of China, they concluded that the best strategy for the time being was to concentrate on developing what lay outside Japanese control.

Their assessment of the international situation was realistic, for in the years immediately following the Tangku truce there prevailed an atmosphere of uncertainty in Western capitals concerning the structure and orientation of Asian-Pacific affairs. The picture became especially fluid after the accession of Adolf Hitler to power in January 1933. He had openly called for revision of the Versailles peace structure, and as soon as he became the new German chancellor he took steps to undermine part of it by withdrawing from the Geneva disarmament conference and denouncing the existing restrictions on German armament. Like the Japanese revisionists, he took the country out of the League of Nations and instituted domestic measures to lessen the influence of those committed to or identified with the postwar order. Hitler's Germany was less expansionist than Japan, at least for the time being. Its immediate aim was to regain some of the territory in central Europe it had lost in 1919, not to add more land. Hitler was, however, keenly interested in restoring Germany's position in Asia, not through joining the Washington system from which it had been excluded, but through unilateral initiatives in approaching China and Japan. Because of the changed conditions in the area, Hitler and his aides judged an aggressive East Asian policy would serve to weaken the position of the United States, Britain, or France in their commitment to the Washington system, and thus indirectly contribute to damaging the Versailles peace structure. It would also strengthen Germany's position *vis-à-vis* the Soviet Union; while the two nations that had been excluded from both the Versailles and the Washington treaties had often acted together, they had become progressively estranged, particularly in view of the intense hostility between Nazis and Communists in Germany. The clandestine military co-operation between the two countries, which they had secretly undertaken in defiance of Versailles, came to an end in 1933.

It was more difficult, however, to define precisely how best to enhance the country's power in Asia. Hitler and some party officials wanted to encourage Japanese alienation from the West by offering to recognize the state of Manchukuo, while the Foreign Office was strongly opposed to such a step, fearing it would prematurely isolate Germany in world affairs. Instead, most civilian diplomats as well as the professional military favoured a policy of close relations with China because the latter offered much-needed raw materials as well as a market for German arms and consumer products.[31] For several years after 1933, this latter view prevailed, and Germany undertook ambitious programmes for expanding trade with China and, more important, providing it with aircraft and aviation experts. Such programmes were incompatible with a policy of befriending Japan, and thus Germany was emerging as China's close partner in Asia. For the Chinese, however, German support was not an unmixed blessing, for other Western powers, as well as Japan, would take exception to the growing German influence in Chinese affairs. Nevertheless, in the period following the Tangku truce, Germany appeared to be more willing than others in offering assistance even at the risk of annoying Japan, and that was the important thing. Chiang Kai-shek repeatedly urged Germany to send General Hans von Seeckt, former chief of the German army command, to China as military adviser, and the appointment materialized over strong Japanese objections. In a sense, Germany was the one country willing to defy openly Japanese wishes, as exemplified by the Amō statement, that no foreign powers come to the aid of China. And yet, German willingness to help China's strengthening did not mean it would be ready to co-operate with China against Japan. Hitler's professed proclivity for Japan would not tolerate it, and besides, German policy in Asia was not designed for reinforcing the existing treaty system. For that reason, China could not completely count on Germany alone in its struggle against Japanese imperialism. It would still need Anglo-American assistance.

Here the picture was not very bright. In London, officials were becoming strongly influenced by their view of the interrelatedness between Asian and European affairs. Their policy towards the Chinese–Japanese conflict would hinge to a large extent on the state of British–German affairs. If, for instance, Germany's threat to European stability increased, it would become necessary to recall much of the navy from Asian waters to areas closer home, making it difficult to take a firm stand towards Japan. If, on the other hand, Britain succeeded in maintaining an equilibrium *vis-à-vis* Germany in Europe, it would stand a better chance of playing an active role in Asia. For these reasons, a cardinal effort by the government of Stanley Baldwin, who headed the cabinet during 1935–37, was oriented towards averting an open crisis in Europe. British strategy was two-pronged. One, the so-called Stresa front, sought to check Germany by means of an agreement among Britain, France, and Italy to preserve the European status quo. The second, a naval agreement with Germany (1935), succeeded in having Hitler agree to keep German naval strength at 35 per cent of British. Both these instruments went beyond the Versailles treaty and indicated a desperate attempt by London to avert an international crisis. The treaty system was not yet buried, but it was modified to preserve the peace, thus undermining the confidence of nations in the durability of the postwar structure of international affairs.

In Asia, too, Britain was willing to come to terms with the new realities. After the League's failure to press Japan to return to the pre-1931 status quo, London no longer sought a solution through the world organization, and instead tried to see if conditions on the Asian continent could be stabilized through some other arrangements. British officials toyed with various possibilities throughout 1933 and 1934: a *rapprochement* with the Soviet Union in order to restrain Japan, co-operation with the United States, unilateral moves to strengthen naval defences in Asia, initiatives to assist China's economic development, and 'a permanent friendship with Japan' (in the words of Neville Chamberlain, the chancellor of the exchequer).[32] This last alternative, which Chamberlain pushed with vigour, even envisaged recognition of Manchukuo. While no such step was approved by his cabinet colleagues, discussion of this and other options indicated a serious search for a fresh approach. Just as they were willing to go beyond the Versailles settlement to conciliate Germany, London's officials were contemplating some new mechanism for preserving the peace in Asia. They were not advocating a departure from the structure of the Washington system; they periodically reminded the Japanese that the nine-power treaty was still in effect. However, Britain would be interested in devising means for ensuring greater stability. And at this time the strategy of working closely with the Soviet Union or the United States against Japan seemed less realistic than that of improving relations with the latter so as to obtain its compliance with stabilizing conditions in China. Out of such deliberations came the mission of Frederick Leith-Ross who, as will be noted, was to contribute to strengthening China's position economically and politically.

The United States, in the meantime, was under the leadership of a new president, Franklin D. Roosevelt. Unlike his predecessor, he was not committed to any specific system of international relations. At the London Economic Conference (1933), he showed a willingness to give up the principle of international co-operation to preserve the gold standard in favour of a more flexible policy that would enable the nation to act unilaterally to regulate the price of gold and the rates of exchange between American and other currencies. Roosevelt was determined to focus on domestic recovery and showed little inclination for becoming bogged down in international issues. He would deal pragmatically with issues as they arose, without necessarily tying their solution into a larger framework. This does not mean that he was indifferent to the fate of the League of Nations or the Washington system; but in comparison with Hoover he was less interested in preserving these formal structures.

His pragmatism and initial indifference to developing a cohesive framework for American foreign affairs were reflected in the policies of the Roosevelt administration towards East Asia. They were not so much policies as *ad hoc* decisions that did not add up to a clear statement. For instance, the president supported the Tydings–McDuffy Act of 1934 which promised independence to the Philippines in twelve years. Such a decision implied uncertainty regarding America's military position in the western Pacific, and the War Department was inclined to write off that region as falling within Japan's sphere of power. Neither Roosevelt nor the Navy Department was willing to go that far, and they pushed with vigour a naval construction programme within treaty limits. The Vinson–Trammell Act of 1934, authorizing just such a policy, was an important first step. Washington also insisted on maintaining the existing treaty ratios, rejecting Japan's demands for parity. As Admiral William H. Standley, chief of naval operations, pointed out, if the United States were to preserve the international system based on the nine-power treaty and the Paris pact, it was imperative to retain a requisite naval strength in the Pacific as specified in the agreements.[33] The contradictory positions of Japan and the United States on this point led to a stalemate at the preliminary naval disarmament conference in London throughout 1934 and 1935. Although their failure to come to terms on the parity question was certain to doom the existing naval agreements, thus destroying one corner of the treaty structure, American authorities preferred such an outcome, laying the onus on

Japan, to approving a modified system in which Japanese power would be strengthened. In the meantime, the State Department responded negatively to the Japanese suggestion for a Pacific agreement to recognize their respective spheres of influence, contending that such a step was contrary to the Washington understanding. In other words, the Roosevelt administration's policies towards Pacific questions showed neither a determined effort to preserve the Washington system nor a strong interest in replacing it with something else. The government was much less concerned with international co-operation than with bilateral issues with Japan which would be dealt with primarily in terms of the perceived needs and interests of the nation.

Much the same tendency can be detected in Roosevelt's approach to the China question. He was by and large willing to leave the new realities alone in Manchuria. While he followed Hoover's policy of not recognizing the state of Manchukuo, he did not want to challenge Japan's position directly. State Department officials had become deeply disillusioned by the failure of the co-operative, internationalist diplomacy to restrain Japan and to uphold the Washington system, and some of them now advocated recognizing the new status quo to preserve what was left of that system. So long as American rights and interests were not openly threatened, and the Japanese kept insisting that they were still honouring the principle of the Open Door in Manchuria, it seemed best to restabilize the situation by restoring some framework of co-operation with Japan and other Washington powers. The president, however, was not very interested in such a scheme, and instead wanted to see if a new stability could be worked out through an approach to the Soviet Union. The recognition of the revolutionary regime in Moscow in November 1933 was a product of many forces, but one significant factor was a perception shared by the two capitals that an American–Russian *rapprochement* might serve to check Japan. While by no means an explicit understanding to that effect, the recognition episode revealed Roosevelt's willingness to go outside the existing framework of treaties and agreements and to experiment with something new.

The administration's lack of concern with a comprehensive approach to foreign policy also characterized its policy in China. On one hand, there was continued sympathy with the plight of the Nanking government and an interest in helping its economic recovery measures. An instance of this was a loan of 1933, totalling a credit of $50 million from the Reconstruction Finance Corporation, which was to enable the Chinese to purchase American cotton and wheat. It was, however, an isolated event, less part of a systematic approach to helping China and more a product of domestic and Congressional pressures to dispose of surpluses. These same pressures severely tested American–Chinese relations when Congress enacted a Silver Purchase Act in 1934, authorizing the Treasury Department to buy silver at rates higher than those prevailing in the world market. Quantities of silver drained out of

China as a result, some through Japanese hands, so that the country's silver reserves dropped from some 602 million yuan in April 1934 to 288 million yuan in November 1935, when it was forced off the silver-based currency system.[34] Nanking's efforts at economic rehabilitation were derailed, and the ability to consolidate its position undermined. This was clearly not a friendly act on the part of the United States, and Chinese officials had desperately tried to dissuade Washington from carrying out the silver purchase policy, but the Roosevelt administration had no overall China strategy in terms of which to cope with the situation. Although this was the very time that Britain was considering an offer of aid to China to help its fiscal modernization, and although silver purchases conflicted with such a project, there was no interest in Washington to co-ordinate policies with London.

Under these circumstances, China could not count on a systematic, co-operative policy on the part of the Western powers as it sought to cope with Japan's entrenched position in Manchuria. That position was being willy-nilly confirmed by the absence of a comprehensive collective response. The upshot was a new stability, not exactly an alternative to the Washington treaty system but a modified version of it. There was no consensus as to what the modification consisted of, or how the modified status quo was to be sustained, and for that very reason each power felt free to pursue its own policies irrespective of those of the others. At least no country wanted an open conflict, so that there was a chance that a new framework might in time emerge.

THE POPULAR FRONT

In July 1935 the seventh Comintern congress convened in Moscow. There a new thesis was adopted: the establishment of a global front against fascism. Characterizing international conditions as a struggle between fascism and anti-fascism, the delegates called on all peoples and countries to establish a popular front against the forces of fascism, defined as dictatorships trying to save capitalism from collapse through a repartitioning of the world. Nazi Germany and militarist Japan were identified as the main forces for aggression and war, so that the Comintern declaration was a call for an alliance of all countries, both in the West and elsewhere, against them. Within each country, the Comintern directed the Communists to co-operate with workers, peasants, urban middle classes, intelligentsia, and non-Fascist political parties to fight fascism. It was not, to be sure, a formal call by the Soviet Union for a global alliance, nor a specific proposal for coping with Germany and Japan. Still, coupled with the Franco–Soviet treaty of alliance that was being negotiated at the same time, the Comintern congress marked the return of Russia to the international community as a supporter of order and peace, not as an isolated advocate of revolution and radicalism. Just as Japan and Germany had begun distancing themselves from the existing treaty frameworks, the Soviet Union was joining them from the opposite direction. But the Comintern thesis indicated an interest in adding to, if not replacing, the Washington and Versailles systems through the establishment of a global popular front which would have the effect of fortifying the former through the participation of the Soviet Union as well as colonial populations struggling against Fascist imperialism. Most important, the Soviet initiative provided some conceptual clarity to a world situation that had been characterized by uncertainty and contradictions. By defining international conditions in dichotomous terms, it sought to cut through the maze of conflicting ideas and policies simultaneously being pursued by the powers, and to urge them to align themselves against violators of the status quo.

The new Soviet approach implied a reversal of the cautious policy towards Japanese aggression which it had pursued after the Mukden incident. Moscow had not interfered with Japanese military operations in Manchuria, and in China it had continued to encourage Communist resistance to the Nationalist regime in Nanking. But the Soviet leadership clearly was worried about the implications of the strengthened Japanese position in the Asian-Pacific region, and began a process of preparing for a possible conflict with Japan. In December 1932 Moscow extended recognition to Nanking; in late 1933 the Soviet Union was recognized by the United States; and in 1934 the Soviet Union entered the League of Nations. In the meantime, while Moscow went through with its sale of the Chinese Eastern Railway to Japan – a formal agreement was signed in Tokyo in February 1934 – it began an active programme of strengthening its defences in the Asian-Pacific region. Along the Manchurian–Siberian border airfields were constructed and four-engine bombers placed there; trenches were dug and scaffolds built; and the Pacific fleet was reinforced by submarines. The second five-year plan, started in 1933, emphasized the building of factories and urban communities in eastern Siberia.[35] All these steps were watched closely by the Japanese, and instances of border collision steadily increased. The Comintern thesis against fascism and imperialism did not mean that the Soviet high command expected a war with Japan or Germany in the near future, but it apparently judged that identifying these countries as the main threat to peace would persuade enough other capitalist countries to take note of the Soviet Union's potential value as an ally and to prod them to take measures against the Fascists.

If these were the Soviet hopes, they were not fulfilled, at least not immediately. Neither London nor Washington was interested in so explicitly opposing themselves to Germany and Japan. For the time being, the two governments would continue to try to stabilize international affairs by working with, not against, these powers. This was revealed when, during the Italian invasion of Ethiopia (1935–37), both Britain and the United States co-operated with the League in imposing economic sanctions on the former, but refused to go further for fear that alienating Italy from the West would only encourage Germany and Japan to come to its defence, thus pitting the three Fascist states against the rest of the world. This the Anglo-American nations wanted to avoid, for it would deal a fatal blow to the treaty structure. For the same reason, they did not accept Moscow's call for an anti-Fascist coalition. Even France, despite its alliance with the Soviet Union and although a popular front government came into existence in 1936, was unwilling to punish Italy so severely that the latter might be pushed towards Germany. When, in March 1936, German troops occupied the Rhineland in violation of the Versailles and Locarno agreements, the Western powers stood by, preferring to believe that this was a minor modification of, and not a deadly challenge to, the international system. The same was true of the Spanish Civil War which broke out in July 1936. It provided a test case for the feasibility of a popular front, anti-Fascist strategy, but Britain, France, and the United States were satisfied with the establishment of a non-intervention committee, an organisation that would coalesce all interested countries in a joint pledge to desist from interference in Spain. The proposal was seen as a way of preserving some semblance of international order, but for that very reason its utter failure was to undermine the structure.

In the meantime, in East Asia Britain continued its effort to restabilize Chinese affairs through economic assistance within the framework of co-operation with Japan. The sending of an economic mission headed by Frederick Leith-Ross exemplified this approach. The mission, designed to contribute to those objectives, reached Japan in September 1935, just after the adjournment of the Comintern congress, and then moved to China, to remain there for several months. Leith-Ross's basic idea, for which he had the support of some high officials in London, was to co-operate with Japan in extending a loan to China, which would help bring order to China's financial situation at a time when it had been thrown into chaos by the American silver purchase policy.[36] In return for such aid, the Chinese might, he believed, be persuaded to extend at least *de facto* recognition to Manchukuo. This scheme, which he presented to Foreign Minister Hirota and other officials in Tokyo, was a bold attempt to confirm the framework of co-operative diplomacy while explicitly recognizing some significant modification of the Washington system. It was based on the assumption that Japan had not entirely left, nor had the intention of leaving, the system, and that China and other powers would be willing to accept the new status quo. Thus the Leith-Ross mission had more in common with Britain's ongoing European diplomacy, in which it was ready to come to terms with German and Italian revisionism so long as it could be kept within bounds, than with the Soviet-initiated call for an explicitly anti-Fascist coalition. Faced with such choices, there was no hesitation to opt for the first.

This was a big gamble, but one that provided Japan with an excellent opportunity to avoid international isolation. By agreeing to co-operate with Leith-Ross, Hirota could have encouraged Britain, and through it possibly the United States, to work with Japan, instead of following the Soviet lead in the strategy of the popular front. But Japanese policy did not favour such an approach. Instead, it focused on strengthening bilateral ties between Japan and China in order to stabilize their relations. One expression of this was Tokyo's decision to raise its Nanking legation to the status of embassy. A symbolic move, the decision was meant to convey to the Nationalist leadership Japan's interest in preserving the status quo. Another was Hirota's eagerness for a diplomatic settlement of outstanding differences between the two countries. Throughout 1935 negotiations were held in Tokyo and Nanking to see if the governments could not improve their relations on the basis of some fundamental principles. While nothing came of these negotiations, since there was an unbridgeable gap between Japan's insistence on Chinese acquiescence in Manchurian independence and China's demand for Japanese adherence to the treaties, they at least were meant as a gesture of goodwill on the part of Japan, indicating its intention not to encroach upon Chinese sovereignty south of the Great Wall, and its hope that China would reciprocate by not turning to the West for help. Under the circumstances, it was perhaps inevitable that Leith-Ross should have encountered only lukewarm responses from Japanese officials. His scheme for a regime of British–Japanese co-operation in China ran counter to the prevailing policy in Tokyo.

Even if Hirota had wanted to be more encouraging to the British mission, moreover, he would have run into strong opposition on the part of the Japanese military. It is true that the military did not speak with one voice. The army was seriously divided at this time over the issue of strategic preparedness. One group, represented by General Araki Sadao (war minister during 1933–35), insisted that everything be geared towards the goal of an effective military build-up against the Soviet Union. Extremely anti-Communist in ideology, this group was particularly alarmed over the implications of the new Comintern offensive and Soviet military reinforcements in Siberia, and argued that all considerations must be subordinated to preparing the nation militarily to fight a war with the Soviet Union which was expected to come within a few years, if not sooner. Another group, however, was more interested in 'total mobilization'. The idea was to mobilize the nation's political, economic, and intellectual resources, not only the armed forces, in preparation for war – war in general, not just a specific war with the Soviet Union. Strongly influenced by what they perceived to be the worldwide trend towards such mobilization, this group, centring around Nagata Tetsuzan (head of the military affairs bureau of the War Ministry till his assassination by an officer belonging to the first faction in August 1935), wanted to work together with civilian officials, scholars, and even businessmen to create a condition of effective preparedness. Compared with the first group, the latter was more 'scientific' and less ideologically anti-Communist. The struggle between the two factions reached a climax on 26 February 1936, when about 1,400 troops led by young army officers belonging to the first faction staged a coup, assassinating several cabinet ministers and seizing the War Ministry, the General Staff, and other governmental buildings. The uprising, however, was quickly suppressed and its ringleaders tried, paving the way for what was to be a long reign by the total mobilization group. Its control over military affairs ensured the army's undisputed influence, and it is this phenomenon which is often implied by the term 'Japanese fascism'.

Despite such factionalism, the two groups were essentially in agreement regarding Japanese policy towards China in the mid-1930s. This was because both recognized the importance of consolidating Japan's hold on Manchuria and Inner Mongolia and of avoiding a major crisis with the Nanking regime. To that extent military thinking was in line with the government's interest in a *rapprochement* with China. At the same time, however, the Japanese army on the continent, especially the so-called Tientsin Army (stationed in accordance with the Boxer protocol of 1901 to safeguard the communication links between Peking and the sea), was intent upon removing sources of anti-Japanese activities in north China by setting up separatist regimes in the area. They were not exactly replicas of Manchukuo, but they enjoyed a degree of autonomy south of the Great Wall, as a buffer between Manchuria and Kuomintang-controlled China. These moves were opposed by some military leaders, notably Ishiwara Kanji, one of the architects of the Mukden incident, who came to the view that in the interest of total mobilization Japan's position in north China should be retrenched and the irritation in Japanese–Chinese relations thereby reduced. Disagreement on the problem had the effect of halting Japan's advances in north China, but the military were virtually unanimous in rejecting the idea of Japanese co-operation with the Anglo-American nations in Asia, and so Hirota could have done little else than give a cool reception to the Leith-Ross mission.

Discouraged but determined to go through with part of his scheme, Leith-Ross worked energetically in China to help its economic rehabilitation and currency reform. Chinese officials were trying to restabilize the currency situation after it had been upset by America's silver purchase policy, and the only way to do so would be to demonetize silver and to issue a new currency not linked to the metal. In order to take such steps, it would of course be necessary for foreign banks and governments to accept the new currency and to surrender their silver reserves in exchange. Britain strongly backed up these measures on the recommendation of Leith-Ross, and thus by November 1935 the Chinese government had been able to initiate a currency reform, entailing the linking of the new *fapi* notes to the pound sterling. Here was an instance where Britain succeeded in strengthening its position in China without identifying itself with the Soviet-led popular front strategy, and without Japanese concurrence. In that sense, British successes did little to resuscitate the moribund Washington system, or to replace it with a radically new alternative.

American policy was much less active than Britain's. Washington was annoyed by Moscow's initiative to establish an anti-Fascist coalition and took little official cognizance of it. The United States government was not interested in joining the Soviet Union to punish Germany and Japan. Nor was it ready for a new diplomatic move of its own. Throughout most of 1935–36, President Roosevelt evinced no serious inclination to deal boldly with Asian affairs. He would not accept Japanese contentions for a new status quo in China or their demands for naval parity. When a formal disarmament conference opened in London in 1935, neither Tokyo's nor Washington's position had changed on this issue, and so the conference adjourned indefinitely in January 1936, indicating that the earlier naval agreements had now lapsed, and that the United States, Britain, and Japan would no longer be bound by them. Even so, the Roosevelt administration was not yet willing to restructure the basis of American policy in the Asian-Pacific region.

It was left up to Japan in 1936 to determine the future of the Washington system. The assassinations in February brought about a change in Tokyo's leadership, and Hirota was named prime minister. He remained as foreign minister till April, when a professional diplomat, Arita Hachirō, succeeded him. Together, Hirota and Arita did much to contribute to the progressive weakening and virtual demise of the Washington treaties. One of them, the naval agreement, had already been abrogated, but the Hirota cabinet was also willing to disregard, if not openly repudiate, the nine-power agreement. In March the Foreign Ministry decided that henceforth Japan would avoid making an explicit commitment to observing the treaty but would aim at its *de facto* nullification. While it would not be prudent to take unilateral steps to abrogate the treaty, the nation would no longer pay lip-service to it.[37] Thus by 1936 it could be said that as far as Japan was concerned, any pretence that it was still acting within the Washington framework was all but gone. Instead, Japan would define a new basis for its policies. It was no coincidence that the government and the military in Tokyo deliberated on policy alternatives in mid-1936, an effort that resulted in the drafting of two key documents, 'The fundamentals of national policy' and 'Foreign policy guidelines', in August. The documents, which were approved by cabinet ministers, called for three basic objectives: maintenance of the nation's position on the Asian continent, resistance to Soviet ambitions, and expansion into the South Seas.[38]

The idea of expanding into the South Seas – the European colonial areas of South-East Asia and the south-western Pacific – was as yet only a vague aspiration, but in 1936 it was written into a statement of national objectives because of two developments: the triumph of the total mobilization faction within the army, and the abrogation of the naval treaties. For the former, preparedness for a possible conflict with the Soviet Union so as to remove its threat remained the army's main concern, but the total mobilization school saw it as only a part of the massive national effort to establish Japanese power in Asia. To that extent it overlapped with the navy's emphasis on preparedness against the United States and Britain, now that the naval agreement had lapsed. The army and the navy disagreed as to which came first – war with the Soviet Union or with the Anglo-American powers – but for the first time the military adopted a defence policy which named the United States, the Soviet Union, China, and Britain as hypothetical enemies. It was not that Japan necessarily intended to go to war against all four simultaneously, although that was what would actually come to pass, but these guidelines indicated a willingness to make a clear break with the Washington framework and adopt an ambitious goal to establish Japan's superior position in the Asian-Pacific region.

As if to confirm such thinking, Tokyo entered into an anti-Comintern pact with Germany in November. Ostensibly a response to the Comintern's call for an anti-Fascist front, it provided for co-operation between the two countries against Communist subversion. But a secret protocol attached to the pact specifically referred to the Soviet Union and specified that in case one of the signatories became involved in a war with that country, the other would refrain from assisting the latter. Even more important, the anti-Comintern pact, signed just a month after the formation of the Berlin–Rome Axis (an agreement between Hitler and Mussolini to co-operate in European affairs), signalled Japan's readiness to associate itself with revisionist powers in Europe. That had significant implications not only for Japanese relations with the Soviet Union but also with the United States and Britain. Japan was definitely alienating itself from the Washington powers.

No sooner had Japan begun reorienting its foreign affairs, than an event took place that seriously challenged the basis of the new policy. That was the Sian incident of December 1936, involving the capture of Chiang Kai-shek in the vicinity of the ancient capital of Sian by the forces loyal to the former Manchurian warlord, Chang Hsüeh-liang. Chiang had been engaged in a campaign against the Communists, who had recently completed their 'long march' out of their south-eastern stronghold. The Communists, following the Comintern's new policy, were calling for an end to the civil war and the establishment of a united front against Japanese aggression. The Manchurian general had fallen under their influence, and he promised to release Chiang in return for the latter's pledge to accept the united front strategy. Chiang could have refused if the Communist minority had been the only faction insisting on a struggle against Japan, but by the end of 1936 Chinese opinion had become much more adamantly anti-Japanese. For one thing, economic reform measures, undertaken through the advice of the Leith-Ross mission, were achieving notable successes, with the new currency widely accepted as legal tender. Militarily, German advisers were laying the basis for a modern Chinese air force; at the beginning of 1937, their head official estimated that the military balance between China and Japan was steadily moving in the former's favour.[39] In the political realm, those who advocated an accommodation with Japan had been subjects of growing criticism, as evidenced by an attempted assassination of Wang Ching-wei in November 1935, and by the establishment of a separatist regime in Canton opposed to the government's policy towards Japan. Some prominent Nationalist leaders, most notably T. V. Soong, regained their influence in proportion as the Chinese economy showed signs of a revival. Even those close to Chiang Kai-shek were buoyed up by the success of Leith-Ross reforms, and questioned the wisdom or the need to maintain buffer regimes in north China. They argued that China would not be whole until those regimes were removed and brought under Nanking's control.

The Sian incident took place against this background, and it was a foregone conclusion that nationalistic opinion would force Chiang Kai-shek to accept Chang's terms for ending his captivity. The Nationalist leader returned to Nanking, pledging to end his anti-Communist campaign and to concentrate his resources on a policy of resistance to Japanese imperialism. After the turn of the year 1937, the Nationalist government and press began reflecting this new attitude, while the Communists responded by incorporating their military units into the Nationalist army. Both factions spoke the language of the united front, thus making China one of the first countries to subscribe to the Comintern's call for a global coalition.

Such developments forced the Japanese leaders to reconsider their policy objectives. Although they had just adopted a series of guidelines, the idea that Japan might find itself in war with China, the Soviet Union, America, and Britain had not yet become fixed as the definition of national strategy, and at the beginning of 1937 some civilian and military officials determined that the time had come to reorient Japan's China policy before it was too late. The General Staff, for instance, was willing to stop encouraging separatist movements in north China. The buffer governments in the area had not worked, and had only strengthened Chinese nationalism. It would not be possible for Japan to prevent Nationalist reunification of China proper unless it were prepared to go to war, and the General Staff judged such a war should be avoided.

The military's search for a new policy was welcomed by the civilian government. In January the Hirota cabinet fell and was replaced by that of Hayashi Senjūrō, former war minister. While it proved to be short-lived – it resigned at the end of May – the new prime minister's appointment of Satō Naotake as foreign minister was significant, for the latter, a professional diplomat who had till then been ambassador to France, was known to be an opponent of the Hirota–Arita approach. Whereas his predecessors had emphasized Japan's special position in China and the need to reduce Western influence from the continent, Satō strongly believed that Japan's salvation lay in an open international economic system in which the nation would promote industrialization and export trade. Japan's acute population problem should be solved, he had asserted, not by resettling a surplus population elsewhere, but by industrialization, which in turn necessitated an unlimited access to the world's raw materials and markets. An open economic system, moreover, depended on close co-operation and consultation among nations, and thus it was essential for Japan to promote a policy of international co-operation.[40]

These views were diametrically opposed to the neo-mercantilistic perceptions of the Japanese military and civilians who had promoted an autarkic empire, and the fact that a diplomat with such ideas should have been appointed foreign minister reflected the prevailing atmosphere of the time. There was a feeling that although Japan had achieved swift successes in Manchuria, that alone had not solved much. On the contrary, it had alienated Chinese opinion and isolated the country in the world. If Japan were unwilling to push the autarkic policy to its limits and risk total international ostracization, then a fresh approach might be desirable. Fully aware that the military, too, were eager for a new policy, Satō pushed for Japan's acceptance of a unified China under the Nationalists. He knew he could do little about Manchuria, but at least in China proper Japan should give up the policy of trying to detach the northern provinces. Such views were adopted as official policy at a meeting of the four cabinet ministers (ministers of foreign affairs, finance, war, and the navy) in April. They agreed that henceforth Japanese policy in north China should be primarily economic, no longer aiming at a political separation of the area from the rest of China.[41] Such a policy was a clear retreat from the grandiose scheme of 1936.

In the meantime, Satō was eager to resume a policy of economic interdependence. During his short tenure in office, he repeatedly and publicly expressed the theme that Japan's survival depended on 'restoration of international commercial freedom and the opening of resources'. World peace would be attained only if the powers recognized these principles and accorded Japan access to raw materials and markets. It so happened that just at this time the League of Nations was sponsoring a conference on access to raw materials. It had established a seventeen-nation committee including, it is interesting to note, Japan, and the committee held a total of three meetings in Geneva.[42] While little came of it immediately, many of the ideas expressed at these meetings would ultimately find their way into official doctrines promulgated by the United Nations during and after the Second World War. In other words, Satō's thinking was reflective of one strand of international opinion at that time, when governments were desperately trying to avoid war and to rescue the world from the morass of excessive economic nationalism.

Most unfortunately, the new diplomacy never had a chance to succeed. For one thing, the cabinet of General Hayashi was extremely unpopular as it contained no ministers representing any of the political parties. More seriously, its willingness to reorient China policy alarmed those in the army who refused to reconcile themselves to the new approach. They were convinced that the policy would merely play into China's hands and weaken Japan's position on the continent. To desist from promoting the separation of north China was particularly galling to the Tientsin Army that had been behind the scheme to set up buffer regimes. Its officers were convinced that if the trends in Chinese politics and Japanese policy continued, the nation would sooner or later be compelled to give up its special position in north China, and possibly even Manchuria. For them, there was only one plausible response: to resist Nationalist revanchism and to try to strengthen Japan's hold on north China.

Given such thinking on the part of the Tientsin Army, it should have been incumbent on Tokyo's civilian and military leaders to promote with vigour their new approach to China. Perhaps if the Hayashi cabinet had stayed in power, or if Foreign Minister Satō had remained in office, the situation might have been different. But Hayashi resigned in June, and Prince Konoe Fumimaro was appointed prime minister. This proved to be a fatal choice. He had been president of the House of Peers, and was best known as an ideologue of Japanese revisionism. He had consistently argued, even during the 1920s, that the League covenant, the nine-power treaty, and the pact of Paris had all defined an international system on the basis of the status quo, which tended to freeze national boundaries and, more important, did nothing to alter the fundamentally inequitable distribution of natural resources. Richly endowed nations such as the United States and the British empire had every reason to support the status quo, but for a country like Japan it spelled perpetual poverty and injustice. 'We must overcome the principles of peace based on the maintenance of the status quo', Konoe had written, 'and work out new principles of international peace from our own perspective.' Whereas officials like Satō believed that the problem of the unequal distribution of resources could best be dealt with through multilateral trade and industrialization, for Konoe something more fundamental was needed. Thus he wholeheartedly supported military action in Manchuria as a necessary step towards making available the area's rich resources to Japan.[43]

The assumption of office by such an imperialist, coming just at a time when Japan was trying to reorient its China policy, was extremely significant. Opponents of the Hayashi–Satō approach must have been encouraged by Konoe's coming to power, and by his statement as prime minister that there was in the world a conflict between 'have' and 'have-not' nations, and that international justice ultimately required redistribution of the globe's resources and land. Although such a goal was unobtainable for the present, Japan, as a 'have-not' country, must secure for itself 'the right of survival'. In the absence of an overall international system of justice, Japan's continental policy was fully justified. Such a statement, combined with Konoe's appointment of Hirota as foreign minister, virtually nullified the effect of the Hayashi cabinet's new China policy; Hirota, as will be recalled, had, both as foreign minister and prime minister, pushed for forging close bilateral ties between Japan and China in order to reduce Western influence on the continent. The return to the Foreign Ministry of such an official was extremely inauspicious for an improved relationship between Japan and China. Konoe and Hirota, perhaps more than any other civilians, were to confirm Japan's tragic isolation in world affairs.

REFERENCES AND NOTES

1. See Akira Iriye, *After Imperialism: The Search for a New Order in the Far East, 1921–1931* (Cambridge, Mass. 1965).
2. See Lloyd E. Eastman, *The Abortive Revolution: China under Nationalist Rule, 1927–1937* (Cambridge, Mass. 1964).
3. For a recent survey of the background of the 1931 crisis, see Akira Iriye, 'Japanese aggression and China's international position', *Cambridge History of China*, vol. 13 (Cambridge 1986).
4. On the impact of the world economic crisis on Japanese policy and politics, see Iriye, *After Imperialism*, Ch. 9.
5. Ibid., pp. 284–5.
6. Usui Katsumi, *Manshū jihen* (The Manchurian incident; Tokyo 1974) p. 24.
7. Ibid., pp. 41–5.
8. Ibid., pp. 48–9.
9. Ikei Masaru, '1930-nendai no mass media' (Mass media in the 1930s) in Miwa Kimitada (ed.), *Saikō Taiheiyō sensō zen'ya* (The prelude to the Pacific war reconsidered; Tokyo 1981), p. 179.
10. See Miles Fletcher, *The Search for a New Order: Intellectuals and Fascism in Prewar Japan* (Chapel Hill 1982).
11. Usui, *Manshū jihen*, p. 55.
12. Ibid., p. 71.

13. *Chung-hua Min-kuochung-yao chih-liao ch'u-pien: tui-Ju kang-chan shih-chi* (Important historical documents of the Chinese republic: the period of the anti-Japanese war; Taipei n.d.), 1.1: 262–85.
14. Ibid., p. 277.
15. Ibid., pp. 282–3.
16. Foreign Ministry, *Nis-So kōshō-shi* (History of Japanese–Soviet negotiations; Tokyo 1942), p. 239.
17. Usui Katsumi, 'Alternative paths: Konoe Fumimaro and Satō Naotake' (unpublished essay, 1985).
18. Justus D. Doenecke, *When the Wicked Rise: American Opinion-Makers and the Manchurian Crisis of 1931–1933* (Lewisburg, Pa. 1984), p. 34.
19. Usui, *Manshū jihen*, p. 127.
20. *Nihon gaikō bunsho* (Japanese diplomatic documents): *Manshū jihen* (the Manchurian incident; Tokyo 1979), 2.2: 12–13.
21. Ibid., p. 14.
22. Usui, *Manshū jihen*, p. 183.
23. Usui, 'Alternative paths'.
24. *Chung-hua Min-kuo*, 1.1: 431–42.
25. Shinobu Seizaburō, (ed.), *Nihon gaikō-shi* (A history of Japanese diplomacy; Tokyo 1974), 2: 384.
26. *Nis-So kōshō-shi*, pp. 241–4, 286–91.
27. *Chung-hua Min-kuo*, 1.1: 644, 651–2.
28. Hosoya Chihiro *et al.* (eds), *Nichi-Bei kankeishi* (A history of Japanese–American relations; Tokyo 1971), 1: 122–4.
29. Ibid., 2: 111.
30. Stephen Lyon Endicott, *Diplomacy and Enterprise: British China Policy, 1933–37* (Vancouver 1975), p. 35.
31. John P. Fox, *Germany and the Far Eastern Crisis, 1931–1938* (Oxford 1982), pp. 38–53. See also William C. Kirby, *Germany and Republican China* (Stanford 1984), Ch. 5.
32. Endicott, *Diplomacy*, p. 72.
33. Dorothy Borg and Shumpei Okamoto (eds), *Pearl Harbor as History: Japanese–American Relations, 1931–1941* (New York 1973), pp. 201–10.
34. Eastman, *Abortive Revolution*, p. 189.
35. Hayashi Saburō, *Kantōgun to Kyokutō Sorengun* (The Kwantung Army and the Soviet Far Eastern Army; Tokyo 1974), pp. 62–74.
36. Endicott, *Diplomacy*, pp. 103–10.
37. Usui, 'Alternative paths'.
38. *Gendaishi shiryō* (Documents on contemporary history; Tokyo 1964), 8: 354–62.
39. Fox, *Germany*, p. 211.
40. For an assessment of Satō's foreign policy, see Kurihara Ken *et al.*, *Satō Naotake no menboku* (The real worth of Satō Naotake; Tokyo 1981).
41. Shinobu, *Nihon gaikō-shi*, 2: 410–11.
42. Usui, 'Alternative paths'.
43. Ibid.

Chapter 2

JAPAN ISOLATED

The outbreak of war between China and Japan in July 1937 came at a critical moment in the orientation of Japanese policy. For some months civilian officials and military leaders had been divided between those who wanted to return to some modified version of the Washington system and those who preferred to push for an alternative – albeit loosely defined – order of Asian-Pacific affairs. Chinese–Japanese skirmishes outside of Peking on 7 July added fuel to the debate, and the internal discord continued until the government decided on seeking a 'new order in East Asia' by expanding the hostilities. Such action compelled other countries to take a stand, to redefine once again their respective positions not only towards the war but towards the whole issue of Asian-Pacific order. Unless they opted to adopt a policy of indifference and passivity, which became more and more untenable because of the increasing gravity of the European situation, they would either have to intervene by force in order to check Japanese aggression in China, or they could try to reason with the belligerents, including the aggressors, to persuade them to put an end to the fighting and to re-establish order and stability. This latter approach, the equivalent of the 'appeasement' strategy pursued energetically in Europe, was, however, never seriously tried in Asia. Instead, the Western powers and the Soviet Union were willing, for at least two years after July 1937, to consider collective and individual measures short of war to punish Japan and assist China. The result was that by September 1939, when a European war broke out, Japan found itself more isolated than ever, even more so than Germany. Why the West was prepared to appease Germany but not Japan is an interesting question, one that is ultimately linked to the issue of the survival of the Washington system.

JAPANESE AGGRESSION IN CHINA

On the night of 7 July 1937, a Japanese company engaging in night manoeuvres was fired at near the Marco Polo bridge in Peking. Seeing it as a premeditated attack by Chinese soldiers belonging to General Sung Che-yüan's 'autonomous' regime, the Japanese army counter-attacked, pursuing them to their barracks and killing some of them. This was an isolated shooting incident and could have been contained if Tokyo and Nanking had early on let the local commanders work out a settlement. The fact that they failed to do so, and that the incident led to full-scale fighting that was to last eight years, can only be explained in the context of developing world affairs.

At first the Japanese cabinet under Prime Minister Konoe Fumimaro adopted a policy of preventing the extension of hostilities. Neither he nor the army supreme command had anticipated such an incident or been prepared for a fresh war with China. At the same time, however, some civilian officials, politicians, business men, and journalists began clamouring for punitive action. They had been frustrated over trends in national politics as their influences had waned, and they seized on the Marco Polo bridge incident to embarrass the national leadership by attacking its indifference to humiliating developments in north China. For them, the 7 July incident appeared to be one more instance of China's growing confidence and arrogance, supported by Western powers, and Japan's retreat. Although public opinion was by no means the only factor, Konoe felt driven by it to do something more than starting local negotiations for settling the incident. After all, he himself had encouraged revisionist thinking and justified Japanese control over China's resources and called for an end to the global status quo defined by the 'have' powers. Thus he supported the army's contingency plan to dispatch three divisions from Japan to the area of the incident. The plan was approved by the cabinet on 11 July, the very same day that a cease-fire was worked out by representatives of the Tientsin Army and the 'autonomous' Peking regime.

Nanking, however, refused to endorse these negotiations and forbade Sung to conclude any settlement. Simultaneously, Chiang Kai-shek appealed to the signatories of the nine-power treaty for help. In taking such action, the Nationalist leader, too, was responding to domestic opinion that had become noticeably more open in assaulting Japanese imperialism after the Sian incident. Had he accepted an agreement between the Japanese army and the buffer government, he would have been accused of betraying the spirit of Sian; already on the day after the Marco Polo bridge incident, the Communists had published an appeal to all Chinese 'to resist the new invasion by Japanese aggressors'. Chiang must have believed that, in comparison with the situation in 1931, China was in better shape, politically, militarily, and economically, and also that Japan's position in the world was more isolated. In the intervening years, not only had Germany and Britain rendered active assistance to China, but the Soviet Union had recognized the Nanking government, and the United States had refused to accept the changes Japan had brought about in Manchuria. These powers were, to be sure, divided in Europe, but at the same time they appeared anxious to prevent a serious breach in their relations, as seen in their agreement, however superficial, not to intervene in the Spanish Civil War. All such considerations led Chiang to issue a public statement on 17 July, calling on the Chinese people to resist Japanese encroachment to the bitter end. He ordered the dispatch of Nanking forces to north China, into the areas that had been demilitarized after the signing of the Tangku truce. That truce, more or less in effect for four years, was no longer valid. For the Nationalist leadership, here was clearly an opportunity to reassert its authority in the Peking region so as to emerge as the undisputed government for all of China (save Manchuria).[1]

The success of Chiang's bold strategy hinged on Japanese reaction as well as responses of the powers. He gambled that the Japanese would be unwilling to risk a military confrontation with Nanking's troops, and that the powers would exert pressure on Japan to retreat. Here the Chinese leader miscalculated, at least in the short run. His calls for action emboldened those in Japan who were advocating stronger measures to demonstrate the nation's determination to uphold its position on the continent. On 26 July, the General Staff, with Konoe's endorsement, ordered the implementation of the contingency plan to send three divisions to China. Soon they were joining forces with troops already in north China to launch a major offensive, and by the end of the month they were in control of the Peking–Tientsin region. Fighting spread to Shanghai in August when a Japanese sailor was attacked and killed by a Chinese security officer. From then on, the war continued to escalate, with both sides mobilizing more troops for combat and calling on their respective nationals to be prepared for a full-scale conflict. The fighting was not called a war, since both Tokyo and Nanking saw advantages in not doing so, particularly in dealing with other nations from which the two countries sought military necessities. But calling it an 'incident' rather than a war did not prevent Japanese and Chinese forces from engaging in fierce combat. At the same time, as will be noted, for the Japanese the war with China contained many ambiguities, and their failure to resolve them was an important aspect of Japan's deteriorating position in world affairs.

In the short run, at any rate, Chiang miscalculated, as his troops were forced to retreat from north China. In the meantime, he did not immediately get the kind of support that he counted on from the powers. Germany, to be sure, was actively involved because of the presence of many military advisers. The Chinese were hopeful that Germany would continue to deliver arms to, and retain military advisers in, China and otherwise help the country with its struggle against Japan. Chiang Kai-shek presumably knew the optimistic view of General Alexander von Falkenhausen, chief of the German advisory group in China, that with the advice of the Germans (totalling over seventy), Chinese forces would be able to drive 'the Japanese over the Great Wall'. But there was a limit beyond which Germany would not wish to go. German caution was in part motivated by the fear of Soviet involvement. If Germany dragged its feet regarding Chinese requests, Nanking might turn to the Soviet Union for help, which would alarm the Japanese and lead them to call on Berlin to invoke the anti-Comintern pact for a joint response. But too much German assistance to China might alienate Japan and weaken the pact. The best way out of the predicament was to maintain neutrality in the war and to promote a peaceful solution of the conflict. That led to the idea of German mediation, which top officials in Berlin began to entertain in late August.[2] This was much less than the Chinese had hoped to obtain from Germany.

The Soviet leadership had its own reasons for involvement in the Chinese–Japanese conflict. The spirit of the popular front strategy would have dictated that the Soviet Union take some action to help China's struggle against Japanese aggression. At the same time, however, Moscow was wary of becoming drawn into the conflict while other countries sat by. A bilateral programme of assistance to China might be viewed by Japan as tantamount to a declaration of war for which the Soviet Union was unprepared. (Joseph Stalin's purges were in full swing at that time.) Under the circumstances, Maxim Litvinov, foreign minister, preferred collective action, in co-operation with the United States, Britain, and France.[3] That would in effect establish a global popular front and prevent Soviet isolation. But during the first phase of the war none of the Western democracies was willing to go beyond deploring the Asian hostilities. Typical was Secretary of State Cordell Hull's statement on 16 July, expressing American support for peaceful settlement of international conflicts. Significantly, the United States sent the message to all the governments in the world, indicating a revived interest in international co-operation, but the gesture did not lead to specific action towards the Chinese–Japanese War. Washington was reluctant to endorse London's proposal at this time for a joint mediation. The most that the United States would do was to desist from applying the Neutrality Act to the Asian war. By not calling it a war, the administration could acquiesce in shipments of goods, including arms, to both combatants, some of which would presumably reach China. This was a haphazard way of assisting it, and even such a modest step was denounced by isolationist and peace groups in America as too provocative.[4]

The Chinese well recognized such passivity on the part of the Western governments and pressed the Soviet Union for support, reasoning that, apart from Germany, Russia was the country most likely to come to China's assistance. In mid-August Chiang Kai-shek forwarded a request to Moscow for 350 planes, 200 tanks, and 236 heavy guns.[5] He was obviously counting on such shipments both to supplement and to balance German supplies. The Soviet Union agreed to send about half of the requested items, but first wanted a non-aggression pact with China; the latter would have to pledge not to use such armaments against Russia. Although a small step, Soviet willingness to become at least indirectly involved in the Chinese–Japanese War was extremely significant, for it served to present Japan with a serious dilemma as to its strategy following the military successes of July and August. For the Japanese were finding it rather difficult to define clearly their war objectives. They had not actively solicited the war, and their stated objective on the eve of the war had been the promotion of 'Japanese–Manchukuo–Chinese co-operation' in combating communism and reducing Western influence. But how could such an objective be achieved if the hostilities continued and aroused an intense anti-Japanese feeling among the Chinese people? How could they be persuaded to work with Japan in fighting Soviet and Western influence when they would surely turn to these countries for help? What was the point of fighting China if it drained resources away from military preparedness against other countries, the goal that Japan's strategists had emphasized, particularly since 1936? More specifically, where and how should the war be ended, and how could a satisfactory arrangement be made so as to restore some sense of stability in Chinese–Japanese relations?

These were issues that Japan's leaders should have pondered before expanding hostilities on the continent beyond Peking, Tientsin, and Shanghai. Instead, they started talking of a prolonged conflict. In early September, for instance, Prime Minister Konoe issued a statement on 'spiritual mobilization', calling on his nation to be united for a long and hard struggle ahead. The 'incident', he said, had resulted from China's consistent disregard of Japan's legitimate rights and interests, and thus Japanese soldiers had been obliged to 'punish' the Chinese. The country's goal remained the same, however: 'to stabilize Asia on the basis of co-operation between the two countries'. Such stability would contribute to world peace. But it could only be achieved if China ceased its anti-Japanese activities and pledged to respect Japanese rights. Konoe stopped short of asserting that Japan was aiming at establishing a regime of Chinese–Japanese 'co-operation' as an alternative to the existing international system, but the idea was behind Tokyo's refusal to let the League of Nations discuss the war. When, on 13 September, China formally appealed to the League to sanction Japan for its violation of the covenant, the nine-power treaty, and the pact of Paris, the Japanese Foreign Ministry responded by asserting that military action in China was merely intended to compel the latter to stop its anti-Japanese policies and was therefore justifiable in the name of justice, humanism, and self-defence. Therefore, Japan would insist on dealing with the crisis bilaterally with China, rejecting League interference.

Thus the situation was analogous to that prevailing after the outbreak of the Mukden incident. As in 1931, the Japanese six years later were determined to prevent third-power intervention and to localize the dispute. In contrast to the earlier crisis, however, in 1937 Japan was less successful in either objective. Not only was the League of Nations not deterred by Japanese objections from convening an advisory committee of twenty-three nations – the first meeting took place on 29 September – but the Soviet Union and Germany had been actively involved in the conflict. The top military in Tokyo were extremely concerned with possible Soviet intervention and wanted to bring the fighting to a stop. On 1 October, the four cabinet ministers agreed that Japan should 'conclude the incident as speedily as possible' through diplomatic means.[6] Ironically, in seeking an end to the hostilities Japanese officials chose to turn to Germany as mediator, thus confessing the impossibility of dealing directly with the Chinese. But German mediation seemed to make sense in view of that country's interest in maintaining friendly relations with both China and Japan. Moreover, Germany refused to participate in the advisory committee being set up by the League, so that for Japan to turn to Berlin for mediation would serve to circumvent the international body. The upshot was that the German ambassador in Nanking, Oskar P. Trautmann, acted as an intermediary between Japanese and Chinese officials to work out mutually acceptable conditions for a cease-fire. He moved energetically throughout October and early November. The situation became complicated, however, since in addition to the League advisory committee, a meeting of the signatories of the nine-power treaty was also being held. This, requested by China in view of Japan's violation of the treaty, and supported by the League and the United States, convened in Brussels just as Trautmann was stepping up his efforts.

The United States had already participated in the League's advisory committee, and when, on 6 October, the Assembly denounced Japan and called for a nine-power conference, the Roosevelt administration quickly concurred, joining in the condemnation of Japan's violation of the peace and of Chinese independence. Moreover, on just the preceding day, Roosevelt had delivered an important speech in Chicago – the 'quarantine address' – indicating America's interest in acting together with other countries to 'quarantine' those that were 'creating a state of international anarchy and instability'. He did not specify which these countries were, but it was clear to his listeners at home and abroad that he had in mind Germany, Italy, and Japan. (He had privately branded them 'bandit nations', in view of what Germany had done in Spain, Italy in Ethiopia, and Japan in China.) Although vague, it was not difficult to see the implications of the speech. The United States, after several years of relative passivity and lack of interest in identifying with an international structure, was once again showing signs of willingness to act together with other nations to 'preserve peace'. Isolation or neutrality, the president said, was no longer the answer. Instead, 'peace-loving nations must make a concerted effort' to 'quarantine . . . the epidemic of world lawlessness'. To give some specificity to the idea, Roosevelt considered the possibility of inviting other governments to join him in establishing some general agreements on the world's political, economic, and security problems. Nothing came of the scheme as Secretary of State Cordell Hull thought it was premature, but both agreed that the United States should participate in the nine-power conference in Brussels.

Thus, just at the time when the Japanese were turning to Germany to help them bring the Chinese war to a close, they learned that the League and the nine-power treaty were still very much alive, both supported by the United States. Under such pressures, German mediation might still have served to prevent the war from expanding and restore some stability to the region. In fact, on 2 November, Foreign Minister Hirota Kōki intimated Japan's acceptable peace terms to German officials for transmission to the Chinese, and these terms might have provided a basis for negotiation: an autonomous Inner Mongolia, a demilitarized zone in north China to be administered by Nanking through a pro-Japanese official, cessation of anti-Japanese activities, co-operation in fighting communism. While these terms clearly infringed upon Chinese sovereignty and were therefore a violation of the nine-power treaty, some sort of cease-fire on that basis might have been viewed as a step towards restabilization. Chiang Kai-shek, however, was not persuaded. He adamantly refused to discuss terms unless Japan first restored the status quo. Besides, he told German mediators, the Western powers meeting in Brussels 'had the intention . . . to work for peace on the basis of the Washington Treaty'.[7] China would rather seek its salvation through the treaty, which had the support of the United States and Britain, rather than through German mediation which might work to the advantage of Japan. The fact that on 6 November Italy joined the anti-Comintern pact must have impressed upon the Chinese that they should not play into the hands of the three Fascist states, particularly when they had just been denounced by President Roosevelt. Here again was an interesting conjunction of movements. The division of the world between aggressive Fascist countries and those upholding the peace as defined by the treaties was becoming more pronounced than ever. China clearly identified with, and wanted to take advantage of, the emerging perception, and seek its salvation within an international framework.

The division, however, was far from rigid. For one thing, the conferees in Brussels failed to adopt an effective programme to sanction Japan. Britain and France, to be sure, were eager for some collective action that involved the United States. Officials in London and Paris reasoned that if the major Western powers, possibly including the Soviet Union, could co-operate in responding to Japanese aggression, that would set a precedent for similar action in Europe. Since the United States had tended to stand aloof from European questions, the Brussels meeting was a test case to see if it was ready to resume a more active policy of international co-operation. In the event, the Roosevelt administration was not ready. The president believed that the American people would not support coercive measures against Japan; they would view such a step as an implementation of the quarantine address, envisaging many similar acts in the future. The country was in no mood for such activism, Roosevelt judged, and he vetoed the suggestions made at Brussels for an economic sanction against Japan. The Brussels conference adjourned on 24 November with only a mild statement of support for China. Disappointed by the failure of the powers to act together, Chiang Kai-shek finally agreed to German mediation. By then, however, the military situation was undergoing drastic change.

The Japanese could have seized the opportunity, when the nine-power conference did not achieve the results China had hoped for, to take speedy steps to conclude the fighting. Had they done so, they might still have been able to return to the fold and avoid international ostracization. Trautmann was as eager as ever to bring the two sides together. Unfortunately, the end of the Brussels conference coincided with a Japanese landing at Hangchow Bay, just south of Shanghai, to attack Chinese forces in that city from the rear. The strategy was a success, forcing them to withdraw *en masse* and retreat towards Nanking. On 1 December a decision was made to pursue them to the capital. Sensing danger, Nationalist authorities left the city, and there was only sporadic fighting as Nanking fell to Japanese soldiers on 13 December. During the following several days they rounded up Chinese soldiers, guerillas, and civilians, killing a large number of them (as many as 200,000, according to contemporary Chinese accounts).[8] The 'rape of Nanking' would make it all but impossible for Japan to be still accepted as a respectable member of the international community, although efforts would continue to be made to persuade the country to desist from further destabilizing the situation in Asia.

The day before Nanking fell, several Japanese military planes attacked a United States navy gunboat, *Panay*, as it was loading American diplomats and residents to evacuate them to Shanghai. It capsized, with a loss of lives and property. Later investigations established that the pilots of the Japanese planes saw the American flag flying on the ship but suspected it was carrying Chinese military personnel and weapons. Without waiting for orders, the pilots fired at the ship and realized only later the graveness of the act. The *Panay* incident sent shockwaves across both sides of the Pacific, for it could lead to a serious crisis between Japan and the United States. It symbolized Japan's disregard of American treaty rights and, coupled with the sack of Nanking, threatened to isolate Japan completely in the world.

Tokyo responded to these events in and around the Chinese capital in two separate ways: a quick settlement of the *Panay* crisis, but the stiffening of terms for peace with China. The former was really the only choice the country had, unprepared as it was for a rupture of relations with the United States. As soon as the news of the *Panay* sinking reached Tokyo, Foreign Minister Hirota received the American ambassador, Joseph C. Grew, and expressed his regret over the incident. It took less than two weeks for the Japanese government to settle the event to Washington's satisfaction; the terms included an apology and indemnity payments to the victims' families. Such quick action, rather uncharacteristic of Japan, was a measure of the extent to which it was willing to go to avoid conflict with a Western power.

Unfortunately, such sensitivity was not applied to Japan's dealings with China. The fall of Nanking – it was celebrated by lantern parades in the streets of Tokyo on the very day that Hirota and Grew worked furiously to minimize the damage done by the *Panay* affair – emboldened the Konoe cabinet to revise the terms of peace that had been transmitted earlier to the Chinese. Chiang Kai-shek, it will be recalled, had rejected them, hoping that the Western powers would render China timely support at Brussels. Now, however, he was willing to accept most of those terms, whereas Tokyo demanded more. As revealed to the German ambassador in Japan, the latter would call for the establishment of demilitarized zones and regimes in northern and central China, an indemnity payment by China, and recognition of Manchukuo. Foreign Minister Hirota also intimated that it would be desirable if China terminated the non-aggression pact with the Soviet Union and instead joined the anti-Comintern pact. In other words, Japan would bring China under its virtual control. China was to accept these harsh terms by the end of December. Clearly, there was no way that the Nationalist leadership would do so.

These events put Germany in a predicament, for it was becoming more and more difficult to mediate between the two combatants and thus to preserve its own position in Asia. Sooner or later Berlin would be compelled to choose between China and Japan. But no decision had yet been made; Hitler had, at a high-level conference held in early November, intimated his plans to conquer Austria and Czechoslovakia, in 1938 if feasible but by 1943–45 at the latest. However, such action would call for stabilizing the situation in Asia, and he was initially in no mood to alter what he regarded as a sensible orientation of German policy in the area. Still, pressures were mounting among his advisers for drawing the nation closer to Japan, a redefinition of policy that would come in early 1938.

Equally significant were signs of change in American policy at the end of 1937. To be sure, the quarantine speech had not resulted in drastic action to punish Japan, nor had Washington favoured trade sanctions at Brussels. However, in the wake of the rape of Nanking and the *Panay* incident, President Roosevelt became interested in the idea of initiating staff talks by American and British naval officers. Britain had suggested such a step as a way of preparing for possible Anglo-American collaboration against the Japanese navy in the Asian-Pacific region. The sinking of the *Panay* made Roosevelt receptive, for he realized that the United States might become drawn into the Asian conflict even against its will. Deeply outraged by the events of mid-December, the president at one point even toyed with the idea of establishing a joint naval blockade of Japan; American and British cruisers would position themselves astride the western Pacific, to contain the Japanese navy and prevent its aggressive action in the direction of the Philippines or Singapore.[9] Nothing came of the scheme, as London was not willing to take so drastic a step which could easily lead to war. But the fact that Roosevelt began thinking of such strategic co-operation was significant, presaging what would eventuate in a full-fledged alliance three years later. In the meantime, the president finally authorized the initiation of staff conversations and sent Captain Royal E. Ingersoll, director of plans for the United States navy, to London to exchange information with his British counterpart regarding signalling, codes, and night manœuvres. Ingersoll arrived in London on the last day of the year 1937, as if to suggest that something momentous was about to happen.

GERMANY'S DECISION TO ASSIST JAPAN

The beginning of 1938 was a crucial moment in the history of Asian-Pacific affairs. First, Germany transformed its policy and now explicitly sided with Japan, forsaking its five-year-old involvement in China. Second, the Japanese government declared its policy of no longer recognizing the Chiang Kai-shek government as representing China and began making plans for establishing a pro-Japanese regime. Third, Captain Ingersoll carried out his secret mission in London, marking the start of strategic co-ordination between the American and British navies. Fourth, strident criticism of Japan began appearing in the Soviet press and indicated a willingness to go beyond the existing policy of modest aid to China in checking Japanese power. All these developments, taken together, implied the internationalization of the Chinese–Japanese War. Hitherto Japan had been condemned by the League and at Brussels, but there had been little overt involvement by other powers in the war. The pattern was about to shift.

Hitler's decision to reverse the long-standing policy of maintaining good relations both with China and with Japan, in favour of the explicit support of the latter, was related to the strategic plans outlined at the November 1937 conference, alluded to above. In order to carry out the premeditated conquest of Austria and Czechoslovakia, it would make sense to forestall British and Soviet intervention, an objective which in turn could be facilitated if Japan were successful in China and expanded its power elsewhere in Asia. Such a development, it was hoped, would tie Britain and the Soviet Union down in the region, immobilizing them in Europe. By January 1938, no immediate peace between China and Japan appeared likely; the Chinese were adamantly refusing to accept Japan's latest terms, whereas the latter would not consider going back to its November proposal. Some, notably Ambassador Herbert von Dirksen in Tokyo, were convinced that Japan was going to win the war and argued that Germany should take advantage of the situation by forging close ties with it. Nazi ideologues, such as Joachim von Ribbentrop, had long advocated such a step. As he wrote, 'strengthening our friendship with Italy and Japan and in addition winning over all countries whose interests conform directly or indirectly with ours' was an important step for preparing the nation for war against Britain and the Soviet Union.[10] Advocates of a *rapprochement* with Japan were aware that it would involve recognition of Manchukuo and the withdrawal of military advisers from China. The impressive German accomplishments in China during the 1933–37 period would be nullified. Yet the risk appeared worth taking in view of the apparent failure of the Nationalists to resist Japanese aggression. These ideas finally won over Hitler who, having hesitated for several months, revealed his agreement with them when he appointed von Ribbentrop foreign minister on 4 February. Sixteen days later, Hitler made the historic Reichstag speech in which he praised Japan for fighting communism and indicated that Germany would soon recognize Manchukuo.

Although formal recognition did not come till May, the decision for it was warmly welcomed by the Japanese, who had found their country more and more isolated after July 1937. Few of them, to be sure, were considering a formal alliance with Germany. When von Ribbentrop, just before being appointed foreign minister, approached Ōshima Hiroshi, Japanese military attaché in Berlin, and suggested that the two countries 'might be brought closer together by means of a treaty or otherwise', the latter considered the proposal so sensitive that he withheld the information from Ambassador Tōgō Shigenori. Still, the idea of transforming the anti-Comintern pact with Germany into closer ties was gaining popularity in some circles in Tokyo. Among civilian officials in the Foreign Ministry, there emerged at this time what would later be known as an 'Axis faction', led by Shiratori Toshio, recently recalled as ambassador to Sweden and formerly head of the information bureau. This group maintained close contact with the army, whose leaders were quite receptive to the German overtures. Both were eager for a drastic reformulation of Japanese policy so as to identify the nation more explicitly with Fascist powers against the Western democracies as well as the Soviet Union. As Shiratori remarked at this time, these latter countries 'stood essentially on the same plane', as they were all based on materialism and individualism.[11] It was time, he and his civilian and army colleagues insisted, for the nation to join forces with other 'have-not' nations and rectify the existing injustices in international affairs. Despite such pleas, and although Ōshima began informal talks with von Ribbentrop in Berlin without the knowledge of Ambassador Tōgō, the Konoe cabinet was extremely cautious in responding to German overtures. It had just weathered the *Panay* crisis, and neither the prime minister nor the military high command wanted to take unalterable steps at that juncture to establish a foreign policy framework that was unambiguously opposed to the Washington powers. Berlin's new Asian policy tempted the Japanese leadership with such a possibility, but it was not yet ready to tie the country's destiny completely to Germany. After all, German relations with the democracies were still in flux, so that the consummation of a formal alliance between Germany and Japan might have the effect of a self-fulfilling prophesy, dividing the world into two camps. Despite his rhetorical support for the ideology of 'have not' nations, Konoe obviously recognized that implementation of such an ideology would antagonize the Western powers. On the other hand, he did little to regain their confidence, let alone friendly co-operation. Such indecisiveness and hesitation were to characterize his leadership till the very end. It could be argued, in retrospect, that he should either have tried to follow up the settlement of the *Panay* crisis by initiatives to improve Japanese relations with the United States and Britain with a view ultimately to restoring some framework of co-operation with them, or acted decisively to take advantage of the new German policy to formulate an alternative approach to foreign policy. He did neither.

In one area, however, Konoe was willing to define policy more resolutely. On 16 January, he issued a statement declaring that henceforth the Japanese government would not deal with the Nationalist government but 'look to the establishment and development of a new Chinese regime, adjust diplomatic relations with it, and co-operate with it in constructing a new, renovated China'. Such a policy meant the end of all mediatory attempts between the two governments, and Japan's decision to encourage the growth of anti-Nationalist and non-Nationalist forces in China. Diplomatic relations between Tokyo and Nanking – or, more correctly, Hankow, as the Chinese government had moved inland after the fall of the capital – were severed, and thus the Konoe statement was tantamount to a declaration of war. The prime minister took the drastic step because of the military successes in December and in response to pressures within and outside the government for a quick victory in China, which was believed unattainable so long as Chiang Kai-shek remained in power.

The repudiation of the existing government of China, which was the only internationally recognized regime, was a momentous step, not unlike the German and Italian rejection of the government in Madrid.

Unlike Spain, there was no Chinese equivalent of Francisco Franco, and the country was much more unified in opposition to Japanese aggression and atrocities. That the Japanese leaders should nevertheless have believed the new policy would work indicated their confidence that, with Germany withdrawing its support of China, and with other countries save perhaps the Soviet Union being reluctant openly to antagonize Japan, the Chinese would soon feel desperate and tire of the fighting. Some of their leaders, it was believed, would then decide to put an end to the devastation and chaos brought about by the war through a *rapprochement* with Japan, rather than hoping for more direct and effective assistance from other powers. Here the Japanese failed to reckon with the possibility that the 16 January statement would make it more difficult than ever for any Chinese to advocate an end to the anti-Japanese struggle; it would now be considered a treasonable offence inasmuch as Tokyo had explicitly repudiated the legitimate government of China. Japan's elusive quest for a Chinese Franco was to last for many more years and end in complete failure.

Chinese politics, in fact, made any *rapprochement* with Japan extremely unlikely. Chiang Kai-shek, driven to Hankow, was committed to the united front, but was trying hard to consolidate his power. The Nationalist Party was being reorganized, and Chiang would soon be named 'president', with Wang Ching-wei as 'vice president'. The two were political rivals, and Chiang's position depended in large measure on his persistence in an anti-Japanese stance. He was bitterly disappointed when Germany informed him of the decision to terminate its military assistance programmes, and he was not confident that China would be able to replace German with British or American support in the immediate future. In the meantime, the nation would have to turn to the Soviet Union for a continued flow of arms across the north-western frontier. Chiang was aware that such dependence could play into the hands of Japanese propagandists who were calling on the Chinese to repudiate their pro-Soviet leaders and join Japan in a joint struggle against communism. But he countered all such propaganda with the argument that any co-operation on Japanese terms was tantamount to Chinese enslavement, and sought to impress the Western nations with Japan's ultimate ambitions in the Asian-Pacific region. It is interesting to note that the Chinese leader frequently referred to the 'Tanaka memorandum', a document allegedly drafted in 1927, as evidence of Japan's intention of conquering the world. Although its authenticity was in doubt – it is now generally agreed to have been a fabrication – the document served to portray Japanese military action in China as but a prelude to turning northward and southward to control the whole of Asia, after which Japan would aim at subjugating the entire world. The only way to deter such ambitions would be for all nations in the world to recognize the threat and co-operate, in particular by coming to the aid of China. Given such thinking, it is not surprising that the Konoe statement only stiffened Chiang's, and through him his people's, resolve to resist Japan.[12]

Had he known of the Anglo-American staff conversations taking place in London in early 1938, Chiang would have felt his confidence in international support was vindicated. He, of course, did not know, but these conversations marked as decisive a turning-point in Asian-Pacific affairs as Hitler's decision to recognize Manchukuo. Both served to internationalize the Chinese–Japanese War. No formal strategic co-ordination emerged from the London conversations, but Captain Ingersoll, the American representative, had the satisfaction of meeting with top British officials, civilian as well as naval, and conferring with them about the two countries' shared interest in checking Japanese power in the Asian-Pacific region. They discussed President Roosevelt's idea of a joint Anglo-American blockade of Japan as well as general co-operative strategy in the Pacific. As if to buttress these talks, on 10 January the president ordered the transfer of major units of the United States fleet from the Atlantic to the Pacific. Such moves by Roosevelt indicated that the United States was finally willing to begin to apply the ideas of collective action that had been contained in the quarantine speech. Coming just at the juncture when Germany was reversing its Asian policy, the initiation of Anglo-American joint action in the Pacific ensured that the Chinese–Japanese War would not long remain a bilateral affair. It would be wrong, to be sure, to single out the Ingersoll mission or the shifting of the bulk of the United States fleet to the Pacific as marking a definite start of Anglo-American co-operation. Even as Ingersoll was winding up his talks in London, Prime Minister Neville Chamberlain was turning down President Roosevelt's proposal for bilateral initiatives for an international conference to discuss armament, trade, and other issues. Britain would like to co-operate with America in Asia, but in Europe it preferred to act on its own to stabilize conditions, particularly through the termination of the Italian–Ethiopian War. Such a stance was to lead to Chamberlain's 'appeasement' diplomacy, as will be discussed. Clearly, Britain and America were not acting in full accord, but the important point is that the two governments were beginning to recognize once again the value of bilateral co-operation in the Asian-Pacific region. Whether such co-operation would take the form of trying to resuscitate the Washington treaty structure or of defining something new remained to be seen.

APPEASEMENT

For a while after February 1938, appeasement emerged as the major theme of international affairs. At one level this was a response to

Germany's move to annex Austria (March) and part of Czechoslovakia (September). Rather than opposing such conquests, Britain and France, with the endorsement of the United States, would acquiesce in the new German boundaries. An implementation of the plans Hitler had outlined at the November 1937 meeting, the annexation of Austria and Czechoslovakia would be in clear violation of the Versailles settlement, although it could be, and was, argued that Germany was simply applying the Versailles principle of self-determination to central Europe. At least until the whole of Czechoslovakia, not just its ethnically German provinces (Sudetenland), was conquered, such an argument had some plausibility and could be seen as not exactly the death-knell of the Versailles system. That was how statesmen in Britain and France chose to view the developments in 1938. Their countries were militarily unprepared to meet the German challenge by force; for the immediate future, they would have to concentrate on military strengthening, and in the meantime acceptance of German expansion in central Europe would avert a war and give the democracies time to do so.

At another level, however, appeasement was much more than a passive acceptance of German-initiated *faits accomplis*. It was also an expression of the interest on the part of the Western nations in restabilizing international order by working with, rather than against, revisionist powers. This was an alternative both to war and to the popular front, and aimed at reintegrating Germany and other Fascist states into the world community. The result would be a modified Versailles system. Perhaps, European statesmen reasoned, the situation could be stabilized by bringing Germany, Italy, and also Fascist Spain into a mutually acceptable framework of international affairs. That would entail, on the side of the democracies, recognition of the German annexation of Austria and Sudetenland, the Italian conquest of Ethiopia, and the government of Generalissimo Franco in Spain. These amounted to accepting the recent developments and to trying to see if a new status quo might not be defined on that basis. But the Western powers would be willing to go much beyond such steps. Time and again throughout 1938, their leaders appealed to Hitler and Mussolini to come together for an international conference to consider jointly 'fundamental causes of war', as Chamberlain put it. The idea was to hold broad discussions on economic as well as political issues of the day so that the nations could identify causes of war and take steps to prevent its occurrence. The democracies were particularly interested in the economic dimension and believed no stable world order could be restored without an international effort to put an end to several years of chaos in trade, raw materials, foreign exchange, and related matters. In return for such overtures, the democracies would expect the Fascist states to reciprocate by affirming their adherence to the modified Versailles system.

Nor were European democratic leaders alone in such an effort. From the outset, President Roosevelt, Secretary of State Cordell Hull, Under-Secretary of State Sumner Welles, and other officials in Washington lent their support to the scheme. After all, as alluded to above, it was Roosevelt who in January toyed with the idea of holding an international conference on disarmament and trade issues, and Welles had proposed a similar idea in the previous autumn. Throughout the year, the president kept in close touch with world leaders through diplomatic dispatches and personal messages in order to put the developing European crisis in a global framework. Such initiatives were in sharp contrast to the earlier expressions of economic nationalism and reflected the sense that, nearly ten years after the start of the Depression, the United States was once again in a position to envisage a desirable international economic order. Germany, Italy, and Japan had begun to refer to themselves as 'have not' nations to justify their defiance of the treaties. Although these countries were far better endowed with resources (natural, financial, technological) than most others, at least in comparison with the United States, the British Commonwealth, or even China and the Soviet Union, they could complain of the lack of space, foodstuffs, raw materials, and domestic markets. The self-styled 'have not' nations, in any event, had resorted to regionalist policies to create autarkic structures, thus threatening to divide the world into economically semi-independent pan-regions. Such a situation might create a stability of its own; there might develop an equilibrium among pan-regions. In 1938, however, the prevailing view in Washington and London was that a world divided into large blocs would enhance, rather than reduce, chances of war. The reasoning here was essentially that which went back to the economic internationalism of the 1920s. Faith in multilateralism, which had been eclipsed by the need to deal with immediate economic issues at home, was gradually returning; at the very least, it came to influence top-level thinking on international affairs and underlay ideas about war and peace.

The idea that war was likely to be occasioned by economic causes was nothing new, but in 1938 it formed a basis of the appeasement strategy. It implied that some of the recent aggressions were understandable, if not excusable, in view of the world economic catastrophe, and that in order to prevent future aggression, the nations of the world would have to be prepared to cope with fundamental economic factors instead of merely responding to crises as they arose. There were few specific proposals at this time for reconstructing the economic order, but clearly it would take the form of reverting to the internationalism of the 1920s, another indication that the world order of that decade had not disappeared altogether. It is in some such sense that appeasement as it was applied in 1938 meant something more than an ignominious retreat in the face of Nazi aggression. It should be viewed as part of a larger phenomenon: an effort to revive, even if in modified form, a shared definition of international order on a basis other than that of the popular front or a Fascist coalition. These two alternatives were seen to be too divisive, whereas appeasement could, it was hoped, embrace most countries of the world, the way the internationalism of the 1920s had done.

What implications did this have for the Asian-Pacific region? For one thing, the kind of international economic order whose survival was being visualized would be incompatible with Japanese aggression and imperialism. If Japan were to participate in an international conference being proposed by Western leaders, it would certainly be told to give up its regionalist policy and return to a more open system like that of the 1920s. In return, the Japanese would be promised a place in the restored system, with the assurance that its needs for raw materials, food, and markets would be met. For the Chinese, such a development would mean a release from war and economic bondage, but they would want more than just a return to the formulations of the 1920s. They would insist on building upon the achievements of the 1930s and on the nation's closer integration, as an independent country, into the world economic system. The Soviet Union, for its part, would be unhappy about the whole appeasement scheme, as it would imply that the West was still refusing to take the threat of fascism seriously and to accept the popular front as the only viable strategy to cope with it.

Throughout 1938, Japanese leaders sought, consciously or unconsciously, to define a response to the West's appeasement policy. It provided them with an alternative to the Chinese war and to the ideology of 'have not' imperialism. On one hand were those who were seriously concerned over Japan's deteriorating balance-of-payments picture. The extension of hostilities was necessitating large amounts of imports of oil, machine tools, and munitions. The nation's dependence on foreign trade, particularly on imports from the United States and the British Commonwealth, was extremely worrisome; it would not only deplete the precious foreign exchange but would place Japan at the mercy of Western countries, the very condition that the Japanese had tried to eliminate by establishing hegemony on the Asian continent. Faced with this situation, some officials advocated the enactment of a national mobilization law that would authorize the government to control, regulate, and utilize the country's human and material resources for the execution of a prolonged war. Such legislation would establish state control over the Japanese people's economic, educational, and cultural activities. Its passage on 1 April could thus be said to have taken the nation a step further along the road towards totalitarianism. Even so, there persisted a nagging doubt that these measures would actually achieve the desired ends, and fear that total mobilization would merely serve to concentrate national resources for the prosecution of the Chinese war and would leave little for anything else. Even if the war were to be successfully waged and won, would this in itself be enough to make the country more self-sufficient and enable it to prepare for future wars, against the Soviet Union and possibly the Anglo-American powers?

Reasoning thus, some in the army as well as the civilian government continued to argue for limiting military operations in China throughout 1938. A good illustration of General Staff thinking was a memorandum written by its operations section on 30 January. It pointed out the importance of bringing the Chinese war to a close as speedily as possible so as to prepare for a possible war with the Soviet Union and for complete national mobilization. It would help, the memorandum noted, if Chiang Kai-shek could change his mind about resisting Japan, or if other countries were able to mediate between the belligerents. Moreover, Japan should aim at maintaining and strengthening friendly relations with the United States. This did not mean that there would be no further military operations in China, but that they would be kept to a minimum so as to adopt a stance of 'passive maintenance', eschewing offensive campaigns.[13] The gist of these ideas was presented at a meeting of the supreme command in the presence of the emperor on 16 February and received approval. Although not exactly a policy of co-operation with the West, it at least implied Japan's willingness to make use of international developments to wind down the war so as to be able to concentrate on preparedness against the Soviet Union. To that extent, this approach was implicitly akin to the West's appeasement strategy.

These ideas were maintained through the spring of 1938, although in reality the war in China kept expanding. The Japanese army in China insisted that it was not enough to control key cities such as Peking and Nanking; these areas were too small to help alleviate Japan's problems of space and resources, and they were surrounded by Chinese forces that were constantly harassing the Japanese. It would, then, be imperative to expand the sphere of action beyond Nanking, to aim at controlling such additional cities as Hsuchow and Hankow. The supreme command in Tokyo succumbed to these pressures and kept sending reinforcements, and after April major campaigns took place in the vicinity of Hsuchow, leading to its occupation by Japanese forces in late May. An offensive against Hankow and even possibly Canton was planned for the autumn. By mid-1938 the bulk of the Nationalist government's personnel, who had left Nanking for Hankow, had moved further inland to Chungking. Thus what the Japanese military visualized was nothing less than control over one-half of China: northern provinces, the Yangtze up to Hankow, and key coastal cities including Canton. Although such planning was totally out of step with the 16 February decision to localize the war, enough high officials of the General Staff and the War Department were persuaded by the argument put forth by the expeditionary army that only military action would lead to a quick settlement of the war.[14]

At the same time, however, the Konoe cabinet was seriously concerned with the costs of such additional campaigns. It therefore was interested in pursuing the diplomatic option simultaneously with military campaigns. Realizing that the Chiang Kai-shek government was far from being defeated, Prime Minister Konoe was willing to reconsider the policy of not dealing with that regime, and to readjust Japanese diplomacy to take advantage of international developments. In order to do so, he reshuffled the cabinet in late May, replacing Foreign Minister Hirota, who had been closely identified with a tough stand towards the Nationalists and the West, by General Ugaki Kazushige, and War Minister Sugiyama Gen by Lieutenant-General Itagaki Seishirō. The last named had been one of the architects of the Mukden conspiracy in 1931, and his selection was not a very wise one, as events would prove. But Ugaki was known to be a pro-Western army officer with strong disagreement with the way the military had conducted the war in China, and his choice by Konoe indicated the latter's eagerness for a modification of Japanese policy and strategy.

Foreign Minister Ugaki lasted in his office for only four months, but it is significant that this period coincided with the high point of the West's appeasement diplomacy. While in office, he pursued two objectives: initiation of peace talks with the Nationalists, thus in effect nullifying the Konoe declaration of 16 January, and improvement of relations with the Anglo-American nations. Both were extremely risky, in view of the supreme command's willingness to enlarge the war and the actual progress of military campaigns in central China, and because War Minister Itagaki was adamantly opposed to the new approach. The latter was not only confident of military successes, and of turning the Chiang government into 'a local regime', but was also convinced that the war should lead to an eventual eradication of European and American power in China. Itagaki was anticipating one strand of Japanese thinking that would gain tremendous influence in the years to come: the view that a fundamental solution of the Chinese war was possible only in an international context. Specifically, Itagaki believed that Japan should put the Chinese war in the framework of a new diplomacy that would tie Japan closer to Germany and Italy and aim at reducing Soviet and Anglo-American influences.[15] Such thinking would emphasize the strengthening of the anti-Comintern pact as the basic orientation of Japanese strategy and, by implication, put an end once and for all to the idea of co-operation with the West and reconciliation with the Nationalists.

Ugaki's was a last-ditch stand against crossing that bridge. He shared with other military men a conviction that Japan's ultimate antagonist remained the Soviet Union, and that in order to prepare for the eventuality of an anti-Russian war, the seizure of Manchuria had been necessary. At the same time, he had been alarmed by the growing power of the military in Japan, as well as by their apparent lack of principle in becoming involved in the needless war in China. He believed that the two countries should co-operate in developing Asia's rich resources, and that they should also welcome the powers' involvement in the task. In particular, he noted in his diary shortly before being named foreign minister, Japan should engage in 'free competition with the powers' in economic and industrial matters throughout Asia, respect their rights and interests, and co-operate with them in the development of resources. Moreover, Ugaki never believed that military successes would bring about Chiang Kai-shek's surrender; it would be much better to co-opt him in establishing a more stable basis for Chinese–Japanese relations.[16]

Konoe was presumably aware of such views held by the foreign minister designate, and in fact he wanted to replace Hirota by Ugaki precisely because of them. He may have reasoned that the prestigious army leader might be able to help him reorient Japan's China policy. Thus the prime minister readily agreed to Ugaki's conditions for assuming his new post: that Japan should begin peaceful negotiations with China, and that the 16 January statement should at some point be cancelled. In other words, both Konoe and Ugaki were intent on improving the situation in China through diplomacy. Even as the Hsuchow campaign was winding down, these leaders reasoned that the time might be ripe to reopen talks with the Nationalists. At the same time, the new foreign minister wanted to improve Japan's relations with the Western powers, in particular the United States and Britain. He judged that they would not want to go to war with Japan over China, but that the best policy was not to irritate them unnecessarily, which could complicate matters. Moreover, Japan would need the co-operation of the Anglo-American nations in the settlement of the war and in 'postwar management', and that the end of the war would naturally lead to improved relations with those countries. This was a grand vision, akin to that earlier entertained by Foreign Minister Satō. Not coincidentally, Ugaki asked the latter to serve as his adviser. The former foreign minister had remained as concerned as ever with the economic basis of national power, and convinced that only through the expansion of overseas trade could Japan solve the financial and raw materials problems that had grown even more acute.[17] At this late hour, he had one more opportunity, through Ugaki, to try to have his ideas implemented in Japanese foreign policy. But time was running out.

Of Ugaki's two main concerns, the first – negotiating with China – was carried out with breath-taking rapidity, but unfortunately it bore little fruit. He suggested, through intermediaries, that the Nationalists designate T. V. Soong to initiate informal negotiations with the Japanese government. Chiang Kai-shek appears to have encouraged such talks for a number of reasons. Obviously the war was not going well, with Japanese forces advancing towards Hankow and Canton. Negotiations might enable the Chinese side to stall such advances and gain time. Moreover, the powers were not forthcoming with their assistance. Only the Soviet Union was still shipping munitions across the north-western frontier, while the democracies were not taking any overt steps to help check Japanese military action. If anything, they were appeasing Germany over Austria and Czechoslovakia, a policy of acquiescence in overt violation of the Versailles treaty, which could have serious repercussions in Asia. Finally, negotiating with Japan would frustrate the latter's schemes for setting up separatist, pro-Japanese regimes all over occupied territory. If a peace could be negotiated between Tokyo and the Nationalists (the bulk of them now in Chungking), that could lead to the latter's returning to the capital of Nanking as the legitimate government of China. For all these reasons, T. V. Soong, the number-two man in the government as president of the Executive Yuan, was authorized to conduct preliminary talks through intermediaries in Hong Kong.[18]

It could have been predicted, however, that barring a miraculous change of heart on the part of both Japanese military personnel and Chinese Nationalists, no compromise peace would be easily achieved. Ugaki could not significantly modify the terms of peace which Hirota had defined after the fall of Nanking – terms which the Chinese had adamantly refused to consider. Their position had not changed, even though they had in the meantime lost more territory to Japanese arms. Ugaki respected Chiang Kai-shek as the symbol of Chinese nationalism, and was willing to help strengthen the Chinese nation, so that the two sides could co-operate against communism and the Soviet Union. But such 'co-operation' entailed, even for Ugaki, Japan's control over north China for security reasons, not to mention the independence of Manchuria from China proper. Chiang might have swallowed his pride and accepted these conditions as preliminary to a formal cease-fire if he had had enough confidence in Ugaki's control over Japanese policy, and if he had felt utterly helpless over the military situation. It so happened, however, that while negotiations were going on, the Japanese army and those civilians opposed to Ugaki's peace talks tried to remove from the Foreign Ministry control over China policy. They proposed the setting up of a separate China Board which would centralize decision-making and policy implementation concerning China. Ugaki viewed such a proposal as interference with his negotiations which, he believed, were going well, and thus when Prime Minister Konoe supported the establishment of the Board, Ugaki promptly submitted his resignation, considering the prime minister's action a breach of the promise he had been given.

While the bureaucratic infighting was going on in Tokyo, there occurred skirmishes between Japanese and Soviet forces in Changkufeng, an area in southern Manchuria that bordered both on the Maritime Province and Korea. Believing that Soviet forces had illegally crossed the Manchurian border and aimed at seizing Changkufeng, the army in Korea was authorized, in early August, to use force to dislodge them.

Small-scale fighting ensued, but before it was enlarged a truce agreement was signed in Moscow. An insignificant event in itself, the incident nevertheless appeared to show Japan's military unreadiness; the Soviet press referred to it as a victory, and clearly the Japanese divison confronting the better-equipped Soviet army was in no position to succeed without reinforcements. Ugaki, for one, opposed the use of force, for he well recognized the folly of starting a serious confrontation with the Soviet Union while the country was deeply involved in the Chinese war. For the Chinese, the war may have given them hope that the Japanese offensive in central and southern China might be dissipated. Such thinking undoubtedly played a role in their unwillingness to accede to Japanese demands.

Simultaneously with his negotiations with the Nationalists, Ugaki held talks with Britain's ambassador, Sir Robert Craigie, with a view to improving the two countries' relations. The foreign minister believed that no workable truce could be arrived at in China that did not have the support of the United States and Britain, and he was particularly interested in coming to terms with the latter. This may have reflected his reading of the European situation where he saw, and applauded, Adolf Hitler and Neville Chamberlain coming together to discuss European questions in order to avoid war. Likewise, Ugaki believed it should be possible to have Britain (and possibly America) accept Japan's special position in China; but he also thought it was desirable to do so in a friendly, co-operative fashion, rather than through belligerent rhetoric or bluffing use of force. Japan could promise to respect British and American interests in China so as to obtain their support of its position on the continent. Thus reasoning, Ugaki held a series of talks with Craigie, trying to sort out where the two countries might come to understandings.

British policy at this time, and to a lesser extent American policy likewise, did not put much faith in Ugaki's diplomacy, but both were none the less willing to let him try. His leadership coincided with the climaxing of the Czechoslovakian crisis, and both Prime Minister Chamberlain and Foreign Secretary Lord Halifax were anxious to avoid an Asian distraction. They aimed at restabilizing relations with Italy and Japan while appeasing Germany, and in the former connection they were ready to recognize the Italian conquest of Ethiopia so as to keep Italy from joining forces entirely with Germany. In the same vein, London would be prepared to come to some understanding with Tokyo. Though unprepared to concede formally the separate existence of Manchukuo, Craigie was authorized to explore with Ugaki ways in which the competition in China could be conducted in a peaceful fashion. Their talks were started in late July, but before they got anywhere, Ugaki resigned.

The United States was not party to the negotiations; Washington at this time was little interested in going beyond strengthening its naval position in the Pacific. On one hand, the army-navy Joint Board revised the traditional war plan against Japan – Plan Orange – in February, in which the blockading of Japan was combined with the older strategy of a frontal assault on its main fleet. At the same time, the new Vinson–Trammel Act was passed by Congress in May, authorizing the construction of sixty-nine more ships, totalling 400,000 tons. To provide logistical support for the expanding fleet, it was considered necessary to control some islands in the Pacific, and in August a Senate report recommended the fortification of Midway, Wake, and Guam. In the meantime, President Roosevelt's attention continued to focus on Europe where, however, he had little specific to propose other than an international conference to consider general problems. He and other high officials were concerned lest Britain and France should become involved in a war with Germany, an eventuality that could ultimately drag the United States into a conflict it was not prepared for. Roosevelt's attitude was best expressed in a message he sent to Hitler on the eve of the Munich conference, in which the president stated that while the United States had no 'political involvements in Europe', it had 'responsibilities as a part of a world of neighbours'. He urged the German leader to settle peacefully all differences over Czechoslovakia. Given his personal, albeit long-distance, involvement in the intricate negotiations, Roosevelt had little time to devote to Asian problems. Neither he nor Secretary of State Hull showed much interest in the Ugaki–Craigie negotiations.

For both Britain and the United States, however, these talks had a symbolic meaning: they indicated Japan's eagerness for improving relations with the Anglo-American powers rather than strengthening ties to Germany and Italy. Officials in both Washington and London were aware that the latter possibility existed, and that both in Berlin and Tokyo there were forces that favoured transforming the anti-Comintern pact into an explicit alliance. The matter was shrouded in mystery, as no formal negotiations were conducted between the two governments. Rather, as noted above, von Ribbentrop and Ōshima conducted their private conversations, and the latter, as military attaché, transmitted the information only to his superiors on the General Staff in Tokyo. In time, however, the Foreign Ministry and other high officials became aware of the German overtures and sought to define a response. They learned that von Ribbentrop was proposing not only a defensive pact aimed at the Soviet Union but a more comprehensive mutual security agreement among Germany, Italy, and Japan. Such a treaty would combine the three powers and obligate them to come to each other's assistance in case one of them were attacked by an outside power – Britain, for instance. High Foreign Ministry officials were adamantly opposed to such an enlarged undertaking, convinced of the need not to antagonize the Anglo-American nations while Japan prepared for a possible conflict with the Soviet Union. They would also object to making the mutual defence obligatory, insisting that the proposed treaty should merely commit the three powers to consult with one another in case one of them were attacked by the Soviet Union. Such a cautious stand was opposed by the army and the navy, which preferred a more flexible response, even including the possibility of German–Japanese military co-operation against Britain.[19] In the event, nothing definite would be decided till 1940.

Against this backdrop, Ugaki's conversations with the British ambassador held importance, for they indicated an interest not to antagonize the Anglo-American nations. Ugaki was not above being impressed with German power and forceful diplomacy, as revealed particularly during the Czech crisis, but he was never captivated by the vision of a German alliance as a basic strategy in Asia. He was keenly cognizant of the need to prevent international isolation of Japan, and of the wisdom of making use of shifting world conditions to settle the Chinese war. It was this sort of sensitivity to international affairs that tended to isolate him from his erstwhile army colleagues. In fact, even some of his new subordinates in the Foreign Ministry began expressing their impatience with his approach. Several of them remonstrated directly with him, arguing that Ugaki's negotiations with Craigie would only result in unsatisfactory compromises with the Anglo-American nations, whereas he should really be concentrating on strengthening Japan's ties with Germany and Italy so as to crush the Nationalists in China once and for all.[20] Thus Ugaki was fighting a rearguard action to prevent Japan from making an inflexible commitment to tie itself to the Fascist countries. From the perspective of London and Washington, therefore, his tenure in office provided them with a breathing space as they focused their attention on Europe.

All in all, then, the spring and summer of 1938 saw little change in the Asian international situation. With Japanese forces continuing their offensive in China, chances for re-establishing stability were remote. But Japan had by no means made an irrevocable choice to establish an alternative to the Washington system. It hesitated. This very hesitation was to make its position unpopular at home and unsatisfactory from the viewpoint of other governments. Unlike the situation in Europe, there was no serious pursuit of an appeasement diplomacy in the Asian-Pacific region.

A NEW ORDER IN EAST ASIA

The Munich conference, convened at the end of September, was the high point of appeasement. Just as Prime Minister Chamberlain returned home joyously waving his agreement with Hitler, President Roosevelt sent congratulatory messages, expressing satisfaction that war had been averted. Under Secretary of State Sumner Welles declared that 'a new world order based upon justice and upon law' was now becoming more possible than ever.[21] They were not deceiving themselves, but were reflecting a widely shared sentiment that it would be possible to stabilize international affairs through reincorporating Germany (and Italy) into a new status quo. That would not be the same thing as returning to the Versailles system: recognizing the territorial changes in central Europe was tantamount to accepting the system's erosion. Still, the regime of European affairs in which Britain, France, Germany, and Italy came to basic understanding, one that had the support of the United States, would retain one essential aspect of the Versailles structure. What was needed now was to revitalize it further through agreements on economic and armament issues. Before anything was done in that direction, however, Hitler would show his utter lack of interest in such a co-operative enterprise by annexing what was left of Czechoslovakia.

In the meantime, having somehow weathered the crisis in central Europe, the democracies might next have turned to Asian-Pacific affairs. Here, however, there was no equivalent to the European appeasement, nothing comparable to the Munich conference taking place. Reasons for this contrast are not as simple as might at first appear. After all, Britain, France, and even the United States were fearful of, and at the same time had to be prepared for, another European war, and would not have wanted to provoke a serious crisis in Asia. The Japanese were enlarging their fighting on the continent, and if any outside pressure was needed to check it, it was the Soviet Union which was providing it. Western democracies might have decided that the time was opportune to induce Japan to negotiate for a settlement of the Chinese war. Without some international agreement in Asia, Munich alone would not have ensured global stability for, after all, the Versailles system had been complemented by the Washington structure, so that its resilience would hinge on what happened to the latter.

That neither London nor Washington was much interested in an Asian Munich, in the wake of the fateful conference, suggests several underlying assumptions on their part. First, the Western governments may have considered chances for an Asian appeasement much more problematical than one in Europe. Second, related to this must have been a tacit assumption that China was not quite the same thing as Austria or Czechoslovakia. Japan could not have used the German argument for a racial *Anschluss*. Japanese military action was much more of a transparent aggression. Third, at the same time, the democracies may have believed that the Asian war was less likely to develop into a world war than the European crisis brought about by Hitler's revanchism. Fourth, they may have reasoned that the Soviet Union would be more successful in checking Japanese than German expansionism, and therefore that an appeasement strategy in Asia would have to involve it as a principal actor; but the latter had not abandoned its popular front policy and would have vehemently opposed any appeasement of Fascist nations at that time. In fact, Munich impressed Stalin as an attempt by the West to mollify Germany, which had the effect of weakening their resolve to stand firm towards Hitler. The Soviet leader would in time respond to this turn of events by approaching Hitler himself for an understanding. But this was in the future, and for the moment the Soviet Union's adamant opposition to an international settlement in Europe made it certain that it would likewise object to an Asian Munich.

A combination of all these factors resulted in the West's lack of initiative to appease Japan in late 1938. But one should also add another significant difference between Europe and Asia. The United States was more prepared to be involved in the latter region. Opinion polls indicated that the American people were far more willing to take a stand on the Chinese–Japanese War than on any European issue at that time. With an overwhelming majority (consistently three-quarters or more of those polled) expressing their sympathy for China, the Roosevelt administration, even if it had wanted to, would have found it virtually impossible to approach Japan for some kind of agreement, unless it included the latter's withdrawal from China, an unrealistic goal. Moreover, the public was becoming alarmed over the fact, which newspapers and magazines began stressing, that American trade with Japan, especially export of arms, was growing. An inference could readily be drawn that the United States was supplying Japan with munitions which the latter used to fight against China. Japan's dependence on American scrap iron and steel was particularly noticeable, and these items could easily be pictured as being turned into tanks and aircraft for use in China. This was an appalling revelation, and a movement to stop shipments of raw materials and arms to Japan began to be organized throughout the United States. It was supported even by some isolationists, such as Senators Gerald P. Nye and George W. Norris, in sharp contrast to the much more cautious and cynical stand they took regarding European issues. One outcome was the founding of the American Committee for Non-Participation in Japanese Aggression.[22] With former Secretary of State Henry L. Stimson as honorary chairman, the organization coalesced individuals and organizations willing to condemn openly Japanese military action and to call for punitive sanctions such as the embargo of war materials. Given such pressures, the Roosevelt administration could not well have sought an Asian equivalent of Munich.

The only conceivable Asian appeasement, under the circumstances, would have been one in which Japan came together with the Western powers for a stable Asian order on the basis of the status quo *ante bellum* including respect for China's integrity and the Open Door. In other words, just as some in the West imagined that Munich would reintegrate Germany into a resuscitated, albeit modified, Versailles system, so

Asian appeasement would have to mean a reconstructed Washington treaty system. The powers, to be sure, might have been willing to forgo consideration of Manchuria for the time being, but at least they would have insisted on a return to the situation prevailing before July 1937. Japan, furthermore, would have had to accept, in principle at least, the concept of economic internationalism.

Japanese diplomacy under the leadership of men like Ugaki and Satō might have considered such an option but, as seen above, the former resigned at the end of September over the creation of the China Board. He was replaced by Arita Hachirō, who had served as foreign minister once in 1936. Together with Shiratori, Arita was viewed as a leader of the 'radical' wing of the Foreign Ministry. (Young 'radicals' sought to pressure Prime Minister Konoe to appoint Shiratori as Ugaki's successor, and when Konoe demurred, Shiratori suggested Arita's name.[23]) It was expected that he would act more boldly than his predecessor in identifying Japanese policy with the cause of revisionism. Moreover, his assumption of office coincided with crucial military campaigns against Hankow and Canton. The latter was occupied by Japanese troops on 21 October, and the former six days later. Thus within sixteen months after the outbreak of the war, all major cities in China had fallen to Japanese forces. Still, there was hardly a feeling of victory on the Japanese side. The Nationalists had moved their government to Chungking and refused to surrender, and Communist and other groups were in control of the vast hinterland, preparing for an eventual counter-offensive.

In such circumstances, a return to the pre-1937 situation was out of the question. The new Konoe–Arita team realized that Japan would either have to continue the war effort, or turn to other countries for mediation. But the latter would certainly insist on Japan's making major concessions, while the former alternative would require further expenditures of national resources, to the detriment of preparedness against the Soviet Union. Faced with the dilemma, the Tokyo government responded by taking two crucial steps. First, it proclaimed a new order in East Asia, making explicit for the first time Japan's abandonment of the Washington treaty structure. Second, it continued to negotiate with Berlin for a military alliance against the Soviet Union. Both steps were intended to help settle the Chinese war to Japan's satisfaction, while preventing the latter's isolation in world affairs. In the event, neither objective was achieved.

On 3 November Prime Minister Konoe issued a public statement, defining the basic national objective as the construction of 'a new order for ensuring permanent stability in East Asia'. This, the statement asserted, was the joint goal of Japan, Manchukuo, and China; all three must co-operate politically, economically, and culturally so as to 'establish international justice, carry out a common defence against communism, create a new culture, and bring about an economic combination' in East Asia. The establishment of a new order was 'derived from the founding spirit of our nation', Konoe declared, but he optimistically coupled such a particularistic statement with the hope that the powers would 'correctly understand' the policy and make adjustments to the 'new situation' in the region. Most important, while the Nationalist government had degenerated into 'a local regime', if its leaders altered their adamant resistance and decided to join forces with the Japanese in the new task, they would not be rejected, for Japan sincerely hoped to share with China the task of establishing the new Asian order.

Clearly, the statement reflected the view that a political appeal to the Chinese must follow military successes so as to bring the war to a satisfactory conclusion. Moreover, it modified the 16 January declaration by offering the possibility of co-operation with the Nationalists if only they gave up their resistance and their pro-Communist policy. But the new statement was also significant for Japan's relations with Western powers, for it harked back to Hirota's and Arita's earlier emphasis on having the West recognize Japan's new position in Asia and, furthermore, on establishing an Asian autarky that would stress the region's political unity, economic interdependence, and cultural uniqueness, all to the ultimate exclusion of Western influence. This latter point became even more unmistakable when Foreign Minister Arita communicated a note to the United States government on 18 November in response to a strong note of protest from Washington concerning infringements on American rights and on the Open Door principle in China. Arita's response was unambiguous:

> It is the firm conviction of the Japanese Government that now, at a time
> of continuing development of new conditions in East Asia, an attempt to
> apply to present and future conditions without any changes, concepts and
> principles which were applicable to conditions prevailing before the
> present incident does not in any way contribute to the solution of
> immediate issues.[24]

In other words, the treaties and principles cited by the United States government were no longer valid and would not be accepted as such by the Japanese. One could date Japan's formal rejection of the Washington system from this point. The Konoe statement and the Arita message showed that Japan, after long hesitation, finally crossed the bridge of no return. Although, as will be detailed, Japanese officials would later equivocate and even try to conciliate Americans by speaking of their co-operation in Asia and the Pacific, as far as Washington was concerned an irrevocable decision had been made by the Japanese leadership, and no reconciliation could now be effected unless these statements were explicitly repudiated.

That would not happen, for the Konoe–Arita leadership was also eager to formalize and bring to conclusion negotiations with Germany for an alliance. As seen above, informal talks had been held in Berlin, and the Foreign Ministry had taken no official cognizance of them, but the Japanese military attaché, Ōshima, who had been engaged in the Berlin conversations, was appointed ambassador to Germany shortly before Arita's assumption of office, so that now for the first time the government in Tokyo would become involved. And Arita was eager for it; he had always been for strengthening ties with Germany and Italy. At the same time, however, he was not ready to countenance the German suggestion for enlarging the scope of the projected alliance to apply to other countries in addition to the Soviet Union. While he had fully subscribed to the ideology of 'have not' nations and defended the policy of steadily reducing Western influence in China, he apparently judged that it would be unwise at that time to antagonize the Soviet Union and the Anglo-American nations simultaneously. Moreover, Foreign Ministry officials were seriously divided on the issue, and he could not express the pro-German viewpoint as representing a consensus. In any event, the navy supported his caution, as did the finance minister, whereas War Minister Itagaki persisted in his espousal of a broadened alliance scheme so that Britain and France as well as the Soviet Union would be covered. There was no reconciliation between the two views, and disagreement on this and other issues led to the Konoe cabinet's resignation in early 1939. Arita, however, was to stay on as foreign minister of the succeeding cabinet.

So an alliance with Germany would not materialize, but the Japanese government had, through its enunciations of November 1938, taken an explicit stand, as if to respond to Germany's bold initiatives that had culminated in Munich. Whereas, however, Hitler had at least paid lip-service to the idea of consulting with Britain and France about modifying the German–Czech boundaries, the Japanese leaders had issued their statements unilaterally, not within any framework of international action. They may have reasoned that just as Germany was getting away with its conquest, Japan could also impose a *fait accompli* on the powers, or even obtain their tacit acquiescence. If so, they were treated to a mild shock when the United States, which had officially approved of the Munich agreement, issued a ringing denunciation of Konoe's 'new order' declaration.

For the Chinese–Japanese War was beginning to create a serious crisis in Japanese–American relations, more notable than the uneasy state of American–German relations. Tension, to be sure, had existed for some time across the Pacific and had grown after the *Panay* affair in the previous December, but it was from the autumn of 1938 onward that the war on the Asian continent became closely tied to vicissitudes of Japanese–American relations. Whether consciously or unconsciously, American officials were coming to the conclusion that the successful consummation of appeasement in Europe would have adverse effects elsewhere. Not only would Japan be emboldened by Germany's successes, but Britain's prestige and position would be perceived as having suffered, with serious implications for its power in Asia. Now more than ever the British would be preoccupied with European questions so as to preserve the precarious balance on the continent, with little time or determination left to maintain the status quo further east. That would leave the United States as the only power, outside of the Soviet Union, to restrain Japan. Russians could do their share in the north, but with the Chinese war expanding into the Canton area, it would be up to America to stand guard and protect Western interests in the rest of Asia. Konoe's and Arita's statements, which were made just as officials in Washington were thus reconfirming their stand, gave them an opportunity to respond in strong language. Castigating the 'new order' note as 'arbitrary, unjust, and unwarranted', the State Department repudiated Japan's right to serve as an 'agent of destiny' or an architect of a new order unilaterally. The United States, on the contrary, adhered to the principles of the Open Door and multilateral economic relations which would conduce to the benefit of all, Japan included. America, in other words, would want Japan to go back to the framework of the Washington conference rather than espousing diametrically opposite ideas of unilateralism and particularism.

It was around this time that some key officials in Washington began contemplating specific measures to sanction Japan. Rather than vaguely formulated contingency plans for naval action which Roosevelt had favoured, these officials were thinking of economic pressure. They were particularly interested in two ideas: the abrogation of the existing treaty of commerce with Japan, and the offer of loans to China. The first began to be urged by some officials as an effective way of sanctioning Japan. The 1911 treaty of commerce and navigation had regulated trade between the two countries, and to abrogate it would mean depriving the trade of American legal protection. It would place Japanese import from and export to the United States at the mercy of the latter. This would be a drastic but necessary step, according to its advocates, now that the Japanese had explicitly repudiated the Washington treaties. The second suggestion was less dramatic: the United States might offer China loans so as to enable it to keep resisting Japan. Secretary of the Treasury Henry Morgenthau emerged as the spokesman for this alternative, pleading with Roosevelt for an initial $25 million loan to China. The 'future of democracy, the future of civilization', he declared, 'are at stake'. Supporting Morgenthau, Stanley K. Horbeck, adviser to Secretary of State Hull on Asian affairs, argued, 'Unless the Japanese march is halted by the Chinese or by some other nation, the time will come when Japan and the United States will be face to face and definitely opposed to each other in the international political arena.'[25] Such a perception was shared by an increasing number of officials in Washington. But they disagreed among themselves as to the specific action America should now take. Hull thought all these proposals were premature and would unnecessarily irritate Japan, but Roosevelt at least approved the loan scheme, and thus the first of what would amount to billions of dollars of credit was offered to the Chinese at the end of the year.

It was a small loan, but of symbolic significance, as it clearly revealed American willingness to support China, and by implication to help stop Japan. With the British and French still preoccupied with European issues in the wake of Munich, and with the Soviet Union becoming alarmed over the implications of the appeasement strategy, it must have been reassuring to the Chinese that the Americans were now more willing than earlier to make known their strong opposition to Japanese policy and their support for China's struggle. Chiang Kai-shek and the Nationalists sorely needed such an indication of help at that juncture, for on 20 December Wang Ching-wei, one of their leaders, secretly left Chungking and flew to Hanoi, there to initiate a campaign for setting up a pro-Japanese regime in China.

The Wang scheme was a product of the Japanese policy, mentioned earlier, that had looked to some political settlement of the war. Since Chiang Kai-shek appeared unwilling to accommodate, Japan's military and civilian officials looked to Wang as the best alternative. To persuade him to turn against Chiang and other compatriots, the Japanese formulated in late November a list of terms that would be offered Wang as inducements for betraying his country. The terms included Japan's respect for Chinese 'territorial integrity and sovereignty' and gradual retrocession of concessions and extra-territorial rights in China, in return for which the new Chinese government to be set up by Wang was to recognize the independence of Manchukuo and the principle of Japanese–Manchukuo–Chinese co-operation against communism and for economic collaboration. These latter principles actually amounted to violating Chinese sovereignty, for they were to be made specific through the stationing of Japanese troops in north China and Inner Mongolia, as well as the establishment of an economic area in the lower Yangtze where China would offer special privileges to Japan. Despite such obvious infringements on Chinese rights, Wang Ching-wei and his supporters judged that, given the fall of Canton and its environs which had been their power base, it would be best to encourage Japanese overtures for an alternative to Chiang's regime and to bring the war to a close. They could at least try to ascertain where Japanese intentions lay, and if the move should result in a reasonable peace settlement, they would be hailed as 'saviours of the nation' and contribute to the goal of combating communism.[26]

On 22 December, two days after Wang reached Hanoi, the Japanese government issued another declaration, expressing a willingness to 'adjust its relations with a new China' – those who shared Japan's concerns and looked to the establishment of a new order in East Asia. That order would be built on the principles of anti-communism and economic co-operation. Wang responded by accepting the Japanese overtures. As he explained in his communications to Chiang and other leaders in Chungking, both Japan and China were having difficulties fighting the war, so that the time was opportune for them to come together for a settlement. While America, Britain, and France had been assisting China, Wang said, they would never send their own forces to fight against Japan. The Soviet Union, too, would be unable to act unilaterally, and as for Germany, it would gladly help bring the belligerents together. Now that the Japanese government had enunciated its policy of respecting Chinese independence and sovereignty, it should be possible to negotiate with it, arrive at a truce, and concentrate China's energies on 'nation-building'. If that were done, the two countries would be able to build the foundation of eternal peace and contribute to order and peace in the Pacific and the entire world. Although Wang was being extremely naïve, it should be noted that he was basing his daring action on a view of international affairs which appeared to rule out any direct intervention by a third power in support of China. Lacking such support, he concluded that it would be worth gambling on the Japanese scheme.[27]

Chiang, on his part, was adamantly opposed to it. He exhorted his countrymen not to be deceived by Japanese propaganda which was a mere cloak to conceal its ambition to subjugate China and conquer the entire world. He castigated the Japanese concept of a new order in East Asia as a policy of ejecting American and European influences from Asia, creating an economic unit out of China, Manchukuo, and Japan, and enslaving China. The so-called 'new China' with which the Japanese were saying they would collaborate was in reality a China that had lost its independence, and their insistence on preserving Eastern civilization amounted to obliterating China's own national culture. Japan's slogans about the two countries' co-operation to fight communism were also a rationalization for retaining its troops in China and controlling the latter's political and cultural affairs. Once again citing the 'Tanaka memorandum', Chiang repeated the charge that Japan was intent upon conquering China as the first step towards conquering the world; already it was trying to eject Western power from Asia and to upset international order in the area. Against such acts of violence and madness, China was engaging in a just war for the entire world. Although, Chiang concluded, most other countries were hesitant to join China in the struggle, the latter was willing to sacrifice all for the fight for justice in the hope that ultimately the world would come to co-operate in the joint effort, for 'virtue is never alone but always acquires neighbours'.[28]

At that time most Chinese politicians and generals stood by Chiang Kai-shek, viewing Wang's behaviour as too quixotic and unlikely to lead to anything. But they too recognized that much would depend on the attitude of the powers. It was gratifying that none of the Western nations except Germany had expressed approval of the several Konoe statements, and that in London, Washington, and Moscow officials were saying that their governments would never recognize the 'new' Chinese regime that Wang might set up through Japanese machinations. In such circumstances, the announcement of an American loan of $25 million must have been especially welcome. However small, it was a clear signal that the United States stood by the legitimate Chinese government. Hitherto, small-scale credits had been extended to China in return for purchases of silver, for stabilizing its finances. The new loan, in contrast, was clearly military aid, intended for enabling the Chinese to obtain trucks and arms from the United States. It showed the latter's willingness to circumvent the Neutrality Act, come to China's assistance, and, by implication, to reprimand Japan. This stance would not change for three years.

A DIPLOMATIC REVOLUTION

On 4 January 1939, Konoe resigned as prime minister. The resignation reflected his sense of frustration over the unending war in China and over the cabinet's division concerning a German alliance. He was succeeded by Hiranuma Kiichirō, a right-wing politician who had been president of the Privy Council. He was a weak leader and had no firm views on affairs of state. He retained both War Minister Itagaki and Foreign Minister Arita, knowing full well that these two had disagreed strongly on the German alliance question. And they continued to differ, the former insisting on accepting Germany's proposal for an alliance aimed at the Soviet Union and the European powers, while the latter opposed such an enlargement of the pact. Clearly the two views could not be reconciled, but the Hiranuma cabinet decided, on 19 January, on a weak compromise: Japan would enter into an alliance with Germany and Italy directed against the Soviet Union, but would accept the possibility of its including other countries, provided that Japan would retain the freedom to decide on the nature of its applicability to the latter. In other words, it would be ready to come to Germany's assistance by force of arms if the latter became involved in a war with the Soviet Union, but it would not promise beforehand how it would react if the war became enlarged to include Britain or France. Such vague assurances were as far as Arita and the Foreign Ministry were willing to go, and they were clearly unacceptable to Germany and Italy.

While inconclusive talks were held in Berlin and Rome, the international situation resumed momentum in Europe as Hitler ignored the Munich agreement and, in March, sent troops to occupy what was left of Czechoslovakia. This was an explicit departure from the arrangements of the previous autumn which the European governments had painfully worked out. Deeply shocked at this breach of appeasement, Prime Minister Chamberlain declared that henceforth Hitler was not to be trusted or appeased, and that, on the contrary, he must be stopped before he undertook further acts of territorial aggrandizement. To frustrate his ambitions, the powers would have to be prepared to make a commitment to uphold the status quo. Thus he declared, within days of the German annexation of the whole of Czechoslovakia, that Britain would guarantee Polish territorial integrity. Poland now emerged as the symbol of the passing of appeasement; Hitler had not concealed his ambition of rectifying the German–Polish boundaries which he declared had been unjustly established in 1919, while Chamberlain committed his government's prestige to upholding them. The French government followed suit. London and Paris also initiated talks with Moscow for a collective arrangement to deter further German aggrandizement.

Under the circumstances, it might have been expected that the United States would openly and vigorously proclaim its support for the British–French position and to assist their negotiations with the Soviet Union to keep Germany in check. The Roosevelt administration, however, was not yet ready to involve the country in the mounting crisis in Europe. To be sure, Roosevelt was willing to countenance a secret sale of military aircraft to France and to prepare national opinion for revision of neutrality laws. As he asserted in the State of the Union message, 'when we deliberately try to legislate neutrality, our neutrality laws may operate unevenly and unfairly – may actually give aid to an aggressor and deny it to the victim'. Clearly, he wanted his nation to build up armaments so as to help democracies against aggressors. He was now freely using words like 'democracies' and 'aggressors', and nobody misunderstood which countries he had in mind. Still, he would not join Britain and France in guaranteeing Polish independence or safeguarding the European peace. He would for the time being focus on neutrality revision, and even toyed with a scheme that recalled the appeasement strategy: on 15 April he sent public messages to Hitler and Mussolini, asking them to refrain from attacking or invading thirty-one specifically named countries for a period of ten years. If they would agree, the United States would organize an international conference on disarmament and trade. Nothing came of this scheme except embarrassment, as Hitler openly ridiculed the Roosevelt initiative. In the meantime, the president saw the Soviet ambassador from time to time in the spring and early summer of 1939, but such talks did not amount to indicating America's strong commitment to upholding the European status quo, or its interest in co-operating with the Soviet Union against Germany.

Such caution was in striking contrast to the resoluteness with which the United States government dealt with Asian affairs. The more alarming the situation became in Europe, the greater the tendency in official circles in Washington to consider strong measures in Asia, such as trade embargoes against Japan, reinforcing British naval ships in Asian waters, and abrogating the Japanese treaty of commerce. Such a tendency confirmed the earlier stance of helping China withstand Japanese pressure, but in 1939 it also came to have global significance. The United States would not simply be helping one Asian country against another; it would also be doing its share in maintaining international order. This was because frustrating Japanese ambitions in China would deter it from attacking British and French possessions in Asia, and also reduce its value as a potential ally of Germany. In this sense the failure of appeasement in Europe signalled the beginning of greater American assertiveness in the Asian-Pacific region. It was not surprising, therefore, that a serious crisis in American–Japanese relations came even before the open rupture in British–German relations.

Washington had good reason to be concerned over the interlinkages between Japanese aggression and German ambitions. For Japanese leaders were beginning to realize that the crisis in Europe could bring about a 'major turning-point' in world affairs, as a senior General Staff officer noted in April. He foresaw a war between Germany and the Anglo-American powers by 1941 or 1942, and asserted that Japan must be prepared to take advantage of such a development. The war in China, too, would become affected; it would now be more than ever imperative to build up national military strength to cope with the crisis of 1941–42, and in order to do so it would be necessary to establish control over China as expeditiously as possible. At the same time, however, prolongation of the Chinese war could sap national resources to such an extent that the country might not be in a position to respond energetically to the anticipated change in the international situation. This was a serious dilemma, but it clearly indicated, for the Japanese army, the wisdom of broadening the scope of the Asian conflict; the war with China should not merely be seen in the context of crushing Chinese resistance or even of establishing a puppet regime; nor would it be sufficient to view the war as a prelude to a more important confrontation with the Soviet Union. The Chinese–Japanese War would have to be seen as an aspect of a significant transformation of global politics.

Though still vague, such thinking indicates the growing tendency among Japanese officials to become fascinated by long-term prospects and to subordinate the goal of settling the war to visions of future power and glory. The tendency was to damage seriously Japan's ability to cope realistically with existing problems. In any event, in the spring and summer of 1939, the Japanese military took some significant steps that seriously complicated Japanese relations with other countries. Most of these steps had little to do directly with the prosecution of the war in

China but were rather designed to improve the country's position *vis-à-vis* the powers in preparation for an anticipated development in international affairs.

First, the navy occupied Hainan Island, off the southern China coast, in February, and in the following month the Spratly Islands, 700 miles south of Hainan, were incorporated into the jurisdiction of the Taiwan colonial government. (A naval office had been established in Taiwan in 1938.) These islands nominally belonged to China, but Chinese forces were unable to put up any resistance. The taking of such territory expressed the navy's interest in extending its sway over the South Seas even at the risk of creating tensions with Britain, France, and the United States, all of which held colonial possessions in the region. Already in 1936, it will be recalled, the Japanese navy had succeeded in having written into key strategic plans the idea of southern penetration, but no specific action had taken place to implement it. Now, however, given the mounting gravity of the European situation, top naval officials clearly judged the time was opportune to take initial steps towards weakening the position of the Western powers, especially Britain, in South-East Asia. While London and Paris made no formal protest, in June the Dutch authorities in the Indies (Indonesia) notified Tokyo that they were reducing their import of cotton textiles and other goods from Japan. This was the first instance where the colonial regime in the Dutch East Indies took action against Japan, and presaged the coming crisis in Japanese–Dutch relations.

The army, in the meantime, decided to test British power by blockading the British concession in Tientsin in June. All who entered the British compound were subjected to a search. Such a procedure, extremely humiliating to the British, again had little to do with the fighting in China, which had moved elsewhere. The Japanese army justified its action by citing the need to suppress anti-Japanese terrorists operating out of the concession, but its real intention was to embarrass Britain and damage its prestige, something that might have favourable repercussions on the ongoing negotiations in Berlin for an alliance. And precisely for that reason, London was unwilling to retaliate. Its officials feared that any military involvement with Japan at that time would only encourage Hitler's moves, probably into Poland. Consequently, they offered to negotiate a settlement. Ambassador Craigie held a series of talks with Foreign Minister Arita, and on 24 July they drafted a tentative agreement in which Britain recognized Japan's special needs during the war with China, and consented to desist from interfering with Japanese measures to maintain law and order. A severe blow to British prestige, the incident nevertheless did not help bring about a speedy conclusion of an Axis alliance. Arita hoped to make use of the hard-line policy towards Britain to persuade the Germans that Japan was willing to exert pressure on that country, but he remained opposed to a formal military alliance against Britain which could involve Japan in a

European war before it was ready. Arita and most of his subordinates understood that making such a commitment would mean loss of freedom and flexibility for Japan and could lead to its diplomatic and strategic isolation. Even if the nation should ultimately aim at driving out Britain and France from Asia, noted a high Foreign Ministry official, the time was not yet ripe, especially because Japan must first cope with the Soviet threat in the north. Rather than joining Germany and antagonizing all the others, it would be much better to manœuvre the European powers to make use of them in order to enhance Japan's relative position in Asia.[29] Such reasoning prevailed through spring and summer, and as a result, no progress was made in the Berlin negotiations. In other words, Japanese action in Hainan, the Spratly Islands, and Tientsin gravely affected Japan's relations with Britain but did not help those with Germany. This was an example of an inept diplomacy which could only create further complications for Japan in the world arena.

To make matters worse, there were also serious crises in Japanese–Soviet and Japanese–American relations in the summer of 1939. The former arose as a result of skirmishes between Japanese and Mongol forces along the north-western border of Manchukuo, adjoining Outer Mongolia. The area, known as Nomonhan, was disputed territory, but the Japanese infantry stationed there judged that several hundred troops of Outer Mongolia had crossed the border and invaded Manchukuo. These troops were repulsed once, but they returned periodically, thus escalating the conflict. Although the area was about 500 miles from Soviet territory, Outer Mongolia had in fact been its protectorate, and soon Soviet planes began flying over the region. The situation threatened to develop into a military confrontation between Japanese and Soviet forces, an eventuality which key officers of the General Staff sought to avoid. But the Kwantung Army, as well as some in Tokyo, were optimistic that the Soviet Union would not be prepared to wage a major battle because of its preoccupation with the European situation. Moreover, in view of the ongoing negotiations in Berlin, Japan would be able to turn to Germany for assistance in case the crisis escalated. Ignoring the supreme command's cautious stance, the Kwantung Army authorized the crossing of the Mongolian border for punitive expeditions, where its forces encountered those of the Soviet Union as well as Outer Mongolia. In this way, from the middle of July until mid-September, Japanese and Soviet forces engaged in a series of battles involving larger and larger forces as well as tanks and aircraft.

Surprisingly stiff Soviet resistance indicated a deliberate policy. In the early months of 1939 Moscow was fully aware of the negotiations in Berlin for a German–Japanese alliance; moreover, after the German occupation of Czechoslovakia, it appeared to be a matter of time before Germany would invade Poland. The Soviet Union then would be faced with a grave situation in the west, even as its relations with Japan had remained tense after the 1938 fighting at Changkufeng. Under the circumstances, Soviet leaders might well have decided to placate the Japanese in order to discourage them from entering into a pact with Berlin, and to concentrate on the defence of the western border. Instead, Stalin gambled on the opposite strategy, to seek a *rapprochement* with Germany and maintain a stiff stand towards Japan. In part this may have been induced by reports from Tokyo through the Sorge spy ring that Japan was not likely to want a full-scale war with the Soviet Union at that time. Even so, to check Japanese advances along the Mongolian border it would be necessary to reinforce Soviet armed strength in the east. Moscow evidently concluded that it would be more practical to deal strongly with the Japanese threat to discourage Tokyo from entertaining any thought of an aggressive war against the Soviet Union in the near future, and in the meantime to approach Germany for a temporary truce in order to stabilize the western frontier.

It is possible to argue that the Soviet Union's strong military action in Asia might have induced the Japanese to redouble their efforts to conclude a German alliance. Already in mid-June, German officials were intimating that unless Tokyo agreed to such an alliance (on German terms), they might turn around and enter into a non-aggression pact with the Soviet Union.[30] Japanese officials, however, remained divided on the applicability of the proposed German alliance to Britain and France; besides, Foreign Minister Arita refused to believe that Berlin would violate the spirit of the anti-Comintern pact and sign a new pact with the Soviet Union. For all these reasons, negotiations in Berlin made little progress, driving German officials to the acceptance of a Soviet agreement. That in turn had the effect of enabling the Soviet Union to concentrate a large force, equipped with fire-power, on the Manchukuo–Mongolian border, even shifting some troops from the European front. Soviet troops turned to an offensive in late August, inflicting severe damage on Japanese forces. This, and the announcement of the German–Soviet non-aggression pact on 23 August, were a double blow to Japanese strategy.

As if this were not enough, another blow was received, this time from the United States government. On 26 July, Washington notified Japan that it intended to abrogate the 1911 treaty of commerce and navigation between the two countries. According to the terms of the treaty, abrogation would take effect six months after notification, namely January 1940. This drastic step, it will be recalled, had been considered in late 1938 as a way of retaliating against Japan's explicit denunciation of the Washington Conference treaties, but several officials had advised caution. Now, however, in the wake of Japan's blatant disregard of British rights in Tientsin and London's meek submission to it, Washington decided the time had come to act. It was no coincidence that the notification came just two days after the signing of the Arita–Craigie agreement. Loss of British prestige was followed by an assertion of American power to influence Japanese behaviour. Just as the Japanese had taken advantage of the European situation to humiliate the British in China, so the Americans were determined to stand in the way, not to let Japan get away with the tactic. As British prestige and power declined in Asia, the United States would step in so that it would have no adverse repercussions in Europe. The Anglo-American powers, in other words, would be as interested as Japan in linking European and Asian affairs.

Japanese officials had not been totally unprepared for the shock of abrogation. Public opinion in America had for some time been calling for such a step, and earlier in the month of July the Senate foreign relations committee had considered a resolution to embargo trade with countries that violated the nine-power treaty. Senator Arthur Vandenburg had also introduced a resolution calling on the government to abrogate the commercial treaty. Despite such warning, however, Tokyo was taken by surprise when the Washington notification came. Few were willing to brush it off as of no consequence, or to go even further and consider retaliatory measures against the United States. Japan simply could not afford to add to its growing list of diplomatic complications, or to antagonize so powerful a Western nation. Besides, Japanese trade with the United States was still substantial; Japan was continuing to obtain scrap iron, steel, oil, and other essentials from America, which had become the most important supplier of these goods outside of Asia. It would be impossible to do without American trade, and officials in Tokyo realized that they had just six months to try to mollify Washington.

By August 1939, then, Japan's international position had seriously deteriorated. It was becoming more and more difficult to avoid complications with third powers while the nation tried to conclude the war with China, and the attempt to take advantage of the European situation for enhancing Japanese power in Asia was not working. In the growingly desperate situation, some in Tokyo, notably War Minister Itagaki, strongly argued that the best way out of the impasse was to conclude an alliance with Germany as quickly as possible, even accepting the latter's terms. Japan would then at least have one reliable ally, whereas otherwise it would be totally alone in the world. But Prime Minister Hiranuma still dragged his feet, unwilling to complicate further Japan's relations with the Anglo-American nations. It was while these leaders were still groping for a sensible policy that Berlin and Moscow signed a non-aggression pact.

The signing of the pact on 23 August marked a reversal of the Soviet Union's popular front strategy, which had provided one definition of international affairs. It had sought to pit all nations of the world against Germany, Italy, and Japan. The latter three, in turn, had joined together in an anti-Comintern pact. But the world had not really become divided into these camps. The United States and Britain, in particular, had stood outside of the Soviet-initiated popular front, and had tried to appease Fascist states, especially Germany. It was only in 1939 that a global coalition that combined the popular front with Anglo-American initiatives appeared to be a possibility: British and French guarantees to Poland, Russian successes at Nomonhan, the abrogation of the Japanese–American treaty of commerce – all such steps suggested a trend on the part of the anti-Fascist nations to act more boldly and collectively than in the past in defence of the global status quo. It was just at that juncture that the Nazi–Soviet pact was announced, to the consternation of the whole world. It put an end to the popular front; and all over the world those who had supported and acted on behalf of the strategy felt betrayed. The Soviet leadership would deny that they had given up the popular front but insist on the contrary that the German agreement was a defensive move to safeguard national security at a time when the imperialists were trying to push Germany and the Soviet Union into war against one another or to appease the former at the expense of the latter. Soviet officials and writers would later claim some kind of moral and strategic victory, arguing that the pact preserved Soviet strength which could have been squandered in a premature military engagement with German power, so that the nation could better save itself, and the West, when war actually engulfed the globe two years later. Communists in other countries would swallow such tortured reasoning, and even hail the Nazi–Soviet pact as a victory for the world proletariat. Even they, however, could not easily deny that the popular front was dead, at least for the time being.

The Western governments had never put too much faith in the popular front, but the Nazi–Soviet non-aggression pact was none the less a surprise. It sealed the fate of a possible arrangement between them and the Soviet Union against Germany, and in fact it seemed to enhance chances of war. Government officials and press commentaries in London, Paris, and Washington agreed that with the possibility of a Soviet counter-attack gone, German troops would march into Poland at the next possible moment. It was now too late to do much about it, and so when, on 1 September, the expected happened, Britain and France automatically countered by declaring war. Another European war began.

The war, to be sure, was initially a local European conflict, involving territorial readjustments in central Europe. At that time there was no certainty that it would draw in outside powers or affect other parts of the world to turn it into a global war. Still, the repercussions of the diplomatic revolution were keenly felt in Asia. Both Chinese and Japanese had taken the state of German–Soviet antagonism as a given factor in Asian affairs; the Chinese had counted on Soviet aid and the global popular front to tie Japan down, whereas the Japanese had been on the point of formulating an alliance with Germany against the Soviet Union, which would have reduced the latter's assistance to China. All such calculations were now thrown overboard. The Soviet leadership, it is true, assured the Chinese that their commitment to an independent China was unaffected, and that they would continue to provide the latter with arms. But for Chinese Communists the German pact was a bitter pill to swallow. While they dutifully reproduced Moscow's propaganda line to explain the pact, they had serious misgivings about what it implied for the popular front which, after all, had been the basis of their united front strategy with the Nationalists.

The Japanese sense of consternation was perhaps the greatest of all. Prime Minister Hiranuma issued the famous statement on 28 August, saying that 'inexplicable new conditions' had arisen in Europe, and proceeded to resign. This was a candid reaction to the diplomatic revolution. What was most frustrating was that the Japanese had not prepared an alternative; they had focused their attention on negotiating a German alliance aimed at the Soviet Union. Almost overnight they were forced to go back to square one and start again, a most difficult task in view of the hardened attitude of the United States. To be sure, to the extent that the German–Soviet agreement meant the demise of the popular front, this was to be welcomed; perhaps there would be less Soviet aid to China. But such a gain was offset by what was seen as Germany's betrayal of the spirit of the anti-Comintern pact, and in fact the pact threatened to nullify this agreement altogether.

Thus the outbreak of war in Europe had profound global implications. It not only signalled the failure of appeasement; it also implied the demise of both the popular front and the anti-Comintern pact. These three schemes had been attempts at redefining international affairs in response to the steady erosion of the Versailles and Washington treaty systems. Now all these structures were gone, and the world was entering a period of anarchy and confusion. If order were to emerge out of the state of uncertainty, another global war might have to be fought. This was why the German invasion of Poland was not simply a local issue of the traditional sort. On the contrary, it showed in stark clarity the absence of structure and definition throughout the world. Whether some order might yet emerge, and what kind of order it would be, were questions in which all nations would be interested. Chinese and Japanese, no less than Europeans and Americans, would be doing their share in providing answers.

REFERENCES AND NOTES

1. A good recent autobiographical account of the Marco Polo Bridge incident and its escalation is Matsumoto Shigeharu, *Shanghai jidai* (The Shanghai years, 3 vols; Tokyo 1975).

The Origins of WWII in Asia and the Pacific

2. John P. Fox, *Germany and the Far Eastern Crisis, 1931–1938* (Oxford 1982), pp. 234, 243.
3. Jonathan Haslam, 'Soviet aid to China and Japan's place in Moscow's foreign policy, 1937–1939', in Ian Nish (ed.), *Some Aspects of Soviet–Japanese Relations in the 1930s* (London 1982), p. 36.
4. Robert Dallek, *Franklin D. Roosevelt and American Foreign Policy, 1932–1945* (New York 1979), p. 147.
5. Haslam, 'Soviet aid', p. 38.
6. *Nihon gaikō nenpyō narabi shuyō bunsho* (Japanese diplomatic documents and a chronology of main events; Tokyo 1955), 2: 370–1.
7. Fox, *Germany*, p. 266.
8. The scale and extent of the Nanking atrocities is a matter of serious dispute among writers. For a recent assessment, see Hata Ikuhiko, *Nanking jihen* (The Nanking incident; Tokyo 1986).
9. James R. Leutze, *Bargaining for Supremacy: Anglo-American Naval Collaboration, 1937–1941* (Chapel Hill 1977), p. 19.
10. Fox, *Germany*, pp. 292–3.
11. Hosoya Chihiro *et al.* (eds), *Nichi-Bei Kankeishi*, (A history of Japanese-American relations; Tokyo 1971), 1: 129.
12. *Chung-hua Min-kuo, Chung-yao chih-liao ch'u-pien: tui-Ju kang-chan shih-chi* (Important historical documents of the Chinese republic: the period of the anti-Japanese war; Taipei, n.d.), 6.3: 33–45.
13. Defence Agency, War History Division (ed.), *Daihonei rikugunbu* (The army supreme command; Tokyo 1968), 1: 532–3.
14. Ibid., 1: 546.
15. Ibid., 1: 549.
16. *Ugaki Kazushige nikki* (Ugaki Kazushige diary; Tokyo 1970), 2: 1235–8.
17. Ibid., 2: 1240.
18. Ibid., 2: 1245–52.
19. Foreign Ministry (ed.), *Gaimushō no hyakunen* (One hundred years of the Foreign Ministry; Tokyo 1966), 2: 402–11.
20. *Ugaki nikki*, 2: 1253–56.
21. Arnold A. Offner, *American Appeasement: United States Foreign Policy and Germany, 1933–38* (Cambridge 1969), p. 269.
22. Wayne S. Cole, *Roosevelt and the Isolationists, 1932–45* (Lincoln, Neb. 1983), pp. 346–8.
23. *Nichi-Bei*, 1: 151.
24. *Foreign Relations of the United States: Japan* (Washington 1943), 1: 797–800.
25. Jonathan G. Utley, *Going to War with Japan, 1937–1941* (Knoxville 1985), pp. 44–7.
26. *Chung-hua Min-kuo*, 6.3: 45–51.
27. Ibid., 6.3: 51–4.
28. Ibid., 6.3: 33–45.
29. *Gaimushō*, 2: 420–2.
30. *Daihonei rikugunbu*, 1: 601.

Chapter 3
THE FORGING OF AN ANTI-DEMOCRATIC COALITION

The year between September 1939 and September 1940 saw Japan engaging in its own diplomatic revolution in response to the European war. As the initial 'phoney' phase of the war came to an abrupt end in the spring of 1940 with German attacks on Scandinavia, the Low Countries, and France, a conscious decision was made in Tokyo to take advantage of the developments and to reorient its policy once again, this time not only to conclude an alliance with Germany and Italy, but also to effect a *rapprochement* with the Soviet Union. Tokyo's grandiose scheme for establishing a worldwide coalition of non-democratic and anti-democratic nations pitted itself against an alliance of democratic powers, led by the United States and Britain, which was also being forged. Thus, within a year after the German invasion of Poland, world politics was once again becoming sharply divided. The upshot was an even more heightened sense of crisis across the Pacific than ever before.

TOKYO AND WASHINGTON

Japan's initial official response to the outbreak of war in Europe, however, was in the opposite direction. When they recovered from their shock and organized a new cabinet under General Abe Nobuyuki, Tokyo's top leaders began yet another search for fundamental guidelines of foreign policy and strategy. Already a few were beginning to suggest that Japan follow the German lead and effect a *rapprochement* with the Soviet Union. They believed that Germany was going to be successful in its expansionist and revisionist policy and would soon establish a new order in Europe. The Soviet Union appeared to be an accomplice, thus in effect dividing Europe into two spheres of influence. Under the circumstances, it would make sense for Japan to join these powers and together establish a new global order. Ideological opposition to communism would, for the time being at least, have to be subordinated to power considerations, particularly in view of the bitter experience of Nomonhan. (A cease-fire agreement was signed in Moscow on 15 September, restoring the status quo *ante bellum.*) Moreover, as the Soviet Union was still the major supplier of war material to Chungking, an understanding with Moscow might lead to the discontinuation of this aid, which passed through the 'north-western route' of Kansu Province, Inner Mongolia, and Sinkiang.

Among civilian officials, several were in agreement with such reasoning. Tōgō Shigenori, now ambassador in Moscow, Shiratori Toshio, ambassador in Rome, and the so-called 'revisionists' in the Foreign Ministry argued that a pact between Japan and the Soviet Union would serve to put psychological pressure on both China and the United States and facilitate the solution of the Chinese war. The emergence of such a view is one of the most crucial factors in the pre-history of the Pacific war. Why some civilian diplomats joined the military in advocating this strategy is a fascinating question. Most fundamental was the sense of frustration with the long, drawn-out war with China. The war was draining national resources, and it was not resulting in any tangible benefits. On the contrary, the Japanese people were being asked to sacrifice more and more of their livelihood for a military undertaking whose purpose was far from clear. Reluctant or unable to face the fact that at bottom the basic cause of the long war was the resistance presented by Chinese nationalism, Japanese leaders persuaded themselves and the nation that what prevented a quick victory was foreign assistance to China. Soviet aid to Chungking was particularly important. It followed, then, that an agreement with the Soviets so that the latter would terminate their shipment of military goods to Chungking would go a long way towards settling the war. The Soviet Union in other words, was being blamed for Japan's failure to win in China. Such an attitude, looking for a scapegoat, would remain with the country's leaders till the entire world turned against them.[1]

Some went beyond tactical reasoning to embrace a vision of a new world order. Since 1931, of course, Japan had steadily defied the international system, and after 1938 made repeated announcements about the need to establish a new order in East Asia to replace the defunct Washington conference system. In the autumn of 1939, however, advocates of a *rapprochement* with the Soviet Union went beyond such a formula and developed a grandiose scheme for a global *entente* of anti-Anglo-American powers, in particular Japan, Germany, Italy, and the Soviet Union. These seemed to have in common their opposition to an international order defined by American and British values such as capitalism and democracy and were in that sense all revisionist powers. They appeared to be on the ascendant and would be able to put an end once and for all to Anglo-American supremacy if they joined forces and acted decisively. While before this time revisionism had taken the form of an advocacy of a Fascist alliance against communism, now it was to be an alliance of all forces opposed to capitalism and democracy.

It is difficult to believe that the Japanese advocates of such a strategy really thought through all the implications. Even as late as 1939, Japan's economic and political systems had more in common with those of Britain or the United States than of the countries with which it would ally itself. After all, despite calls for national mobilization and stringent controls over domestic consumption and especially in the areas of education and entertainment, Japanese industry and commerce were still predominantly in private hands. In spite of repeated enunciations of the principle of self-sufficiency, the country was if anything more dependent than ever on the importation of oil, copper, scrap iron, as well as machine tools, most of which came from the United States.[2] In politics, too, at least there were still political parties in Japan, and nothing remotely resembling the National Socialist Party in Germany or the Communist Party in the Soviet Union had emerged. Although restricted by censorship regulations, the press was not inactive, and the criticism of the government was tolerated so long as it did not pertain to raising questions about the emperor institution. The Japanese fascination and even obsession with the idea of distancing themselves from the Anglo-American nations and identifying with Germany or the Soviet Union was an emotional response to the frustration of a long war, and had little to do with a specific programme for solidarity with revisionist forces in the world.

If nothing else, the German–Soviet division of Poland, followed by the Soviet invasion of Finland in November, might have given the Japanese revisionists second thoughts. However, they appear to have taken these events as further evidence that German and Soviet power was on the ascendance, and that Japan should join and emulate them. Those who had advocated that Japan aim at southward expansion were emboldened by the German and Soviet moves which they believed would weaken the position of Britain, France, the Netherlands, and other European countries and make it that much easier for Japan to move into their colonies in Asia. Moreover, it was felt that a combination of anti-democratic powers would facilitate Japan's control of China, which would succumb to Japan just as Poland did to the combined forces of Germany and the Soviet Union. But it was far from clear how the nation could achieve so easily what it had tried and failed to do in many years. The strategy assumed that the Chinese would give up once the Soviet Union forsook them, and that the United States and Britain would also abandon them. It did not occur to the Japanese advocates of an anti-democratic coalition that such an *entente* might strengthen, rather than discourage, the ties between China and the Anglo-American powers, making the task of subjugating the former that much more difficult.

These problems were clearly recognized by the new prime minister,

Abe. Coming to office on the heels of Hiranuma's abrupt resignation following the signing of the Nazi–Soviet pact, Abe sought to reorient Japanese foreign policy. His appointment of Admiral Nomura Kichisaburō as foreign minister was a clear sign that this reorientation would take the form of an accommodation with the United States, as the admiral was known as a moderate, someone knowledgeable about America. He agreed with Abe that it would be a dangerous thing to follow the suggestion of Tōgō, Shiratori, and others and to effect a *rapprochement* with the Soviet Union before all efforts had been exhausted to improve relations with the United States. A premature *rapprochement* with Germany and the Soviet Union would most certainly harden America's policy against Japan. Washington had already indicated its determination to stand firm by notifying the intention to abrogate the treaty of commerce. Such an eventuality could lead to a total cessation of trade between the two countries, a disaster which would not be made up for by a hasty *entente* with Berlin and Moscow. Thus reasoning, the Foreign Ministry under Nomura initiated a series of talks with the United States, through Ambassador Joseph C. Grew in Tokyo, for a new treaty of commerce.

At bottom was Nomura's perception that the nation was once again at a crossroads. It could either follow Germany and the Soviet Union, or return to the earlier policy of co-operation with America and Britain. There was no assurance that either would work to Japan's satisfaction, but having tried the German option and failed, the country would have no choice but to try to conciliate the United States, upon which Japan was so heavily dependent economically.

The trouble was that the war in China and that in Europe made such reorientation difficult, if not impossible. Even Nomura accepted the need for asserting Japan's special rights in Manchuria and part of China. The nation was in China to stay. What Nomura thought possible was some understanding with the United States so that Japanese–American relations would not be exacerbated because of the Chinese conflict. He well recognized that the continuation of the war would be incompatible with a fundamental reconciliation with America, but he somehow was optimistic that the United States would tolerate Japan's presence in China so long as it did not directly threaten American interests. Thus reasoning, he offered Ambassador Grew certain concessions in return for a new treaty of commerce; Japan would honour and respect American rights in China, and more specifically agree to reopen the lower Yangtze river to foreign shipping – such shipping had been forbidden since 1937.

Such modest concessions were all that the Japanese government could offer in view of the military's adamant opposition to more drastic steps. Moreover, a slight modification of policy towards China was not meant to alter the search for a 'new order' in East Asia. Even as the Abe ministry rejected the alternative of a *rapprochement* with Germany and the Soviet Union, it never abandoned the preceding cabinet's doctrine of a new order. In fact, at the end of December Nomura put his signature on a document signed also by the war and the navy ministers, enunciating the same doctrine; it asserted the need to make use of Japan's neutrality during the European war so as to help settle the Chinese conflict and construct a new order 'in East Asia, including the south'.[3] That implied expanding Japan's empire southward, beyond the China coast. Such an objective would clearly affect Japanese relations with Britain, France, and the United States, and there was every likelihood that these powers, in particular America, would resist Japan's expansion in South-East Asia and the south-western Pacific. Nomura's efforts at conciliating the United States, in other words, would be useless so long as Japan held on to its existing position in China and did not give up its southern schemes.

Washington well understood the situation and responded only coolly to Nomura's overtures. In the last months of 1939 American policy was also in the process of redefinition, with hard-liners arguing for more and more stringent measures against Japan and for greater assistance to China. They had won their first victories in December 1938 (aid to China) and July 1939 (abrogation of the Japanese treaty), and they were not about to let up. They – including Secretary of the Treasury Henry Morgenthau, Secretary of the Interior Harold Ickes, and several, if not all, of the State Department's Asia specialists – were more convinced than ever that Japan was on the defensive and could be pushed further. They were particularly determined that the United States should be prepared to do more to come to China's assistance now that there was a chance of the Soviet Union's reducing its commitments because of the recent reorientation in its foreign policy. The vision of a close relationship between the United States and China as the key element in Asian order had been entertained by generations of Americans, but now it was gaining acceptance among high officials of the Roosevelt administration, and the president himself supported it. For him it was less a sentimental attitude than a pragmatic policy, induced by the realization that for its own security the United States would once again have to play a role in world affairs. National defence hinged on the maintenance of a global balance, which in turn required that American power be brought into the scale. That meant closer ties with Britain and France in Europe, and with China in Asia.

Given the uncertain state of the 'phoney war' as well as the existing neutrality laws, President Roosevelt had to tread gingerly, and he was not prepared to enter into a formal military pact with any of these countries. But he let it be known to his aides that he expected England and France 'to be our first line of defense' against an attack from Germany, and was thus willing to consider sales of aircraft to the democracies. That would necessitate a stepped-up increase in the production of war planes as well as other types of arms. The president's request for an additional $500 million for defence submitted to Congress at this time was but the first in a series of measures he would undertake to deter aggression. 'Deterrence', in fact, became a key concept of American strategy at this time.[4] Only through a military build-up would the United States and its friends be able to frustrate hostile powers' ambitions. And there was little doubt that American arms were going to be needed by the friendly powers. By expressing its willingness to supply the latter with weapons, the United States would be able to show its determination and thereby deter hostile action on the part of Germany and its allies.

The same reasoning applied to Asia. There deterrence would entail an effort to prevent Japanese attacks on South-East Asia and on American territory in the Pacific. In late 1939 the most obvious way of ensuring such deterrence was to weaken Japan's control over China and to strengthen the latter's military capabilities. The threatened abrogation of the treaty of commerce with Japan was a trump card in this process; the United States could agree to a new treaty only in return for Japan's good behaviour in China. Thus, to Foreign Minister Nomura who was desperately trying to find a compromise solution, the American government turned deaf ears, insisting on Japan's acceptance of the principle of equal opportunity as a precondition for any negotiation for a commercial treaty. What that meant was an end to Japan's assertion of special rights and privileges in China, in fact an invitation to Japan to return at least to the status quo of 1937 and to deal once again with the government of Chiang Kai-shek. From Tokyo's point of view, such a drastic solution was unacceptable, and Washington well knew it. The latter was in no hurry to negotiate a new treaty, and thus the talks between Nomura and Grew reached an impasse in late December, with the result that the abrogation of the existing treaty would go into effect a month afterwards.

Not every official in America agreed that such a tough stand would be beneficial. Ambassador Grew and some of his aides continued to think Japanese–American relations could best be dealt with in the framework of the Washington treaties, envisaging a return to some degree of co-operation across the Pacific. They believed that the best way to ensure Japanese good behaviour was to keep them within that framework so as to detach them from Germany or the Soviet Union. Otherwise, Japan would be forever alienated and pushed further into the arms of these potential antagonists of the United States. Moreover, in the view of Grew and his supporters, China was not worth the trouble with Japan. The country was too disunited, too amorphous to be a reliable partner of the United States. Japan, on the other hand, was a better-known quantity, and America had once worked with it to their mutual benefit. The strategy, then, should be to reciprocate Nomura's overtures and initiate modest steps towards improving Japanese–American relations. Such ideas, however, were out of touch with the emerging global strategy of the Roosevelt administration with its emphasis on deterrence and on reinforcing potential allies such as China, Britain, and France. To conciliate Japan might, as a purely tactical measure, buy time, as the earlier appeasement policy towards Germany had, but ultimately it would not preserve the peace any more than Munich had.

China, on its part, was a beneficiary of these developments. Although its leaders had to worry about the adverse implications of the Nazi–Soviet pact, they had every reason to be satisfied with America's hardening stance towards Japan. They judged that the Japanese army's offensive strategy had been dulled, and that it was time for Chinese forces to shift from defensive to offensive moves. Thus reasoning, Chiang Kai-shek ordered a frontal assault on Japanese troops throughout the country in the middle of December. The resulting battle, the fiercest of the war, was inconclusive, but was instrumental in persuading the Japanese military of the need for yet another reconsideration of the war effort. Much of the first few months of the year 1940 would be taken up in a futile attempt to break the impasse in China.

TOKYO AND NANKING

On 16 January 1940, the Abe cabinet resigned, taking responsibility for lack of progress on the diplomatic front. Abe was replaced as prime minister by Admiral Yonai Mitsumasa. Arita Hachirō returned to the Foreign Ministry to head it for the third time. Both Yonai and Arita were in basic agreement with their respective predecessors regarding the need for preventing a crisis with the United States. Yonai, a retired admiral, was much like Nomura in outlook, and Arita was known for his opposition to a German alliance directed against the Anglo-American nations. The new leaders would be seriously interested in improving Japanese relations with these countries, but there was little hope that they could accomplish what others had failed to do. The United States certainly gave them no chance, formally abrogating the treaty of commerce with Japan ten days after the formation of the new cabinet of Tokyo.

Not surprisingly, the Yonai cabinet then turned to China, the only area where Japan could undertake some initiatives. If a reconciliation with the United States as a way of solving the China impasse was not going to work, obviously the only alternative left was to deal with the latter directly. But there were many ways of doing so, and as many as four were tried at this time, with no significant result.

One alternative was strategic reorientation. It involved reducing the level of Japanese army strength in China, numbering 850,000 at the end of 1939. Chinese forces far outnumbered them, amounting to over 1 million in the Wuhan area alone. In the view of the supreme command in Tokyo, Japan was simply not in a position to prepare against the Soviet Union while at the same time engaging in an extensive war in China. Some army officials, to be sure, had begun advocating a *rapprochement* with the Soviet Union, as was seen above. But that had not yet been accepted as a national policy, and a hypothetical war with the Soviet Union remained the key assumption of Japanese strategy in early 1940. For this reason, it was agreed in Tokyo that future military action in China should be confined to a few key areas so as to prepare Japanese resources for a possible confrontation with the Soviet Union. As worked out by the General Staff, the new plan called for reducing the size of the Japanese army in China to 500,000 by mid-1941, to be concentrated on the Shanghai–Nanking–Hangchow triangle as well as north China and Inner Mongolia. That would entail withdrawing from the Wuhan and Canton areas.

No sooner had the General Staff adopted the strategy of reducing commitments in China, than the Japanese army on the continent raised fierce objections. They agreed with their superiors in Tokyo that the war in China should be settled soon, but insisted that this could be done only by reinforcing, not reducing, the size of the combatants. Japanese military in China argued that the reduction of forces would become possible once Japan won a decisive victory, which could be attained by sending more divisions. This argument was based on the same reasoning that had led to the escalation of the conflict in China since 1937, with no decisive result. But as in the past, the supreme command bowed to pleas from the field, and agreed to send two more divisions to the theatre of war, one from Japan and the other from Manchuria. It was hoped that the reinforced army would then engage in a final knock-out battle in the autumn and achieve victory, after which the force level would be reduced, perhaps to 700,000. All that such planning amounted to was to confirm the stalemate in China, for there was no realistic reason to believe that victory was any more in sight now that it had been before 1939. In fact, the episode forced Japanese strategists to the realization that it would be next to impossible to try to settle the Chinese war while at the same time preparing for war against the Soviet Union. Such thinking would soon come to reinforce arguments by advocates of a pro-Soviet strategy for effecting a major reorientation of Japanese policy.

In the meantime, Japan pursued two other approaches in early 1940, both of a more political than military nature. One was to finalize the Wang Ching-wei scheme by having him establish a new government in Nanking. Wang, it will be recalled, had secretly left Chungking for Hanoi at the end of 1938, there to engage in negotiations with Japanese officials for an honourable end to the war. He had also sought to persuade other Chinese leaders to join him in the effort, but that had been a total failure. Only a handful of personal confidants would join him, whereas the Kuomintang regime in Chungking remained steadfast in its opposition to any compromise with Japan. Moreover, various organizations at home as well as Chinese communities abroad reacted strongly against Wang's machinations, calling him a traitor, a madman, and worse.[5] He was deprived of his membership in the party and branded a national enemy. In negotiating with the Japanese, then, he represented only himself, an outlaw in China.

Wang and his tiny band of followers nevertheless continued to believe they were doing the right thing in order to spare the country more bloodshed. Given the overwhelming presence of Japanese power, they reasoned that the only way to mitigate its impact was to stop the war and concentrate on economic and political reconstruction. Otherwise, more fighting would only lead to the extension of Communist and Soviet influence. As he told a group of followers who proclaimed themselves to be the Nationalist Party of China, the country was in danger of being transformed into a province of the Soviet Union; the Communists were fighting not for China but for that country. But for their opposition the war with Japan would have ended much earlier. The Chinese Communists, however, were taking orders from Moscow, and they never had the good of China in mind. In August 1939 Wang pointed to the Nazi–Soviet non-aggression pact as an instance of Soviet duplicity and untrustworthiness. Moreover, he noted that the Chinese Communists, who had followed the Moscow line in denouncing Germany, had now begun praising it. That sort of subservience was why he and his comrades were trying to awaken their countrymen to the danger of succumbing to Soviet influence, and to negotiate with Japan for an end to the fighting.[6]

Unfortunately, his negotiations with Japanese officials were far from satisfactory. His hope that 'peace will lead to nation-building on an anti-communist basis' was frustrated as Japan refused to make substantial concessions to him beyond bringing him to Nanking in early 1940. Prior to his inauguration on 30 March as 'acting president' of a 'reorganized government', he held a meeting with officials of the 'north China political council', the separatist regime set up in Peking under Japanese control. It was not clear how these regimes in Peking and Nanking would be merged, but it was generally agreed that a central government would be established in Nanking that was committed to the principles of Chinese sovereignty, independence, economic development, anti-communism, and permanent peace in Asia. It would also co-operate with Japan in establishing a new order in East Asia.[7] These ideas were presented as an affirmation of Sun Yat-sen's fundamental doctrines, and thus the inauguration of the new 'central' government was to mean a return of the Kuomintang government to Nanking from Chungking; in other words, the reorganized regime was to be the legitimate Nationalist government, and the one at Chungking under Chiang Kai-shek a 'false' one, still persisting in a pro-Communist, anti-Japanese policy. As the true heir to Sun Yat-sen, the leaders assembled at Nanking were to carry forward the task of national reconstruction through co-operation with Japan. As Wang's regime was inaugurated, he reiterated the theme that he was acting thus in order to bring peace to China and to enable it to emerge as an independent nation. 'China must maintain the independence of her sovereignty and her national freedom before she is able to carry out the principles of good neighborliness, of a common anti-Comintern front and economic co-operation and, further, share in the responsibility of building up the new order in East Asia', he declared.[8]

Such a statement sounded hollow against the background of the war; the idea that China could be independent while 850,000 Japanese troops were stationed on its soil was fantastic. Of course, Wang visualized that sooner or later the bulk of them would be withdrawn, and the government of China entrusted to him in a spirit of co-operation with Japan; and he would continue to hold such an illusion till his death in 1944. The tragedy was that for the Japanese army he was even less than an instrument of their aggression. He was a mere tactical expediency, to be discarded if they hit upon a better alternative.

Nothing showed Japanese cynicism better than the fact that Tokyo did not recognize the Wang regime right away. Despite the pomp and ostentatiousness of inaugurating a legitimate Kuomintang government at Nanking, Japan's main concern was to use the event as a lever in approaching Chungking, to see if the latter would now be more willing to accept a negotiated settlement of the war. Thus simultaneously with the three other decisions – to reduce the force level in China, to augment it for one final time, and to inaugurate a Wang government – Japan initiated a series of secret talks with a Chinese who represented himself as a younger brother of T. V. Soong (thus a brother-in-law of Chiang Kai-shek). This clutching at straws is instructive in a number of ways. It shows how pessimistic the Japanese army was becoming about its ability to settle the war through military efforts alone. Second, it reveals the existence of a number of individuals and agencies representing the Japanese army, working at cross-purposes. The secret talks began, for instance, as a result of a chance encounter between a junior intelligence officer of the Japanese army and the alleged brother of Soong. Third, the episode also indicates that there were contacts at all levels between Chinese and Japanese, not just Wang Ching-wei and some pro-Japanese factions, but many other groups willing to talk with the Japanese. Most important, the abortive negotiations reveal that Chungking was adept at playing the game of deception. Postwar testimonies established that the highest authorities at Chungking were aware of the secret talks, which were carried on to frustrate the Wang scheme and confound the Japanese. The man impersonating T. V. Soong's brother was an imposter, but was taking orders from Chiang Kai-shek. Thus the negotiations were bound to fail. But the episode showed Japan's lack of consistent strategy: anything would do that eased the burden on Japanese resources, short of a humiliating withdrawal from north China and Manchuria.[9]

For that was what the Nationalists would insist on as a condition for settling the war. To Chiang and his aides, it made sense to encourage Japanese hopes for a settlement if only to gain time. The longer these talks dragged on the more likelihood there would be of American aid reaching Chungking. It might not hurt, either, to engage in some negotiations with the Japanese to impress on the Americans the urgency of more substantial assistance. At bottom, in any event, Chungking's leaders welcomed the growing strain in American–Japanese relations and counted on the former's commitment to the global status quo. Aid from the Soviet Union could no longer be taken for granted, but at last the United States appeared ready to replace it as the major outside power in defence of China. Under the circumstances, the Nationalists could afford to take a firm stand on north China and Manchuria. Any agreement with Japan would have to include the principle of Chinese integrity; the separate state of Manchukuo would have to be abolished. At most, the Chinese might be willing to live with a semi-autonomous Manchuria, but not an independent one.

From Japan's point of view, however, Manchuria and north China were the crux of the matter. They were ready to retrench in China proper so as to concentrate on a possible war with the Soviet Union in which Manchuria would be of vital strategic significance. Even more important, solid control over the region was part and parcel of the design for self-sufficiency. The first months of 1940 were already showing the impact of the European situation in that supplies from Europe, particularly machine tools and industrial machinery from Germany, had stopped because of the war. That was making the Japanese economy more dependent than ever on the United States.[10] If, in addition, Japan lost its control over the resources of north China and Manchuria, it would be back where it was before 1931. That could not be contemplated, and thus the Yonai cabinet found itself constrained from all sides as it sought to steer Japanese policy away from potential dangers.

The more precarious the situation for Japan, the better it looked from the perspective of Washington and London. Officials there, it is true, were still trying to see if the 'phoney war' might be continued indefinitely without breaking into full-scale fighting. As best exemplified by Roosevelt's sending of Under-Secretary of State Sumner Welles to Rome, Berlin, Paris, and London, there was a lingering hope that a serious war could be postponed, if not avoided altogether. Welles was authorized to discuss peace on the basis 'of disarmament and an opening of trade', a formula of inter-war internationalism.[11] Such a mission indicated that as far as the United States was concerned, any restoration of world stability would have to be on that basis. Translated into policy terms, it implied America's continued determination to insist on the restoration of a long-gone status quo. This would apply to Asia as well as Europe. No wonder, then, that the United States government showed little interest in the formation of the allegedly more co-operative Yonai cabinet. After the abrogation of the treaty of commerce in late January, the two nations conducted their trade on an *ad hoc* basis, with no legal framework to protect their respective rights. The state of uncertainty served American policy well, for it would keep up the pressure on Japan for improving its behaviour.

The Japanese government would have liked to do so, but what could it do to please the Americans, short of terminating the war in China on the latter's terms? Besides, Tokyo's contradictory strategies in China only irritated American officials and gave them no reason to trust in Japanese sincerity. The Wang Ching-wei scheme, in particular, was the last straw as far as the United States was concerned. Committed as it was to the survival of the Nationalist regime in Chungking, Washington dismissed the new Nanking government as just a desperate effort by the Japanese to achieve what they could not gain on the battlefield. About all that the Wang scheme did was further to stiffen America's resolve to bolster Chiang Kai-shek's forces.

Britain was a partner in the policy, but was already a junior one, for its attention had to focus on matters closer home. The Chamberlain cabinet did not cherish the prospect of a frontal war with Germany, but by late winter, optimism was fading, and the Royal Navy took steps such as placing mines off the Norwegian coast, to prepare for a German offensive. In the meantime, it would have to defer to the United States to take the lead in formulating an Asian strategy. Britain simply did not have enough ships to divert to Asia, and would not be in a position to defend its imperial position without American assistance. The two navies, to be sure, had not gone much beyond preliminary stages in co-ordinating their Asian-Pacific strategy. For instance, American officials were reluctant to share with their British counterparts cryptographic secrets concerning Japanese codes; those codes would in time be broken and provide valuable information to the American government. On the British part, not all its technological innovations in naval warfare were divulged to Americans.[12] Still, there was now far more extensive and regular communication between the two countries' naval officials regarding the European situation and its implications for Asia than two years earlier, at the time of the Ingersoll mission. Moreover, in China the two governments remained in essential agreement and often reiterated their adherence to the nine-power treaty. When Under Secretary Welles was in London in March, they confirmed this position and told the Chinese ambassador that America and Britain pursued identical policies in Asia.[13] When the Wang regime was established in Nanking, the United States and Britain both immediately proclaimed their continued recognition of Chungking as the only legitimate representative of the Chinese people. Japan's various manœuvres in early 1940, then, were not working, but on the contrary, further alienating the powers. Had the European stalemate continued, Tokyo's leaders might have been compelled to undertake a much more drastic reorientation of their China policy. Once again, however, European events intervened, leading to a more direct linkage between international affairs in two parts of the globe.

THE GERMAN SPRING OFFENSIVE

The 'phoney war' came to an abrupt end when, starting in April 1940, German forces carried out a lightning attack on democratic Europe: Norway and Denmark first, Holland and Belgium next, and finally France. Within two months, all these countries had fallen. Only Britain remained free, apart from neutral countries such as Sweden, Switzerland, and Spain.

Hitler's offensive was a well-calculated gamble. His ultimate objective of crushing Slavic power in the east had not been given up, but he first sought to subjugate the rest of Europe in preparation for that struggle. The fall of Scandinavia, the Low Countries, and France should, he reasoned, so demoralize the British that they would be prepared to give up and 'co-operate' with him in the supreme task of combating the Russians. If they refused, Germany would have to employ force against the Royal Navy and bomb English cities to induce them to surrender. They would do so unless they received substantial aid from across the Atlantic. For this reason it was important to prevent American interference in the war, and the best way of ensuring this, it was believed, would be to make sure that Germany did not provoke the United States. Hitler would assure the American people that he harboured no ill feelings towards them, and that the two countries could maintain a peaceful relationship even while war raged in Europe. To encourage a pacifist or at least a non-interventionist sentiment in America, Hitler would make use of propaganda disseminated by pro-German groups there.

The Soviet Union, in the meantime, was not idle. Having, in the previous autumn, incorporated Latvia and Estonia into its domain and invaded Finland as well as Poland, it now took advantage of Germany's victories in the west by finalizing its absorption of Lithuania and invading Bessarabia. (The Soviet Union and Finland signed a truce just before Germany's spring offensive began, specifying the cession to the former of the Karelian isthmus.) While Hitler's troops marched westward, there were predictions that Stalin's would help themselves to Romania and the Dardanelles. The Soviet Union thus was matching Germany in self-aggrandizement while the rest of the world looked on, dazed.

Obviously, the big question mark in the spring of 1940 was Britain. Whether it would hold out or succumb to the German onslaught would determine not only the outcome of the war but the future of German–Soviet relations. The emergence of a National cabinet under the leadership of Winston S. Churchill, on the very day that German forces began their assault on the Low Countries (10 May), signalled the British resolve not to give up. The new prime minister reiterated that his people would fight to the bitter end rather than see their country occupied by Hitler's agents. But Churchill was convinced that Britain could survive only if the United States were ready to give it massive aid, short of war if not by going to war itself. From this time on, the forging of a more solid alliance between the two English-speaking nations would become a fundamental objective of Churchill's strategy.

In President Roosevelt he found a kindred spirit. Their secret correspondence by letter, cable, or telephone, would come to number in the hundreds, documenting a rare instance of close co-operation between two countries even before they both became involved in war. For Roosevelt, a declaration of war against Germany could not be contemplated. Not only would public opinion react negatively, but America's own defence capabilities were still inadequate. The first priority in the spring of 1940 was to shore up defences and then to provide Britain what 'surplus' arms there were. Still, there was no doubt in Roosevelt's mind that the United States would become steadily more involved in the war. After the fall of France, to be sure, some of his advisers warned him that American assistance of Britain might be wasted and, worse, utilized by German forces should they occupy the British Isles. But Roosevelt chose to couple America's destiny with Britain's. As he declared in his commencement address at the University of Virginia on 10 June, the United States could not be 'a lone island in a world dominated by force'. The entire world was interrelated, and the United States must help those struggling against 'the gods of force and hate'.

These remarks indicate self-consciousness about America's role as a democratic power, the last hope of freedom for mankind. At a time when nations were struggling for survival and giving priority to military defences and strategies, Roosevelt held to the view that a country such as the United States could remain true to its democratic traditions even while it armed itself. He did not agree, he said, that 'only by abandoning our freedom, our ideals, our way of life, can we build our defenses adequately, can we match the strength of the aggressors'. Here he had in mind the domestic and foreign critics of American preparedness, particularly the isolationists and pacifists who, though dwindling in number after the spring of 1940, vociferously argued that a warring democracy was a contradiction in terms. Such pessimism was being attacked not only by the Roosevelt administration but by prominent leaders in the business, academic, and journalistic world. Henry Luce, for instance, wrote in *Life* in early June that, should Britain and France fall, 'we know that we and we only among the great powers are left to defend the democratic faith throughout the world'. The United States must be prepared 'to meet force with superior force'. The theologian Reinhold Neibuhr entered into the fray with his *Christianity and World Politics*, a ringing enunciation of the idea that in a world dominated by totalitarian dictatorships, pacifism was untenable, and that Christian duty called for involvement, even going to war.[14]   Given the spreading perception of America as the last bastion of democracy, it followed that aid to Britain was an obligation that the American people had to undertake. To be sure, they would not, at this time, support going to war. But more and more of them were lining up behind the administration's policy of doing whatever was practicable to help Britain. In the bleak days after the fall of France, Roosevelt and his advisers began preparing specific plans for doing so. The appointment of Henry Stimson and Frank Knox, pro-British Republicans, as secretaries of war and the navy, respectively, signalled that his advisers would be even more forceful in this task than in the past.

Aid to Britain inevitably entailed consideration of the fate of the British empire and the Commonwealth, far flung from Africa through the Middle East, all the way to East Asia and Oceania. The defence of Australia, Singapore, Hong Kong, and Burma was particularly important because of their strategic locations and the rich mineral resources which the Japanese coveted. Japan, it was widely feared in Washington as well as London, would seek to take advantage of the German victories to penetrate South-East Asia and the south-western Pacific, through diplomatic pressures if possible, but through military force if necessary. Should the region, or even a portion of it, fall to Japanese control, the western Pacific would become a Japanese lake, cutting off the Commonwealth from the mother country. Manpower and resources would no longer reach the British Isles, making their defence that much more problematical. Britain, moreover, would have to divert its resources to this area to defend it, or else concentrate on fighting the Germans and give up Asia and the Pacific.

Here again, the destiny of the region came to hinge upon the United States. It was no longer a question of upholding the status quo. It was more a matter of whether the United States would become involved in order to prevent Japanese takeover of the region, or whether the latter would succeed in doing so before America had a chance to pre-empt it. The two countries that had already sharply diverged in China would be engaged in a struggle for control of South-East Asia and the south-western Pacific. Or else they would tacitly agree to a condominium over the Pacific, an idea that went back to Tokyo's 1934 proposal but one that could be considered this late in Washington only as a last-minute tactical move.

For the time being, however, American policy did not go beyond the earlier strategy of deterrence. President Roosevelt obviously did not want Japanese penetration of South-East Asia, but he was not ready to involve American force actively in the region which would surely result in a war with Japan. Such a war would be premature and divert resources from the Atlantic. The best strategy, he reasoned, was therefore to do something to prevent Japan's southward expansion. In the spring of 1940 the most obvious means open to him was to keep the bulk of the United States fleet in Hawaiian waters. The ships, the majority of which were normally kept on the west coast, had completed their annual exercises in the vicinity of Hawaii, but instead of sending them to their home bases, Roosevelt decided to keep them in the central Pacific. That, he thought, would give the Japanese a signal of American determination to prevent their rash action in Asia. Beyond this, however, he was not ready to go. For instance, there would be no formal economic sanctions, and aviation fuel would continue to be shipped to Japan, and trade allowed to be carried on even without a formal treaty of commerce. In other words, before the summer of 1940 American policy focused on deterring Japan from taking advantage of the European war to establish a larger sphere of control in the Asian-Pacific region.

The strategy was one of calculated bluff, and it did not work, as will be seen. In the meantime, the United States government was careful not to antagonize the Soviet Union. Policy towards that country was an extremely sensitive issue. When the Soviet Union invaded Finland in late 1939, there was fear of a German–Soviet division of Europe, and American opinion of the latter reached the lowest point, perhaps even lower than that of Germany. (A *New York Times* editorial sarcastically noted, 'Workers of Finland, unite: you have nothing to bury but your dead.')[15] Now, however, in the spring of 1940, public criticism of the Soviet Union became much more muted; in fact, the press generally refrained from attacking the Soviet takeover of Bessarabia or its purported plans to conquer Romania and other parts of the Balkans. This change was clearly brought about by the realization that the growth of Soviet power would restrain Germany and, as *The New York Times* predicted, eventually benefit Britain.[16] Here the key concept was power, not ideology. American officials and the press alike had been impressed with 'Bolshevik imperialism', as a reporter put it, which appeared to transform the Soviet Union into a practitioner of power politics regardless of its ideological orientation. It would be difficult to consider co-operation with such a country on political or ideological grounds, and there was obviously no way the Soviet Union could be fitted into the developing idea of a global struggle for survival of democracy. But at least its power could be useful as a means for saving Britain and other democracies. For these reasons, Washington became extremely interested in the possibility that the Soviet Union might come to play a crucial role in determining the fate of Europe. By implication, President Roosevelt was also beginning to sense its potential usefulness in maintaining the power balance in the Asian-Pacific region. Although little would come of such thinking for a while, at least it is to be noted that the Soviet factor was beginning to be perceived as relevant to the future of Asia as well as Europe. To that extent, it would become very important to prevent either a possible Japanese assault on the Soviet Union, or a close relationship between those two. America should do its best to avoid complications with it and welcome, without condoning, its growing power.

In the Soviet Union, too, there was no wish to create unnecessary trouble with the United States. As in the past, Stalin and the Red Army were concerned over the possibility of a two-front war with Germany and Japan. Through the spy ring in Japan headed by Richard Sorge, Moscow was learning of the moves for a German–Japanese alliance in the spring and summer of 1940 which, if consummated, would surely enhance chances for such a war. Moscow had to determine how best to avoid it. One way was through encouraging the idea of a Japanese–Soviet *entente* to ensure at least a truce in northern Asia while the latter prepared for a potential conflict with Germany. Foreign Minister V. M. Molotov frequently sought out Ambassador Tōgō to broach the idea of a *rapprochement* between the two countries. But too friendly a gesture in the direction of Tokyo might further antagonize the United States. From Moscow's standpoint, any increase in the tension between Tokyo and Washington was welcome, as this would have the effect of preoccupying the Japanese with a possible conflict with the United States and turn them away from the north, but too transparent a move by the Soviet Union to encourage Japan's southern expansion would earn America's enmity. So it was best to maintain a reasonably good relationship with Japan without giving the impression of anti-American collusion. Just as the United States needed to retain Soviet goodwill, the latter had to keep in view the possibility of co-operating with the former against a common danger. The potential power of the two countries was such that in combination, it would make a significant difference in world affairs in the months ahead. Both Washington and Moscow realized this. It had nothing to do with ideology or principles; it was much more a matter of survival.

While Britain, France, the United States, and the Soviet Union agonized over their next steps in the Asian-Pacific region, Japanese leadership for once showed little hesitation in taking advantage of European developments. The sense of uncertainty and frustration over an unending war in China now gave way to optimism that the time had come to assert Japanese power boldly in the area and to aim at creating a large Asian bloc under its control. The Yonai cabinet took the first step in that direction when, in late May, it put pressure on the Dutch authorities in Batavia to guarantee to Japan a supply of specified quantities of tin, rubber, petroleum, and other materials from the Indies. That of course, would enable Japan to reduce its dependence on the United States and the British Commonwealth. Clearly, the presence of the United States fleet in Hawaii did not deter Japanese action. There was, to be sure, at this time no plan to use force to move into the Dutch East Indies. Instead, Tokyo insisted on maintaining the status quo over the Dutch colony, fearful that American and British forces might occupy the islands after the fall of Holland to Germany. If Japan could receive certain quantities of essential materials from the islands through negotiation, it would avoid complications with the Anglo-American powers and serve Japan's purposes for the time being.

The next step was to try to settle the Chinese war by taking advantage of German victories. Believing that France and Britain would be helpless in Asia, the Yonai government demanded in June that these countries stop sending aid goods to Chungking through Indo-China and Burma. Such shipments had dwindled to a trickle, but the Japanese were determined to shut them off completely by pressuring the French and the British to close the Indo-China border and the Burma route, respectively. It is to be noted that such high-handed policies were adopted by the allegedly moderate Yonai cabinet. Neither Yonai nor his foreign minister, Arita, was above using such a method to solve the Chinese war and to ensure for Japan a guaranteed supply of essential raw materials. This shows their belief that the old order of Asian international affairs was past resurrection, and that Japan must take the initiative to establish a new.

By then it had become axiomatic that the only power that could prevent the Japanese scheme was the United States. Both Britain and France turned to Washington to see if the latter would be willing to stop Japan from dictating to them in Indo-China and Burma. The European nations wanted specific American commitments such as the sending of the United States fleet further west to Singapore, or imposing economic sanctions on Japan. The United States government was put on the spot. It fully shared the French and British view that America alone stood between Japan and South-East Asia. But the Roosevelt administration was unwilling to risk provoking Japan at a time when the situation in Europe looked so gloomy.[17] This did not mean that the United States would condone Japanese acts, or that it would encourage the European governments to enter into a *modus vivendi* with Tokyo to placate the latter and avoid an Asian conflict. The United States, instead, would retain its firm attitude, keep its fleet in Hawaii, and see if this would not in time serve to restrain Japan. In the meantime, it would not come to France's or Britain's assistance in Asia. The European powers had no choice but to accept Japanese demands. The upshot was that the French government under Marshal H. P. Pétain, which had been established just preceding the Franco-German truce on 21 June, agreed to the closing of the Indo-China route to China and the stationing of a Japanese observer mission in the border area. The Churchill cabinet, on its part, decided to acquiesce in the closing of the Burma Road for three months starting in July 1940.

These were humiliating setbacks for the West; Alexander Cadogan, permanent under-secretary of foreign affairs in London, called the closing of the Burma Road 'our far eastern surrender'. He had opposed giving in to Japanese demands, arguing that the nation should even risk war to do so, for otherwise 'Americans will give us up, with hopeless results, not only in [the] Pacific but also on this side'.[18] Events would prove his pessimism to have been premature. For the United States, although its strategy of deterrence had not prevented Japanese moves in South-East Asia, refused to accept the new developments, viewing them as temporary setbacks, to be rectified once its arms were built up to a sufficient level. The darker the situation looked in Europe and in Asia, the greater grew the determination of Roosevelt and his aides for rendering more decisive and concrete assistance to Britain than had hitherto been considered. The 'destroyer deal', involving the transfer of some fifty American destroyers in exchange for the use of British naval bases in the Caribbean, was only the first dramatic step in what would develop into a *de facto* alliance of the Anglo-American powers. This could have only one implication for Asia: the United States would persist in opposing Japanese action in China and South-East Asia. The only question was what form such opposition would take. At what point would American military intervention come about? Put another way, what would be the point of no return? Should Japan seek to control the whole of Indo-China and, perhaps, the adjoining areas such as Malaya and the Dutch East Indies, would that have to be prevented by force? What would best keep Japan from undertaking such further acts of aggression? Could America continue to count on the Chinese to tie Japanese forces down on the Asian mainland? How should the United States weigh the Soviet factor in its strategic calculations? These were serious questions to which urgent answers were needed, but very difficult to define because of the rapidly changing circumstances of the European war. But however those questions were to be answered, one thing was entirely certain: America would oppose Japanese domination of China and any other parts of Asia in the name of the new order. There would be no reconciliation with Japan unless and until the latter returned to the spirit of the Washington system. The irony was, of course, that in order to re-establish that framework the United States itself would have to become deeply involved in Asian affairs, thus significantly transforming the Washington system in the process.

The Japanese understood the same logic, and sought on their part to prevent United States intrusion into Asia. How could this be done? War games and strategic planning in the spring of 1940 indicated that Tokyo's military leaders had two interrelated ideas. One, a short-range plan, was to prepare for a speedy expedition to the Dutch East Indies, particularly Borneo and Celebes, before the United States or Britain had a chance to intervene, thus establishing a *fait accompli*. A meeting of staff officers of the War Ministry and the General Staff in late May is said to have been the first occasion when an operational plan against the Indies was discussed. A draft war plan of 18 June, written by Lieutenant-Colonel Nishiura Susumu, assumed that it would be necessary to establish air bases in Indo-China and Thailand and then carry out a lightning attack on the Dutch East Indies. Two, at the same time, Japan should consider a long-term plan in the event that the Anglo-American powers came to the assistance of the Dutch. It was expected that sooner or later Britain and the United States would use force to eject Japan from its position of dominance, and war plans must be worked out to meet that contingency. One key question was whether or not the two powers could be separated. The Nishiura plan expressed hope that they could. If there was a likelihood of British obstruction, it pointed out, Japan must attack Singapore. But it would leave the Philippines alone, unless it became impossible to separate Britain and America.[19] By early July, with the German invasion of Britain considered to be a matter of days, Japanese strategists believed it would not be too difficult to put an end to the British empire in Asia as part of the 'southern operation'. An army policy statement adopted on 3 July mentioned Hong Kong and Malaya as possible targets. As for the United States, 'war with America was to be avoided as much as possible', the paper noted, 'although preparations must proceed in anticipation of a probable military clash'.[20]

In the meantime, it would be best to readjust Japanese relations with the Soviet Union through a non-aggression pact. The army was particularly interested in such an approach but, given Foreign Minister Arita's fear that it would result in a further deterioration of Japan's position *vis-à-vis* the Anglo-American powers, Tokyo's military and civilian officials concluded that the best alternative would be a treaty of neutrality between Japan and the Soviet Union. Such an arrangement would ensure the latter's neutrality in the event the former became involved in a conflict with the Anglo-American nations, while at the same time putting an end to Soviet assistance to China. This was a transparently selfish proposal on Japan's part, but at that time Moscow encouraged these overtures as it was anxious to prevent a serious crisis in northern Asia when the future of German strategy, and of Anglo-American policy, was so uncertain. Before negotiations for a neutrality treaty were completed, however, the Yonai cabinet was replaced by one headed by Konoe Fumimaro. It is crucial to note, however, that it did not take the onset of the second Konoe government to initiate a shift in Japanese strategy away from the north (the Soviet Union) to the south. As an army spokesman explained at a joint army–navy meeting on 4 July, Japan could not wage a two-front war, particularly when the end of the China war was not in sight. It was tactically imperative to maintain stability in Japanese–Soviet relations while the southern operation was carried out. The army justified this strategic reorientation by arguing that the establishment of an economically self-sufficient zone was an imperative necessity for the nation; this was because Germany and Italy were creating their own blocs in Europe and Africa, and the Anglo-American powers were likely to follow suit and seek to establish a huge southern bloc linking the Western hemisphere, the southern Pacific, Australia, and India. Should that come about, Japan would forever be denied a chance to become self-sufficient and instead perpetually depend on America and Britain economically. 'We are aiming to put an end to seventy years' dependence on Britain and America commercially and economically', declared an army spokesman.[21]

It was against this background that the idea of a Japanese–German alliance was revived in the spring and summer of 1940. Its supporters increased within both the army and the navy; they were joined by diplomats, journalists, and intellectuals who were dazzled by the European war. German victories in Europe appeared to be just what Japan had been waiting for, frustrated as the country had been by the long, inconclusive war with China. Advocates of a German alliance believed that the Yonai cabinet was not sufficiently enthusiastic about the idea and talked openly of replacing it with a cabinet more to their liking. This was unfair criticism, inasmuch as Yonai and his foreign minister, Arita, had already taken advantage of the European war to act in Indo-China, Burma, and the Dutch East Indies. But they were as yet undecided on the wisdom of tying Japan militarily to Germany, and this indecision cost Yonai his cabinet. The army, determined to bring it down, had the war minister, General Hata Shunroku, resign from the cabinet, a standard tactic to signal the army's displeasure with an existing government. Unable to function any longer, Yonai resigned on 16 July.

DOMESTIC NEW ORDER

The army memorandum of 3 July had mentioned the need for 'the establishment of a strong political structure at home'. It was no accident that the same document that called for a southern strategy included such a statement. Both the strategy of southern advance and the establishment of a domestic new order were expressions of a determination to free Japan from Anglo-American influence. Just as the nation would create a zone of economic self-sufficiency in the Asian-Pacific region, it would also eradicate residues of Anglo-American democracy and liberalism and replace them with a system more congruent with the external task. In short, imperialism abroad would be matched by fascism at home. This had been an idea that had fascinated Japanese strategists and intellectuals for some time, but they had never been able to envisage its actual implementation. Now, for the first time, the opportunity seemed to have arrived – again because of German victories. Japan, as it were, would do what Germany had done domestically as well as externally.

The rhetoric was there in abundance, and all eyes turned to Konoe Fumimaro as the leader of the new domestic structure. He had, in 1938 while he was prime minister, talked of the need for a novel political movement, but that had not yielded anything specific, and Japanese politics had not been significantly transformed in the interval. Now, however, Konoe was being looked upon as the logical choice to resume the struggle. His own ideas were rather vague, but he shared the widely held view that the existing parties had outlived their usefulness, and that the nation needed a new structure to mobilize its resources fully without encumbrances and interference by factions and rivalries.[22] In this sense, Konoe became a symbolic figure; he would do domestically what the army, with the support of the navy, would try to carry out externally. Both inside and outside, Japan would define itself as an embodiment of a new order free from the taint of Anglo-Americanism.

Japan's struggle against Anglo-American influence became official on 22 July, when the second Konoe cabinet was launched. The Japanese leadership viewed itself as facing a moment of opportunity which it would seize boldly, or else, it was feared, Japan would never be able to achieve the status it so ardently aspired to. There were several aspects to the self-conscious espousal of a new order at home and abroad, and it is worth examining them. First of all, according to Yabe Teiji, a political science professor at Tokyo Imperial University and a close confidant of Konoe's, the latter was critical of the emperor for persisting in 'old-fashioned liberalism' and in holding no novel views on foreign policy other than that of co-operation with America and Britain. He, Konoe, was going to be different, for he believed nothing remained permanent and that Japan must reorient its politics and policies in accordance with changing circumstances. He even believed that the Meiji constitution itself needed to be revised to enable the state to exercise a greater measure of control over the nation's economy. He also had in mind the importance of avoiding army–navy rivalries that had plagued Japan's decision-making. He wanted greater governmental control over military affairs, putting an end to the tradition of the independent right of supreme command which, he was convinced, had done irreparable harm to Japanese politics and foreign policy.[23] He did not stop to think that perhaps the best way of checking the power of the military or to mobilize national resources more fully might be to go back to and reaffirm democratic values, as the British and Americans were doing. Because, by 1940, the governments in London and Washington had regained their confidence in democracy, liberalism, and capitalism, Konoe's appointment made it inevitable that the ideological opposition between the two sides would become sharper.

This did not mean, however, that Konoe was sold on fascism or Nazism, not to mention communism, as a viable alternative to liberal democracy. This was his problem. While opposed to Anglo-Americanism, he was also unhappy with these other alternatives. His opposition to the Anglo-American system was thus much less strident and more innocuous than the German or Soviet rejection of it. Economically, it is true, Konoe showed greater conviction. Here he shared the belief of many leaders at the time that a free capitalist system would only increase Japan's dependence on an international economy that was controlled by the British and the Americans, and that, if nothing else, the needs of the war against China necessitated greater governmental control for mobilizing national resources. The idea was not new, but Konoe wanted to couple it with an explicit call for the establishment of an economically self-sufficient Asian bloc. Theoretically, such a bloc would enable the nation to free itself from relying on Britain and the United States for resources, markets, capital, and technology, thus reversing a seventy-year-old pattern. But how could this be done? In 1939, for instance, Japanese production of steel and iron fell substantially below expectation – for example, only 85 per cent in regular steel and pig iron – so that the balance would have to be made up by imports.[24] An aggressive move southward would require even more steel, iron, and other materials, but where were they going to come from? Obviously, spoils of war in South-East Asia could be anticipated, but could Japan execute the southern strategy without having to fight a costly war with the Anglo-American powers? Konoe was not so sure, but was convinced that if Japan were really to establish a new economic order in Asia, it would have to be prepared to fight the United States, should the latter intervene by force.

A third element in Konoe's anti-Anglo-Americanism was an extremely naïve view of Japanese relations with China. He believed that the Chinese shared Japan's resentment of Anglo-American domination and that, if the Japanese showed enough goodwill and conciliatory spirit, they would join the latter in the task of building a new Asia. Even Chungking, it was felt, was at heart against the Anglo-American powers, so that it should not be difficult to persuade the Nationalist leadership to give up its resistance to Japan and co-operate with the latter to realize the dream of a new Asian order. Why Konoe and his supporters were so blind to the reality of China's anti-Japanese sentiment is difficult to understand, but it was another reflection of their infatuation with the idea of an anti-Anglo-American system. Because it was to be built in Asia, and because China was an Asian country, it followed that the latter would co-operate with Japan. The dismal beginnings of the allegedly pro-Japanese regime in Nanking should have indicated that the reality was far otherwise, but Konoe was not thinking of Nanking alone. In fact, he was willing to sacrifice the Wang government if Chungking proved more pliable – another indication of a lack of consistency and of wishful thinking.

Finally, related to such wishful thinking was Konoe's fascination with the possibility of an alliance with Germany and a possible *entente* with the Soviet Union. He believed that these powers were fundamentally opposed to Anglo-American democracy, capitalism, and internationalism, and therefore that Japan should enter into a partnership with them to end, once and for all, the Anglo-American domination of the world. Such ideas, it will be recalled, had begun to attract some Japanese officials at the time of the signing of the Nazi-Soviet non-aggression pact, but now Konoe was willing to make them a basis of his foreign policy. Because, both in 1941 and again in 1945, Konoe would express his grave misgivings about and fear of communism, it is surprising that in 1940 he should have so easily succumbed to the allure of a partnership with Russia as well as Germany and Italy. He did so, it would seem, only because he firmly believed in what he had been saying for years, that the new order in Asia that Japan was to build must aim at establishing an alternative system of international affairs to one that had been defined in terms of Anglo-American interests and ideas. Even Soviet communism would help in the process. Although eventually Japan might have to face the possibility of a war with the Soviet Union, the most urgent need for the immediate future was the elimination of Anglo-American influence from Asia.

Although Konoe had been unable to do much about implementing his conception of an Asian new order when he was prime minister during 1937–39, this time he sensed the situation had vastly improved, both domestically and externally. His appointment of Matsuoka Yōsuke as foreign minister indicated confidence that he could proceed with his scheme. Matsuoka, a former diplomat and president of the South Manchuria Railway, was well known for his outspoken espousal of revisionism. He had castigated the Washington Conference system as a peace defined by 'have nations', and openly talked of an inevitable clash with the United States unless the latter recognized Japan's *fait accompli* in China. As he wrote in an essay published in May 1940, the United States and Japan were the two leading Pacific powers, and thus it was 'an historical inevitability' that they should collide. The only way to avoid it was for the two to respect each other's spheres of influence. America and Japan could still 'co-operate', Matsuoka asserted, by frankly recognizing the power realities in the world. But it was possible that two nations that should 'co-operate' might in fact come to blows.[25] In any event, it was crucial for Japan to enter into an alliance with Germany; it would enable Japan to gain an advantage over the United States and force the latter to take Japan more seriously. Given such views, his appointment as foreign minister was strongly supported by army and civilian advocates of the German alliance. Although the emperor apparently remained committed to the idea of maintaining friendly relations with the Anglo-American nations, the political atmosphere in Japan at the time was such that only the appointment of a pro-German foreign minister would have been acceptable to the army.

Before Konoe organized his cabinet, he invited Matsuoka along with General Tōjō Hideki and Admiral Yoshida Zengo, whom he wanted to appoint war and navy ministers, respectively, to his residence at Ogikubo in order to consider foreign policy objectives. Matsuoka prepared a draft statement and argued for the strengthening of the Japan–German–Italian Axis 'in order to establish speedily a new order in East Asia'. Towards the Soviet Union he advocated the signing of a non-aggression pact for five to ten years in order to give Japan time to prepare for an eventual confrontation with that power. The British, French, and Dutch colonies in Asia should be incorporated into the regional new order, while Japan should be determined to reject America's intervention in this process. Finally, Japan should be ready to effect a *rapprochement* with the Nationalists in Chungking, should they be willing to come to terms with it and agree to co-operate in the establishment of an East Asian bloc.[26] These ideas were discussed and became the basis of the new Konoe cabinet's foreign policy. The key document was a cabinet decision of 26 July, entitled 'An outline of fundamental national policies'. Its preamble noted that the world was 'at a major turning point', since 'new politics, economy, and culture are being created on the basis of the emergence and growth of several groups of states'. Clearly, Japan was to develop one such group, now referred to as 'a new order in Great East Asia'. The new order would still have at its core 'three solidly united' nations – Japan, Manchukuo, and China – but it would embrace other parts of Asia in order to create an economically self-sufficient bloc. This document was rather vague as to what was contained in the new order, but other statements and policies adopted at the time revealed that Tokyo's new leaders were thinking of a large region 'east of India and north of Australia and New Zealand', according to an explanation given by a high official of the army General Staff.[27]

Believing in the imperative need to unify decision-making in Tokyo, Konoe resurrected the liaison conference between the cabinet and the supreme command. This institution had been created when the Chinese war broke out, but it had not met since January 1938. Now Konoe intended to make use of it as the final authority on strategic and diplomatic matters. At its meeting on 27 July, the liaison conference approved a list of guidelines to implement the above cabinet decision. It should be noted that the emphasis at that time was on diplomatic initiatives – new approaches to Germany, Italy, the Soviet Union, and possibly China – rather than military action. Army–navy differences on strategy were serious, with the latter reluctant to consider a war against the Anglo-American powers at that time, while the army insisted such a possibility had to be faced. The fact is that there was as yet no specific operational plan for using force against the European colonies, let alone Britain and America, at that point. It was as if the Japanese were anxious to obtain the rich resources of the Asian-Pacific region without much effort, merely by counting on a favourable international environment to pressure the British and Americans psychologically to reduce their commitments in Asia.

Actually, Japanese calculations were unrealistic. Far from impressing Britain, the United States, and China with the hopelessness of their stand, the onset of the Konoe cabinet and loose talk of southern expansion only strengthened their will to stay united. In Washington, President Roosevelt was reaffirming the policy of aiding Britain so as to prevent the latter's defeat by Germany and to ensure the survival of the Royal Navy. Survival of Britain was considered to be of fundamental importance in the Asian-Pacific region since Japan could be expected to hesitate before it used force until Britain's situation appeared hopeless. American strategy in Asia, then, was an integral part of that in Europe. To discourage Japan from acting rashly, Roosevelt also decided, in addition to keeping the United States fleet in Hawaiian waters, to implement economic sanctions of Japan. In late July, aviation gasoline and lubricating oil were embargoed, along with a certain grade of scrap iron.

These measures did not mean that the United States was contemplating a war against Japan. Its strategy was still primarily oriented towards Europe, and before the outcome of the German–British struggle became clearer, it was to persist in a defensive policy in the Pacific. Still, there was no chance that America would back down in the region in the face of Japanese pressures. It was simply that the Roosevelt administration did not want a Pacific war. A combination of firmness, as exemplified by the aviation fuel and scrap iron embargo, and flexibility, enabling Japan to procure low-octane fuel, for instance, would, it was hoped, keep it from resorting to force in South-East Asia.

It was extremely difficult, however, to dissuade Tokyo from turning once again to Germany. To prevent a German–Japanese alliance from materializing, the United States would have to show that Tokyo had more to gain by not committing itself to such a policy. But it had little tangible to offer in return for Japan's desisting from an Axis pact, and it had to fall back on the obvious strategy of ensuring Britain's survival so that the Japanese would not become convinced of the wisdom of a German connection. The signing, in early September, of a 'destroyers-for-bases' agreement was a clear demonstration of Anglo-American solidarity.

British officials were delighted at such evidence of the two countries' co-operation, which had obvious implications for Asia. Britain obviously did not want a war with Japan, but should it come, it would have to rely on American help. The problem was that in the summer of 1940 the United States was disinclined to become militarily involved in Asia, giving top priority to hemispheric defence and then to assisting Britain in its war against Germany. Under the circumstances, Britain would have been put in an extremely difficult position if the Japanese had undertaken an invasion of British possessions at that time. Their hesitation in this regard saved the Anglo-American powers embarrassment and predicament.

This reluctance was in part related to uncertainty regarding the Soviet Union. Although the Konoe cabinet was committed to improving relations with Moscow, it was far from clear what form that would take. Stalin wanted to encourage Japanese overtures for some sort of an *entente* between the two countries, but he did not want such an *entente* to be part of a four-power agreement, among Germany, Italy, Japan, and the Soviet Union, for it would tie the latter too closely to the destinies of the Fascist states. This conflicted with Japanese intentions, and its effect was to prolong German–Japanese negotiations, one factor that made the Japanese hesitate in South-East Asia.

Another was the China question. An essential part of the new Konoe strategy was to continue his predecessor's efforts to de-escalate the Chinese war through whatever means. Among possible strategies, the most obvious, namely, to make use of the puppet Wang regime in Nanking, appealed the least to Japanese leaders. The regime, it will be recalled, had been established in March, but no country, not even Japan, had recognized it as the legitimate representative of China. Towards the end of the Yonai ministry, a mission headed by former Prime Minister Abe was dispatched to Nanking to negotiate a 'basic treaty' preliminary to diplomatic recognition, but the terms Abe carried with him were extremely harsh. Before the negotiations were concluded, Konoe replaced Yonai, but the terms did not change. Wang Ching-wei reminded the Japanese of Konoe's proclamation of 22 December 1938, in which the latter had expressed Japan's readiness to respect Chinese sovereignty and independence, but Abe, under instruction from Tokyo, kept insisting that Japan's first task was to eradicate anti-Japanese and anti-Nanking forces in China. Such a task would necessitate the continued presence of Japanese troops and various measures to ensure law and security in occupied areas. Despite Chinese protestations that these provisions would place the Nanking regime in an awkward position and subject it to attack from the rest of China, the Japanese held their ground, and the draft treaty as finally agreed upon at the end of August combined some high-sounding rhetoric about the two countries' eternal friendship and co-operation with specific measures allowing indefinite Japanese military presence in China. Even so, the ratification of the treaty and Tokyo's formal recognition of Nanking would be put off till the end of November.[28]

The reason for the rather dilatory way of dealing with the Wang regime was that the Japanese leaders never gave up hope of persuading the Nationalists under Chiang Kai-shek to come to terms. The Wang scheme was essentially a tactic to persuade these latter to take Japanese overtures for ending the war more seriously. Prime Minister Konoe was particularly anxious to try this approach. He and the army high command assumed that there was enough war weariness among the Nationalist leaders and that they would be interested in a cease-fire proposal from the Japanese army. Konoe and Chiang, according to this plan, were first to exchange letters and arrange for a meeting of the two armies' representatives. On 22 August Prime Minister Konoe actually wrote a letter addressed to Chiang Kai-shek, stating his confidence that the two countries would be able to 'readjust their relations'. The Japanese expected that the sending of the letter would be followed by a high-level cease-fire agreement in September, and a final · peace conference by the end of the month.[29]

This was a rather fanciful plan. Why the Japanese should have thought that the Nationalists would agree to a peace in such a short time, when they had been struggling against Japan for over three years, is difficult to say, but it certainly showed a naïvety and wishful thinking about Chiang Kai-shek and his comrades. For the latter would never have agreed to a cease-fire unless it were to lead to a complete evacuation of Japanese troops from China, if not from Manchuria as well. Japan was still insisting on an independent Manchukuo and on its right to retain forces in northern China, and under those conditions Chungking could not have been expected to reciprocate the Japanese overtures. In early September, Chungking declared that the Konoe letter was a forgery and refused to accept it.

In taking such a firm stand, the Nationalists were clearly counting on continued support on the part of Britain, the United States and the Soviet Union. To be sure, Chungking was disappointed by the British decision to yield to Japanese pressures to close the Burma Road for three months (July to October); it was estimated that about 10,000 tons of material a month had crossed Burma into Chungking. To lose these shipments, along with the closing of the Indo-China route, would all but choke off the Nationalist stronghold from outside assistance. The only avenue open was the north-western route, via Sinkiang, through which Russian goods had been sent. But the volume of this shipment had steadily diminished, so that in June only about 500 tons were reaching Chungking.[30] The Nationalists would somehow have to make do with sharply diminished goods and war material. Nevertheless, the Chinese could only be encouraged by the unmistakable signs of Anglo-American co-operation. The two powers' open commitment to frustrate German ambitions implied that they would not tolerate Japan's move southward. Equally important, they would do what they could to tie Japan down in China, in order to prevent its thrust southward. America's partial embargoing of aviation fuel and scrap iron was evidence that the United States would make it more and more difficult for the Japanese to crush China. Given such a trend, it would have been foolhardy for Chiang and his supporters to reciprocate Japanese overtures. Faced with a choice between joining the Japanese blueprint for an anti-Anglo-American coalition and staying closer to the latter powers, the Nationalists unhesitatingly chose the latter alternative.

As for Chinese–Soviet relations, both Nationalists and Communists had profound misgivings about the Nazi–Soviet pact and about the reputed Japanese moves for a *rapprochement* with Moscow. Although the Soviets kept assuring the Chinese that they would continue to help their war efforts, from Chungking's perspective Soviet policy with regard to the Chinese–Japanese War was much less clear-cut and less unambiguous than American. For this and other reasons, the Nationalists turned more and more to the United States for support. In the summer of 1940, America was the only remaining power strong enough and explicitly opposed to Japan. There was already a quasi-partnership between China and the United States, and the former was moving fast to identify its destiny with the latter's. Japan's struggle against China was thus developing into a struggle against Anglo-America plus China. Despite all the rhetoric about a new order in Asia emanating from Japan, only a handful of Chinese succumbed to its allure, whereas the rest of the country would have none of it. They would rather entrust their survival to the hands of Anglo-America than Japan.

REFERENCES AND NOTES

1. Hata Ikuhiko, 'Shiron: 1930-nendai no Nihon' (An essay on Japan in the 1930s), in Miwa Kimitada (ed.), *Saikō Taiheiyō sensō zen'ya* (The prelude to the Pacific war reconsidered; Tokyo 1981), p. 32. See also Hagihara Nobutoshi, *Tōgō Shigenori* (Tokyo 1985), pp. 241–82.
2. *Gendaishi shiryō* (Documents on contemporary history), 43: xl (Tokyo 1970).
3. *Nihon gaikō bunsho narabi shuyō bunsho* (Japanese diplomatic documents and a chronology of main events; Tokyo 1955), 2: 421–4.
4. Robert Dallek, *Franklin D. Roosevelt and American Foreign Policy, 1932–1945* (New York 1979), pp. 172, 174.
5. *Chung-hua Min-kuo chung-yao chih-liao ch'u-pien: tui-Ju kang-chan shih-chi* (Important historical documents of the Chinese republic: the period of the anti-Japanese war; Taipei n.d.), 6.3: 55–62.

6.   Ibid., 6.3: 157–8.
7.   Ibid., 6.3: 163–83.
8.   John Hunter Boyle, *China and Japan at War, 1937–1945: The Politics of Collaboration* (Stanford 1972), p. 294.
9.   Ibid., pp. 290–1.
10. Ishikawa Junkichi, *Kokka sōdōin-shi* (History of national mobilization; Tokyo 1978), 7: 1280–4.
11. Dallek, *Roosevelt*, pp. 216.
12. James R. Leutze, *Bargaining for Supremacy: Anglo-American Naval Collaboration, 1937–1941* (Chapel Hill 1977), p. 65.
13. *Chung-hua Min-kuo*, 6.3: 199–202.
14. Dallek, *Roosevelt*, pp. 224, 228; *Life*, 3 June 1940.
15. *New York Times*, 1 Dec. 1939.
16. Ibid., 28 June 1940.
17. Dallek, *Roosevelt*, p. 237; Jonathan G. Utley, *Going to War with Japan, 1937–1941* (Knoxville 1985), p. 93.
18. The Diaries of Sir Alexander Cadogan, 1938–1945, David Dilks (ed.) (New York 1972), pp. 310, 314.
19. Defence Agency, War History Division (ed.), *Daihonei rikugunbu* (The army supreme command; Tokyo 1968), 2: 42, 48.
20. Ibid., 2: 49–50.
21. Ibid., 2: 51–3.
22. Yabe Teiji, *Konoe Fumimaro* (Tokyo 1952), 2: 97–107. See also Gordon Berger, *Parties out of Power in Japan, 1931–41* (Princeton 1977).
23. Yabe, *Konoe*, 2: 106.
24. *Gendaishi*, 43: 240–2.
25. *Matsuoka Yōsuke* (Tokyo 1974), pp. 726–7, 730–6.
26. Ibid., pp. 747–8.
27. *Daihonei rikugunbu*, 2: 55–7.
28. *Chung-hua Min-kuo*, 6.3: 358–66.
29. *Daihonei rikugunbu*, 2: 85.
30. Ibid., 2: 44.

Chapter 4

THE FAILURE OF AN ALLIANCE

The Axis alliance, consummated among Germany, Italy, and Japan in September 1940, was to have been Japan's trump card in implementing its vision of a new Asian order directed against the Anglo-American nations. It would augment Japan's potential power by tying the nation's destiny to German military accomplishments in Europe, and to Soviet neutrality in Asia, and thereby expel Anglo-American influence from Asia. Time was soon to show, however, that this influence, if anything, grew steadily during the months following the formation of the alliance so that, by mid-1941, the Japanese would feel even more insecure than before. They would find themselves surrounded by the ABCD powers – America, Britain, China, and the Dutch East Indies. Rarely did a diplomatic initiative end in a more complete fiasco.

THE AXIS ALLIANCE

The tripartite alliance was signed in Berlin on 27 September 1940. It had been negotiated in Tokyo, between Foreign Minister Matsuoka and Heinrich Stahmer, special envoy of Germany who arrived on 7 September.

The timing of these negotiations was crucial. It coincided with a number of important decisions by the United States government. First, the establishment (in mid-August) of a joint Canadian–American defence board, coupled with the 'destroyers-for-bases deal', meant that the United States was unmistakably involving itself in Britain's war. Second, the Roosevelt administration, with the support of the Republican presidential candidate, Wendell Willkie, called for and obtained Congressional enactment of a military draft. The selective service law, passed in mid-September, established a draft for men between the ages of twenty-one and thirty-five. It again was a demonstration of America's determination to resist German ambitions. These steps, combined with the constant exchanges of views between

Roosevelt and Churchill, assured the British of America's commitment to their survival, and in fact by September it appeared as if the worst was over. Despite the merciless assault by the German air force, Britain had not surrendered, and morale remained high. The very fact that the United States was willing to transfer so many ships to Britain revealed confidence that they would not fall into enemy hands, and that the American leaders had concluded Britain would survive the German assault.

Given these developments, a belated conclusion of a German–Japanese alliance did not have the impact that it might, had it been signed a month or two earlier. An Axis pact in May or June, for instance, might have been psychologically more devastating to the British, who might have been compelled to accede to further Japanese demands in Asia to mitigate its impact. By September, however, Britain could be assured of continued American support, and the United States had already implemented some of its embargoes against Japan. Under the circumstances, there would have been no way in which an Axis pact would cause the Anglo-American powers to soften their stand. On the contrary, the pact could be expected to give them added resolve to stand firm. This was exactly what happened.

Japanese and German negotiators were fully aware of the developing ties between America and Britain, and for this very reason they hoped their alliance would serve to check and reduce the effectiveness of American intervention. By then, as Matsuoka explained at the time, it was becoming obvious that the United States was steadily involving itself not only in European but in Asian-Pacific affairs as well. It was tying itself not just to the British in the Atlantic but to the Commonwealth in Asia and the Pacific. The United States, in fact, would establish itself as a global power, with its influence in the Atlantic, Canada, the Western hemisphere, the Pacific Ocean, and Asia. It followed, then, that henceforth it would be an American-led coalition that Japan had to confront and be prepared to fight. It would no longer be China in isolation, but China assisted by the Soviet Union, Britain, and especially the United States. It would also be unrealistic to single Britain out as the next hypothetical enemy.

Such thinking was evidenced in a number of policy memoranda prepared on the eve of the German alliance. Konoe and the ministers of foreign affairs, war, and the navy agreed, just before Stahmer's arrival, that, given American policy towards, and military preparedness against, Japan, the latter would have to be ready to use force against both Britain and the United States to achieve its objectives. This was a tall order. Unlike a hypothetical war against Britain alone, which could conceivably be executed with some expectation of success, a war against the combined force of Britain and America would be an enormously difficult undertaking. Matsuoka realized this, and for that very reason he welcomed the opportunity to draw Germany into the equation. His hope was that an explicit alliance between Tokyo and Berlin would either deter American belligerence in Asia or, if war should come, assist Japan in its struggle against the United States.[1]

German calculations were somewhat different. Hitler wanted to finish off Britain before the United States intervened militarily, and he certainly did not wish Japan to trigger a crisis with America in such a way that the latter would become involved in a global war. What Germany wanted of Japan, Stahmer told Matsuoka, was that Japan should do everything possible to 'restrain' the United States and to prevent its intervention in the European war. An Axis pact would, it was hoped, serve these purposes by demonstrating the determination on the part of Germany, Italy, and Japan to stand together. While the three should be prepared for the worst and be ready to join forces together to fight against America should that become necessary, Germany intended to do all it could to prevent a Japanese–American collision, Stahmer stated. Moreover, Germany would be glad to serve as 'an honest broker' to mediate differences between Japan and the Soviet Union so that an Axis pact would soon be followed by a Japanese–Soviet *entente*. These ideas revealed Berlin's determination to focus on the defeat of Britain as the immediate objective. It hoped that this could be achieved before American intervention if a German–Japanese pact were signed expeditiously, to be followed by the Soviet Union's joining them in an *entente*. The United States would be left alone in the meantime, in the hope that it would also leave the other powers alone.[2]

Such German thinking impressed Matsuoka as indicative of the possibility that Germany and the United States might come to terms after Britain's defeat in Europe. Should that come about, Japan would be isolated once again, with both Germany and America unwilling to let Japan establish its new order over Asia's colonial areas. To prevent such a development, Matsuoka stated at a meeting of Japan's top civilian and military leaders on 14 September, Japan had either to tie itself to Germany and Italy, or to America and Britain. Returning to the position of co-operation with the Anglo-American powers was still an option, he admitted, but to do so Japan would have to give up its dream of an Asian new order, accept American terms for settling the Chinese war, and 'be dominated by America and Britain for at least half a century'. Should that come about, not only would Japan be back where it had been after the First World War, but it would also face a stronger China, with Chiang Kai-shek's anti-Japanese policy confirmed. These would be the consequences of the policy of reconciliation with the United States, and if Japan did not want it, the only choice left would be co-operation with Germany and Italy. Such co-operation, in Matsuoka's thinking, transcended merely diplomatic collaboration but entailed joint military action, should that become necessary.

By then the Japanese navy had come to accept the possibility of war with the United States. Its leaders were realistic and continued to insist that in a long, drawn-out war Japan would have little chance of success. But the top naval officials appear to have concluded by this time that a German alliance might possibly make the difference in such a conflict. It might enable Japan to establish itself in South-East Asia, which in turn would provide oil and other necessary resources. If this could be arranged, then even if war should come with America, Japan would be in a much more fortified position. The German allies could also be expected to supply Japan with military equipment and oil from their conquered territories. These, plus the possible participation of the Soviet Union in the pact, might immobilize the United States. The army shared such reasoning. Although its strategists hoped that Britain and America could still be kept separate, they recognized that if Japan were to use force against British possessions in Asia, it might have to encounter American opposition. In such an eventuality, the German alliance, combined with an *entente* with the Soviet Union, would prove essential.

Matsuoka explicitly stated at a meeting of Japan's leaders in the presence of the emperor on 19 September, that the Axis pact was 'a military alliance aimed at the United States'. There is little doubt that Japanese–American relations entered another stage of crisis. Although it would be another fourteen months before war broke out between them, Japan's struggle against the Anglo-American nations was clearly confirmed in September 1940. Japanese diplomacy and strategy would henceforth be conducted in that framework. Although there was some hope that the alliance would actually prevent a war between Japan and the United States, Japanese leaders now realized such a war was a genuine possibility. The emperor himself expressed the thought that an American war appeared unavoidable, and that Japan might be defeated. Hara Yoshimichi, president of the Privy Council, stated that the United States would be expected to react to the signing of the Axis pact by tightening its economic sanctions against Japan, in effect engaging in an economic warfare with the latter. Matsuoka's view was that even in such a situation, the German alliance would be useful as Germany could be counted upon to provide Japan with necessary resources. Hara also remarked that the United States might establish bases in New Zealand, Australia, and elsewhere, in order to encircle and contain Japan. Should such moves be considered an act of war, to be responded to by force and thus obligate Germany to come in? Matsuoka said this was a matter that had to be decided by the supreme command. These and other exchanges of views indicate that Japan's top leaders all recognized the definite passing of an era and the arrival of another in the country's foreign affairs. The choice, as they saw it, was between succumbing to American pressures or resisting them; the former would imply accepting the American definition of the Asian-Pacific status quo – one that had the support of China, Britain, and the Soviet Union as well – while the latter would lead to the establishment of an entirely new regional order.[3]

This was also the way American officials viewed the situation. The signing of the Axis pact only confirmed their perception of Japan as ambitious, intent upon establishing a hegemonic position in South-East Asia and the south-western Pacific. Contrary to what Matsuoka expected, and more in line with Hara's misgivings, the United States did not soften its Asian policy in response to the Axis pact. On the contrary, the Roosevelt administration retained its economic sanctions of Japan and confirmed its support of Britain and China. There were, to be sure, differences of view among Roosevelt's top aides as to the wisdom of imposing more stringent sanctions on Japan. Secretary of War Henry L. Stimson, Secretary of the Navy Frank Knox, Secretary of the Treasury Henry Morgenthau, and Secretary of the Interior Harold Ickes were emerging as the leading exponents of the tough approach, believing in pushing and punishing Japan till the latter yielded. Others, notably Secretary of State Cordell Hull, believed little would be gained by such action except to bring about a war which every key official thought should be avoided for the time being at least. Roosevelt sided with the moderates, but this was a difference of views regarding tactics. No one was accepting the Japanese logic that the Axis alliance was creating a new situation to which the United States would have to adjust itself. On the contrary, officials in Washington, including Hull, agreed that Japan should be warned that it could not expect America to be impressed with such an alliance and that the best response to it was to confirm the commitment to preserving the status quo. But since the status quo could not be maintained without American involvement, the situation continued to be that of pitting Japanese power against American power in Asia and the Pacific.[4]

This became clear at this time as the United States responded to related developments in South-East Asia. Simultaneously with German–Japanese negotiations on an Axis pact, small-scale fighting broke out between Japanese and French forces in Indo-China. It will be recalled that towards the end of the Yonai cabinet, the Japanese government had forced the French authorities to close off the Indo-China route to Chungking. Not satisfied with this, the Konoe cabinet decided to seek further concessions, such as the use of Indo-Chinese airfields by Japanese forces, which were to have the right of transit, as well as the supply of provisions for these forces. While negotiations were conducted in Tokyo and Hanoi, Japanese troops stationed along the border crossed it on 23 September and engaged in skirmishes with French forces. Two days later the French surrendered, and Japan's occupation of northern Indo-China became a fact. Unlike some earlier instances, the crossing of the border had been approved by the top cabinet officials; as they said, Japan was to carry out a 'peaceful occupation' of Indo-China, but if the French resisted, force would have to be used.[5] In the event, French resistance was minimal, but it did not change the story. The Japanese had invaded and occupied another country. Although the Axis alliance had not yet been concluded, Washington reacted at once, embargoing the export of all types of scrap iron to Japan.

A parallel development was the series of negotiations between Japanese and Dutch officials concerning the supply of East Indies oil and other resources. Kobayashi Ichizō, minister of commerce, was sent to Batavia for the talks in mid-September, but negotiations dragged on as the Dutch counted on American support and refused to grant Japanese demands for oil concessions in the colony. The most they would do would be to offer Japan a certain quantity (1.3 million tons was mentioned in October) of oil to purchase.[6] That fell far below what the Japanese were asking, as they obviously were in great need of aviation fuel after the American embargo, as well as other items that would surely be added to the list. Dutch authorities in Batavia worked closely with European and American oil companies in the Indies, which in turn were in constant contact with the government in Washington. The upshot was that even Japan's 'peaceful' advance was being met with stiff opposition linked to a hardening American policy.

As if that were not enough, Britain too was showing its intention of following America's example. Whereas in July London had agreed to close the Burma Road for three months, by September Churchill and his cabinet judged that the situation in Europe and Asia had changed for the better and therefore that they should refuse to keep the Burma Road closed. With American resolve daily becoming clearer, there was no point in continuing to submit to Japanese pressure. The three-month closing of the Burma Road would end in mid-October, and London decided to reopen it then so as to resume shipments to Chungking.

For the Chinese, all this was good news. The Axis alliance, far from impressing them with the fearsomeness of a German–Japanese combination, actually reassured them that Japan would further alienate the Anglo-American powers, a development that would be to China's advantage. When American Ambassador Nelson T. Johnson in Chungking reported around that time that 'Chinese morale is now higher than at any time since the start of the Sino-Japanese conflict', he was undoubtedly observing the Chinese view that the Axis alliance had the effect of linking European and Asian affairs closer together so that the United States and Britain would reconfirm their determination to oppose Japanese aggression in China.[7] There was, to be sure, one consequence of the German–Japanese alliance that would be troublesome; Berlin would be pressed by Tokyo to recognize the puppet regime in Nanking as the government of China. Nothing was happening yet, however, as German officials hesitated to take so drastic a step which would serve no useful purpose except obtaining Japan's gratitude. Their primary concern was Europe, and they feared that Germany's support of Wang Ching-wei against Chiang Kai-shek would further complicate its relations with the United States and the Soviet Union.

Thus, with even Germany hesitating to support Japan on the Nanking. question, the Nationalists could feel the consummation of the Axis alliance made little immediate difference in their struggle against Japan.[8]

One area where the Chinese showed some concern was the implications of the new alliance for Soviet policy. Soviet officials continued to reiterate that their policy towards assisting China would not change, but at the same time the press was giving prominent coverage to the Chinese–Japanese negotiations in Nanking, as if to create the impression that China was becoming divided.[9] This was troublesome from the Nationalist point of view, as was the explicit provision in the Axis pact that it was not aimed at the Soviet Union. From these instances, the Chinese could draw the inference that there might be an improvement in Japanese–Soviet relations and that the latter's support of China's war effort might weaken. To some extent such misgivings were justified, as Moscow was encouraging Japanese overtures for an understanding so as to divert Japan's ambitions away from the north. Much of this, however, was derived from concern with a possible rupture of German–Soviet relations. In the autumn of 1940 German and Soviet forces were converging on Romania and elsewhere in the Balkans, creating a tense atmosphere. Foreign observers were already predicting a clash between the two powers, breaching their non-aggression pact. The *New York Times*, for instance, printed several news analyses by its staff throughout October, emphasizing the possibility, even the imminence, of a German–Soviet conflict. An editorial entitled 'Russia in the dark' (16 October) endorsed such analyses and claimed that the Russians had not been consulted about the Axis alliance and other matters by Germany, and explained that although Stalin would not immediately switch his strategy while 'profits are to be squeezed out of the devious partnership with the other dictator', he was becoming more and more uncomfortable with the German partnership. At the very least, the future of German–Soviet relations was uncertain, and under the circumstances the Soviet Union had good reason to encourage Japan's initiatives for a *rapprochement*. That in turn would be cause for worry to the Chinese.

Given such a situation, one thing that the Chinese could count on was the unswerving position of the United States and Britain *vis-à-vis* Japan. They would have been heartened if they had known that in early October Prime Minister Churchill confided that nothing compared 'with the importance of the British Empire and the United States being co-belligerents'. He believed that American entry into the war against the Axis powers would be 'fully conformable with British interests'.[10] Plans were made for staff talks both in Asia and in Washington among British, American, and Dutch officials for a joint strategy against Japan. It is true that at this stage neither London nor Washington was envisaging full strategic co-ordination with Chinese forces, but the implications were clear; the coming together of Germany and Japan, and even possibly of the Soviet Union and Japan, was only confirming the solidarity of America and Britain, so that the Chinese would find themselves part of a coalition just as the Japanese were trying to establish a global alliance of their own. The Chinese–Japanese War was turning into a conflict between two groups of nations.

TOWARDS AN ANGLO-AMERICAN ALLIANCE

This became confirmed in the late autumn of 1940, when President Roosevelt ran for and won re-election. Both before and after the 5 November presidential election, he explicitly supported Britain's war efforts, making public his policy of selling the latter airplanes and all types of war material. This was not the issue in the campaign, since Willkie also supported such a policy. But Roosevelt's third victory had the effect of strengthening his hand domestically so that he would now be even bolder in devising ways of helping the British.

And they needed American help desperately, since their purchases were fast depleting their funds at home and abroad; it was estimated in December that London had only about $2 billion available, whereas it was placing orders totalling $5 billion. Under the circumstances, obviously the United States would have to step in and finance British purchases. How this could be done without violating existing legislation and involving the United States directly in the European war was the key question with which Roosevelt and his aides grappled in late 1940. The answer came in the form of 'lend-lease'; the United States would 'lend' Britain the arms it needed to crush German–Italian ambitions, such arms to be returned to the United States when the fighting was over. The transaction would not involve normal sales or loans, but would create for Britain 'a gentleman's obligation to repay in kind', as the president said. In order to implement the policy, it would of course be necessary for the United States to step up arms production, even diverting productive capacities from consumer goods. As he declared in his famous 'fireside chat' on 29 December, the United States must become 'the great arsenal of democracy'. America's position was now unmistakably clear. It would help Britain with all means short of war; but 'short of war' was a loose enough expression to contain a variety of options. Except for the fact that American soldiers were not yet fighting, the country was on a war footing. The new Office of Production Management, established in late December to co-ordinate civilian and arms production; the lend-lease idea; and the statements being issued daily by the White House and other agencies, all left no doubt of that. As Roosevelt himself noted in the above speech, 'this is an emergency as serious as war itself. We must apply ourselves to our task with the same resolution, the same sense of urgency, the same spirit of patriotism and sacrifice as we would show were we at war'.[11]

When the president talked of 'war', he did not confine its meaning to the German–British War. Although his speech referred to 'people of Europe ... defending themselves', and did not mention Asians fighting against Japan, he called on his countrymen to 'support the nations defending themselves against attack by the Axis'. Since the Axis alliance had recently been concluded, there could be no mistaking the message. While the survival of Britain would be the top priority for the United States, this goal alone would entail defending British interests in Asia as well as Europe. Even more clearly, such an objective could be achieved only through America's own strengthening, something that would involve fortifying its position in the Pacific as well as the Atlantic. Roosevelt's definition of America as the arsenal of democracy also implied that the United States would aid all those countries that were democratic and struggling for their liberty. These again were loose concepts, so loose that eventually even the Soviet Union would fall within the definition. In late 1940 there was no question that China fitted the picture. The mere fact that it was struggling against an aggressive power which tied itself to Germany was enough to qualify it for special consideration.

The only issue at the end of 1940 was one of strategic priorities. Granted that America was involved in a global struggle against the Axis powers, it needed to establish a sense of where to place its emphasis in the immediate future. Assuming that it could not do everything all at once, the government in Washington would have to decide the most effective ways of implementing the aid policy. Here all-out aid to the British home isles took precedence. Whatever London asked, Washington would provide. China came next. After the reopening of the Burma Road, shipments from America, and smaller amounts from Britain, were resumed. An agreement with Chungking for a loan of $100 million, announced on 30 November, was the most massive given China by the United States. The funds were to be used at Chiang Kai-shek's discretion. Equally important, the United States would provide him with fifty pursuit planes, and American citizens would be allowed to serve in China as aviators and aviation instructors. The planes and aviators would be assigned to a volunteer air force which Colonel Claire Chennault would create in Chungking. The air force, officially called the American Volunteer Group but popularly known as the Flying Tigers, would be in place in the autumn of 1941.[12]

America's top military strategists, however, were unwilling to go much further at this time. They all shared Roosevelt's perception that the nation was engaged in a quasi-war, and that it must be prepared for a real war as well. But they were not yet ready to fight a two-front war, against both Germany and Japan. Although ultimately the nation would have to fight them both, the strategists at this time generally agreed with Admiral Harold R. Stark, chief of naval operations, and General George C. Marshall, army chief of staff, that the United States should first concentrate on the Atlantic theatre. Defeat of Germany would take all the nation's resources and manpower, which should not be diverted to a Pacific war with Japan. The United States should be on the defensive in that part of the world at least until the situation definitely improved in Europe.

The strategy of concentrating on the European war first, and giving the Pacific lower priority, was pushed with vigour by Stark and Marshall. An extension of one of the earlier Rainbow plans, it came to be known as Plan D (or Plan Dog). The problem was that the strategists were not entirely in agreement as to what was involved in a defensive posture in the Asian-Pacific region. Would it entail a defence of the status quo, or would it mean redefining the status quo so that the line of defence would be pushed back to the Hawaiian Islands? That option would, of course, amount to not reinforcing, even abandoning, the Philippines, not to mention Hong Kong, Singapore, and other British possessions which would not be defended by American forces. Such a strategy would have to assume that the British possessions would be defended by Britain, but this was rather unrealistic in view of the latter's struggle for survival at home. Thus a defensive strategy in the Pacific could mean, at least for the time being, conceding the region west of Hawaii to Japan.

Such thinking was clearly incompatible with the official policy of standing firmly opposed to Japanese aggression and assisting China. The two positions were never fully reconciled. President Roosevelt accepted both, the policy of opposing Japan as fundamental, and that of assigning higher priority to Europe as necessary in the short run. He, and civilian advisers like Stimson, Hull, and Morgenthau, believed that a policy of firmness in Asia, backed up by evidence of material support for China, should deter Japan's further aggression so that war with it would not occur. The United States, if at all possible, should avoid precipitously provoking Japan or engaging its forces prematurely; but otherwise it should employ the tactic of deterrence by other means, such as diplomatic warnings to Japan, the presence of the fleet in Hawaiian waters, encouragement to British and Dutch authorities in Asia to reject Japanese pressures, and assistance of the Nationalists in Chungking. Beyond these, little specific could be agreed upon. Even as the president approved Plan D in mid-January 1941, its implications remained unclear. At least, the strategy would not be pushed to its logical conclusion as contemplated by the military; its acceptance by Roosevelt would not mean the United States would reduce its commitments in the western Pacific or South-East Asia. On the contrary, even within the parameters of Plan D, the United States would encourage the emergence of an alliance system among the nations opposed to Japanese expansion in Asia. That was inevitable, given the global nature of American policy at the time. Even if a defensive strategy were to be undertaken in the Asian-Pacific region, its action would be defined in the larger framework of an international coalition. Staff conversations initiated by British and American officials on the defence of Hong Kong and Singapore, while they failed to produce an agreed plan, were themselves evidence that American strategy would be couched in that larger framework. The same was of course true of China and the Dutch East Indies. Chennault was in daily contact with Chinese leaders and was, in November, in Washington to plead for more aid, and in the meantime British and Dutch officials in Asia were discussing a joint strategy, on the assumption that the United States would come to their assistance. Although there was no formal coalition, the constant contact and communication among Chinese, American, British, and Dutch officials and strategists was laying the groundwork for an eventual alliance.[13]

Japan, in other words, found itself more isolated than ever. The German alliance had not helped, and under American leadership a federation of countries opposed to Japan was coming into being. Even a development like the cancellation of the Olympic Games, scheduled to take place in Tokyo in the autumn of 1940, enhanced the sense of isolation. Of course, the cancellation was a result of the European war, but Japan had tied itself to its fate, and the consequences had not been beneficial. There were few new initiatives that the Japanese could now contemplate, and still fewer alternatives that they would be willing to accept.

In the last months of 1940, they fell back on a tactic that had been tried and found wanting: a political settlement of the Chinese war. As in the past, it entailed a two-pronged approach, one towards Chungking and the other towards Nanking under Wang Ching-wei. On 1 October the ministers of war, the navy, and foreign affairs agreed that Japan should conclude a basic treaty with the Nanking regime and at the same time conduct peace negotiations with Chungking. The former would involve formal recognition of Wang's government, but if the latter negotiations were to succeed, some kind of a 'Wang–Chiang coalition' would become necessary. This dual approach was to be carried out in October, with a view to bringing it to successful conclusion by the end of the month.[14] Why Tokyo's leaders should have been so optimistic, if not totally naïve, is difficult to say. Unless they were being cynical, adopting a policy which they knew had no chance of success, they must have been terribly misinformed of the situation in China. Like their predecessors, they little appreciated the force of Chinese nationalism and innocently believed that the majority of Chinese, whether under Kuomintang influence or not, would rather identify their destiny with Japan than with the Western democracies. Japanese leaders were becoming captives of their own illusions. At least these recommendations indicated that they had little genuine hope for the stability of the Nanking government which they had helped bring into existence. But even here, they could not make up their minds whether or not to terminate the experiment once and for all, which would have been a condition which Chungking would have insisted upon prior to any settlement with Japan. Instead, Nanking had to be nursed along just in case negotiations with Chungking fell through. Such a haphazard approach had no chance of success.

Japan's desperate situation can be seen in the fact that despite all these problems, and despite the fact that no progress had been made by the end of October, the above recommendations were approved at a meeting of Tokyo's highest officials in the presence of the emperor on 13 November. They reiterated the idea that peace talks with China must be built on a reunion of Wang's and Chiang's governments, which was to be effected before the Nanking government was formally recognized by Japan. In return for such a reunion, the Nationalists would have to recognize Manchukuo, give up its anti-Japanese policy, agree to the continued stationing of Japanese forces in Mongolia, Sinkiang, north China, and the lower Yangtze Delta, accept the presence of Japanese naval ships in south China, and co-operate with Japan in developing resources necessary for national defence. If no agreement on this basis was reached by the end of 1940, Japan would have to be prepared for a protracted war so as to bring Chungking to its knees. That would entail a continued large-scale occupation of China by Japanese troops and the economic development of the occupied areas so as to maximize the production of war-related materials.[15]

Clearly, a peace settlement on such a basis would have signalled China's capitulation and transformation into Japan's semi-colony. There could have been no chance that it would be accepted by the Nationalist authorities. The Japanese were wasting their time pondering such an approach, and the discussions at the above meeting indicated that they sensed it. Army and navy spokesmen stated that either alternative – a speedy settlement of the war through a Nanking–Chungking reunion or a protracted war against Chungking – was extremely difficult to carry out, but that the recent changes in world affairs, including the Axis alliance, gave the nation a real opportunity to emerge as the leading Asian power. It was hoped that the Chinese leaders would share this perception and realize the futility of persisting in their resistance. In other words, the war in China would have to be solved as part of a new global strategy. Somehow, the changed conditions of the international environment would conspire to enable Japan to end the war to its satisfaction. All such thinking reveals profound confusion regarding strategy. It was as if the Japanese had forgotten Clausewitz's maxim that in war the most important thing is to know who the enemy is. Even while fighting in Manchuria and north China earlier in the decade, they had thought their ultimate enemy was going to be the Soviet Union. That remained the case even after 1937. But now, it was becoming clear that the enemy might not so much be the Soviet Union as the United States and Britain. If so, a global strategy of coalition warfare in the framework of the Axis alliance would become relevant. The war in China would in itself be less significant. Japan, therefore, would be justified in seeking a political settlement of the war so as to minimize its commitment in China and, if possible, to obtain the latter's co-operation in the global struggle.

The Chinese would not have disagreed with the idea that the war with Japan was becoming part of a larger conflict. But such realization had the effect of further emboldening them, as they became more confident than ever that they would be able to obtain support from Britain and America, particularly the latter. It would be nothing short of foolishness in such a situation to accept the Japanese terms for a political settlement. Although Chiang Kai-shek was not above taking advantage of Japanese overtures to alarm Americans so that the latter would give him more aid, from the beginning it was a foregone conclusion that he would reject any peace with Japan unless it restored Chinese sovereignty.[16] Manchukuo might be negotiable, but certainly not the continued stationing of Japanese forces or the existence of a Nanking regime. So the Nationalists gave Japan little encouragement, and the latter finally decided, at the end of November, to go ahead with formal recognition of Wang's government.

On 29 November, Wang Ching-wei assumed the presidency of the Nanking regime, and on the following day the basic treaty with Japan was signed. The treaty, as seen above, had been negotiated since July, but its final signature had to wait until the puppet regime was installed. While pledging their mutual support and co-operation for the establishment of a new order in East Asia, the signatories also provided for the stationing of Japanese forces in certain parts of China for a period of time – up to two years after the conclusion of the war. Even then, they would be kept in parts of north China, Mongolia, and Sinkiang to ensure against Communist subversion. Wang's inauguration as head of the new Chinese regime was dependent upon acceptance of such humiliating terms, a fact that augured ill for its future. As if to underline his subservience to Japanese dictates, he also agreed to the issuing of a joint declaration by Japan, Manchukuo, and 'China', for tripartite economic and political co-operation. In other words, the Nanking regime was officially recognizing the independence of Manchukuo, and joining it and Japan in an alliance directed against the rest of China. No wonder, then, that the Nationalists in Chungking immediately retaliated by publishing a list of Wang and seventy-six other 'traitors', threatening them with severe punishment for betraying their country. Chungking offered a prize for Wang's head, and Chinese communities throughout the world cabled their outrage at Wang's 'madness' in 'selling his country'.[17] Here again was evidence that by its attempt to find allies, Japan was promoting its own further isolation. Certainly the formal recognition of the Wang regime, coupled with the basic treaty, sealed the fate of any possible negotiation for a reconciliation with the Nationalists and ensured the prolongation of the Chinese–Japanese War.

To make matters worse, the Japanese could not bring themselves to concentrate on that war alone, for the last months of 1940 saw a flurry of planning activities on the part of Tokyo's supreme command. By then, naval officers in Tokyo had come to accept a Japanese–American war as all but inevitable. This was not because of the Chinese war, but was simply a corollary of the southern strategy. The former was primarily an army affair, and the navy assumed that it would go on for a long time to come. The southern strategy, on the other hand, would have to be carried out on its own terms, and there the navy would play a major role. Not China but the Dutch East Indies were the navy's main concern. As Admiral Yamamoto Isoroku, commander-in-chief of the combined fleet, explained, Japan needed the Indies' rich natural resources. If they could be obtained peacefully, so much the better. But if not, Japan would have to use force not only against the Dutch but also against Britain and the United States. This was because the Dutch authorities would succumb to Japanese pressures and offer Japan its resources unless they knew they could count on the support of the Anglo-American powers. In that case the Dutch would resist Japanese demands, but then the resulting Japanese–Dutch war would by definition lead to a Pacific war. Thus, Japan would either have the Indies' resources peacefully, or it would have war with the three countries. In the latter case, Yamamoto argued, it would be best to take the initiative and attack the Philippines first, to gain an initial tactical advantage, and then be prepared for a counter-offensive by the American fleet. In November the naval fleet was reorganized with that strategy in mind, and plans were drafted for commandeering civilian ships in an emergency. At the end of the month, a war game was conducted at the Naval War College under Yamamoto's direction. It was concluded that in case of war with the United States, Japan should attack the Philippines, seizing Manila and turning it into a base of operations against the American fleet. Equally crucial, it was noted, would be the use of the Marshall and Bismarck Islands.[18]

The army still had the Chinese war to carry on, and would have to be prepared for a possible conflict with the Soviet Union. In such circumstances, army leaders felt they could not undertake the responsibility of engaging American forces. They pointed out in their talks with their naval counterparts that Japan was not yet in a position to fight a war with the United States. Like the navy, none the less, the army began operational planning for a southern strategy, and in

December the General Staff undertook specific studies of army reorganization, intelligence, and the administration of occupied territory in preparation for a 'southern war'. But the 'southern war' was conceived to be aimed at Dutch and British possessions first, and the emphasis was on attacking Indonesia and Malaya. Although at the end of December the army and naval planners jointly prepared a 1941 war plan and obtained the supreme command's endorsement, it noted their disparate ideas, and there was no final comprehensive strategy with a definite list of hypothetical enemies.[19]

About the only area of specific agreement between army and navy strategists at this time was a policy towards Thailand. Both believed that Japanese strategy, whether it entailed the use of force against both Britain and the United States or only one of them initially, would be helped considerably by entrenching Japanese influence in Thailand, situated just west of Indo-China which was already partially occupied by Japanese forces. For some time there had existed a border dispute between Thailand and Indo-China. Thai leaders, anxious to take advantage of Indo-China's diplomatic distress because of German victories and Japanese pressures, turned to Japan to help them annex some disputed border territory. The Japanese government and military were easily persuaded; by assisting Thai expansionism, Japan would strengthen its position in the area and be able to induce Thailand to enter into a military agreement. The country was in a strategic location in the event of Japan's executing its southern strategy. At the same time, Japanese officials wanted to ingratiate themselves with French authorities in Indo-China by offering Japan's good offices in the territorial dispute. In return for moderating Thai demands, they reasoned, Japan could press the French to grant further concessions in southern Indo-China. The use of force to compel the French to accept Japanese mediation was not yet contemplated, but the idea of establishing Japanese influence in southern Indo-China and in Thailand, countries that had hitherto been under European and American influence, reflected Japan's commitment to a southern strategy. Although the Japanese believed such moves could be taken without their resulting in a military clash with British or American forces, the decision to establish 'close and inseparable relations' between Japan and Thailand, as Matsuoka stated at the end of December, was another milestone in implementing Japan's new Asian order. As of that moment, it could be said that the new order would consist of Japan, Manchukuo, China, Indo-China, and Thailand. Whether the zone of Japanese influence would be expanded would depend on various factors, in particular the European war and American policy, and Japan would have to be prepared for an eventual confrontation with the Anglo-American nations, but at least it seemed possible to extend the new order more or less peacefully to cover Indo-China and Thailand. Consolidation of this bloc would in turn make it possible for Japan to withstand Anglo-American pressures and to seize an opportune moment to try to reduce their influence.[20]

The focus on southern strategy, which had become confirmed through all such developments, had the corollary that Japan's 'northern strategy', aimed at the Soviet Union, would be put on the shelf for the time being. For the army, to be sure, preparedness against that nation remained a fundamental principle, and some were even concerned that Japan might sooner or later have to go to war against all the principal nations in Asia and the Pacific, including the Soviet Union, the United States, Britain, and China. But for the immediate future, it appeared desirable to stabilize Japanese–Soviet relations. The Japanese army in Manchuria, numbering some sixteen divisions at the end of 1940, would have to be maintained, but otherwise no military engagement with Soviet forces would be contemplated.[21]

In addition to the passive policy of avoiding trouble with the Soviet Union, the Konoe cabinet reactivated its predecessor's attempt to effect a *rapprochement* with it. It will be recalled that just before the Yonai cabinet fell in July, it had approached Moscow with that goal in mind and that the Soviet Union had responded by indicating its willingness to negotiate. But the Japanese government now wanted to go beyond merely maintaining stability across the Russian–Manchukuo frontier, and to bind the two countries closer together. As Foreign Minister Matsuoka reasoned, the signing of the German–Italian–Japanese alliance, coupled with the 1939 non-aggression pact between Germany and the Soviet Union, provided an excellent opportunity for Tokyo and Moscow to reassess their relationship in the larger context of world affairs. Harking back to an earlier theme. Matsuoka argued for an *entente* among Japan, Germany, Italy, and the Soviet Union as a bloc of revisionist powers opposed to the Anglo-American domination of the world. Such an *entente* would help Japan establish its new order in Asia; it would not only entail the end of Soviet assistance in China but could also lead to an Anglo-American withdrawal from the Asian-Pacific region. Specifically, Tokyo now proposed a non-aggression pact with Moscow which would be comparable to the German–Soviet non-aggression treaty and in effect divide up most of Asia into two spheres of influence: Japan would grant Soviet supremacy in Outer Mongolia, Sinkiang, and, if necessary, Afghanistan, Iran, and India, in return for which the Soviet Union would recognize Inner Mongolia and north China as Japan's spheres of influence, and acquiesce in future Japanese advances into French Indo-China and the Dutch East Indies.

To implement these ideas, Matsuoka appointed a new ambassador, Tategawa Yoshitsugu, to replace the veteran diplomat, Tōgō. Although the latter had been a strong exponent of a *rapprochement* with the Soviet Union, the foreign minister undertook a sweeping change of diplomatic personnel to indicate the coming of a new age in Japanese foreign policy. Tategawa had been one of the conspirators during the time of the

Manchurian incident in 1931. A professional soldier, he had also headed an 'association for the construction of East Asia', established in 1939 to propagate anti-British and pro-Russian ideas. He shared Matsuoka's view that Japan and the Soviet Union had much to gain through an understanding that clarified their respective spheres of interest, and believed the two nations could co-operate for the establishment of a new international order on such a basis. These ideas were presented to Foreign Minister Molotov in late October. The latter, however, demurred, especially as the Japanese proposal was silent on the issue of Sakhalin. The Russians wanted to regain South Sakhalin which they had ceded to Japan in 1905; at the very least, they sought a cancellation of the oil and coal concessions in North Sakhalin which had been given to Japan in the 1920s. Negotiations dragged on for several months.

Matsuoka's idea had been to incorporate the Soviet Union into a four-power *entente*, so it is not surprising that he should have turned to Germany to help break the impasse. He instructed Ambassador Ōshima in Berlin to seek German intercessions, but nothing came of it. In November, when Molotov visited Berlin and conferred with von Ribbentrop, the latter did mention Japanese–Russian relations and proposed a four-power *entente*. But these issues were overshadowed by German unhappiness over Soviet action in Finland and the Balkans. The two failed to reach agreement on defining respective spheres of influence, and the meeting ended in failure. Soon thereafter, on 18 December, Hitler decided on an anti-Russian war, code-named Barbarossa. The decision for such a war had already been made in July, but he had waited for the right moment. If he could get what he wanted – land and resources in eastern and south-eastern Europe – without a fight, he would be willing to maintain a truce with the Soviet Union. But sooner or later, he believed Germany was destined to struggle against Slavic peoples. Seeing the Soviets taking advantage of the non-aggression pact with Germany to extend their own influence in the Balkans and elsewhere, he reasoned that he would have to renounce the Russian agreement. The war with Britain had not been won, as he had hoped, and as winter set in he knew it would continue well into the new year. But he reasoned that the longer he waited, the greater would become Soviet power. Confident that the United States would not intervene right away, Hitler thought the British war could be continued in high gear even while he shifted the bulk of his troops eastward. In fact, if he should strike a lightning blow at the Soviet Union and bring it to its knees, a colossal empire would become Germany's, and all the resources and manpower could be brought under its control, the better to enable it to meet the British and, ultimately, American challenge.

Barbarossa was to be carried out in the spring of 1941. Hitler ordered that all preparations be completed by 15 May. He did not, however, give any inkling of the secret order to the Japanese. Although the Tokyo embassy was informed in general terms about a coming break with the

Soviet Union, information that was immediately picked up by Richard Sorge and transmitted to Moscow, the latter did not accept it at its face value. Any such news could be a fabrication by unfriendly hands to confuse the Russians and sow the seed of discord between the two countries. Stalin did not want to reorient his policy on the basis of what he considered flimsy evidence. It would be better, he thought, to continue to court Germany by shipping it the arms and material it requested, rather than risk a premature breach in their relations. The fact that Stalin did not take the rumours of war seriously can be seen in his lack of enthusiasm at this time for a Japanese *entente*. If he had been more strongly convinced of an impending war with Germany, he would have tried to secure the eastern front by entering into such an understanding right away, even conceding some of Japan's demands. But he rejected them out of hand, particularly because the Japanese were not offering any concessions on the Sakhalin question. From their point of view, it was out of the question to retrocede South Sakhalin to the Soviet Union or to give up the oil and other concessions in North Sakhalin; to do so would mean returning to the situation before the Russo-Japanese War – something the army could never accept. As a possible way out of the impasse, Matsuoka offered to purchase North Sakhalin rather than dallying in negotiations on its oil concessions, but the Soviet government adamantly refused to entertain such a proposal.

The Japanese bargaining position might have been strengthened if Tokyo had had definite information regarding Barbarossa, but of course this was not the case. Through Sorge his Japanese collaborators found out about German intentions, but they kept the information to themselves. Tokyo's top military and civilian officials, to be sure, never believed that German–Russian relations would long remain cordial. Already at the end of 1940, some diplomats abroad started sending reports of a growing rift between the two powers. Nevertheless, Matsuoka was wedded to his four-power *entente* idea. The Axis alliance was for him but one part of the edifice, his favourite new order which must include active Russian participation. Should German–Soviet relations sour, the foundations of his diplomacy would collapse. He did not want to believe in such a possibility, and he persisted in his belief that a Japanese–Soviet understanding would serve to consolidate the four-party partnership, thus countering any threat of a deterioration in German–Russian relations. If the scheme seemed to have trouble, then he would go to Berlin and Moscow himself to finalize the building of the edifice. He would truly be the architect of a new world order. Thus at the end of December he conveyed to Germany his intention of visiting Europe early in the following year, and Berlin duly extended its invitation. His trip would show if his grand strategy had any basis in reality, or if it was only a product of his wishful thinking.[22]

TOWARDS A JAPANESE–SOVIET *ENTENTE*

Matsuoka did not leave for Europe till 12 March, 1941. And when he did, a high officer of the army General Staff privately recorded, 'There was a huge crowd at Tokyo station. But he is leaving for Europe without any definite idea. He will meet with Hitler and with Stalin, but nobody knows what he will come back with.'[23]

It was a fateful trip, one that was to have been the climax of Japan's struggle for a new, anti-Anglo-American order. In the event, it was to coincide not only with the final break in German-Russian relations but also with the formation of an *entente* among America, Britain, China, and the Dutch East Indies – the so-called ABCD bloc – the very developments that the Japanese had tried desperately to prevent.

The fact that Matsuoka's trip, initially scheduled for early 1941, was postponed till mid-March, indicated indecision on the part of Tokyo's leaders. As will be seen, even as late as March they had not reached consensus as to what Matsuoka should be authorized to tell his counterparts in Berlin and Moscow. Equally pressing were the issues of Indo-China and Thailand, left over from late 1940. The early months of 1941 were taken up by deliberations for finalizing Japanese intervention in the Thai–Indo-China border dispute, and by the signing of a Japanese–Thai treaty. The border dispute had resulted in clashes between Thai and Indo-Chinese forces, both on land and at sea, and the Japanese feared British intervention to support the French. To forestall it, Tokyo's supreme command and government decided on 19 January to offer Japan's good offices to the two countries, and to back this up by a demonstration of force in and around northern Indo-China. The idea was to establish Japan's 'commanding position' over the region as part of the Great East Asian Co-prosperity Sphere, as it was noted in a 31 January decision.[24] This may have been the first time that the phrase, 'Great East Asian Co-prosperity Sphere', was introduced into an official governmental document. It indicated that the strategy of establishing Japanese domination over the Indo-China–Thai region was becoming solidified. It should be noted that at that time little was said of the Dutch East Indies; Japan would proceed piecemeal, and the only region where force might be used was limited to Indo-China and Thailand. In order to carry out the project, it would be necessary to 'prevent Anglo-American machinations', the 31 January document noted, but 'we should avoid provoking them by acting impetuously in areas under their control'. It was expected that the Thai–Indo-China strategy would be completed by March or April.

Ironically, Japan's mediation efforts proved successful, depriving it of an excuse for military intervention. Both Thailand and Indo-China accepted the offer of good offices, and sent delegates to Tokyo to negotiate a border settlement. The talks lasted for over a month, between 7 February and 11 March, as the two sides were adamant about their respective positions. Both Thai and French officials counted on outside support – British and American pressures to mitigate Japanese influence – but in the end they accepted a compromise settlement and signed a new peace treaty on 9 May. The border settlement was a compromise, with Thailand gaining more than Indo-China, but by no means all that it had demanded. What is notable is that Japan failed to seize the opportunity to occupy parts of Thailand or southern Indo-China. All that its intercession in the border dispute had accomplished was some sense of gratitude on the part of Thai leaders; but certainly this was a far cry from any initiation of a serious southern advance.

On 11 March Foreign Minister Matsuoka met with the French ambassador, Charles Arsène-Henry, in Tokyo, and both put their signatures to a document ratifying the Thai–Indo-China border agreement. The following day the foreign minister left on his European trip. He had a sense of accomplishment because of the border settlement, but that in itself was of little use as he prepared to deal with the high officials of Nazi Germany and the Soviet Union. As mentioned earlier, Japan had failed to interest them in a quadruple *entente* including Italy, an idea that was derived from Matsuoka's view that the world was becoming divided into four blocs: East Asia, Europe, the Americas, and the Soviet bloc. Apparently he believed that such a division of the world would create a balance, although he was not entirely certain that a durable peace could be maintained between the Soviet bloc and a Europe under German–Italian domination, or between the Soviet Union and an East Asia under Japanese domination. In any event, it appears that for Matsuoka such a perception was a way of persuading himself and his colleagues that the United States would acquiesce in the proposed division, and that for this very reason it was imperative for Japan, Germany, and the Soviet Union to establish a solid working relationship.

Incoming reports and available intelligence already indicated, however, that German–Russian relations might not remain stable, and that there might soon be a rupture. Matsuoka obtained intimations of such a possibility not only from German officials in Tokyo but also from Japanese diplomats in Europe. But he chose to believe that there were some shared interests binding Japan, Germany, and the Soviet Union together. As he explained to Stalin on his way to Berlin, these countries were all struggling to reduce Anglo-American influence in the world. That was the meaning of the new order, and since Britain and America stood in the way of its construction, Japan and the others must resolutely reject their intervention.[25]

Some of this was sheer rhetoric to impress Stalin. Matsuoka had been specifically enjoined by his government not to promise Japan's support of Germany in the event the latter went to war against the Anglo-

American powers, so that all his talk about a struggle against these powers did not amount to a proposal for a military alliance. Nevertheless, he clearly wanted an understanding with the Soviet Union within the framework of the Axis pact so as to impress Britain and the United States. When he reached Berlin, he held conferences with Hitler and von Ribbentrop in order to obtain their blessings for his grand design, but they intimated that German–Russian relations were deteriorating rapidly and that they might clash soon. Although the German leaders did not specifically confide that they were just then making plans for a Russian invasion, Matsuoka could have guessed at it. The German high command's strategy called for a lightning attack on the Soviet frontier and a push to the major bases and cities before winter; in the meantime, it would count on Japan to attack Singapore and the British empire in Asia. Both steps would, it was believed, immobilize the United States and prevent the latter's intervention.

Matsuoka was unable to commit Japan to any plan of attack on Singapore. Nor was he successful in convincing the Germans of the wisdom of his quadri-partite scheme. In other words, neither the Germans nor Matsuoka achieved anything solid as a result of his visit. Ironically, the deteriorating condition of German–Russian relations impelled the Soviet leadership to be receptive to the idea of an understanding with Japan. When Matsuoka returned to Moscow in April, he was greeted by Stalin and Molotov with an expression of serious interest in a neutrality treaty between the two countries. The Russians were clearly worried over a possible German–Japanese combined attack and hastened to draw up a five-year treaty of neutrality with Japan, binding the latter to neutrality in the event of Soviet involvement in a German war. The treaty was signed on 13 April. An accompanying declaration stated that Japan would respect the territorial integrity of the Mongolian People's Republic, and the Soviet Union would do likewise in 'the empire of Manchuria'. In other words, the latter was now recognizing the Japanese conquest of Manchuria, a severe blow to China, particularly to the Communists and others who had looked to the Soviet Union for leadership in a global coalition of anti-Fascist peoples. From Stalin's perspective, however, the neutrality treaty was a price he had to pay in order to ensure Japanese good behaviour. Moreover, just then the Soviet government was initiating an approach to Britain and America. Still extremely tentative, such a step was in response to the mounting crisis in the Balkans, where German forces were invading Yugoslavia.

Given such developments, Matsuoka's grand design fell flat. The neutrality treaty he obtained in Moscow was not to be a corner-stone of a new world order but was a fatal step that would enable the Soviet Union to concentrate on a coming war with Germany, while at the same time preparing for a reconciliation with the Anglo-American nations. In other words, far from ensuring a solid global coalition for the protection and expansion of the Japanese empire, the Japanese diplomatic initiative would end up further isolating the nation. This became clear in the spring of 1941 when London and Washington further solidified their co-operative framework. The Anglo-American staff conversations in Washington met on fourteen different occasions till they produced a final report – ABC-1 – on 29 March. The report was a compromise between the British insistence on a joint defence of Singapore and other bases in Asia and the American stress on a defensive strategy in the Pacific in order to concentrate on the European situation for the immediate future. It adopted the policy of a strategic defensive in the Asian-Pacific region, concentrating on preventing Japan's southward aggression through economic means and through the stationing of the United States fleet in the Pacific. On the basis of ABC-1, American, British, and Dutch officers conferred in Singapore in late April, confirming the three powers' military co-operation in the event of war with the Axis nations. Moreover, they would incorporate China into their strategy; they would place military aircraft in China, give financial aid and equipment to the latter's regular forces, and assist its guerrillas. Though not yet approved by the highest governmental officials, such plans further confirmed the emerging coalition of the ABCD powers. The same month that saw the signing of the Japanese–Soviet neutrality treaty thus witnessed further con- solidation of the ABCD *entente*, designed to isolate Japan just when the latter was intent upon creating a global coalition against the Anglo- American powers.[26]

Confrontation between the two sides was thus already quite asymmetrical. The United States was fast augmenting its military power and establishing *de facto* alliances in Europe and Asia, whereas Japan was unable to make good its scheme for an anti-Anglo-American global coalition. Given the situation, there was good reason for confidence in Washington that Japan would sooner or later succumb to pressure and realize the folly of its Asian ambitions. On the Japanese side, the growing spectacle of a coalition against the nation necessitated steps to prevent its complete isolation. Either the Axis pact should be fortified to match the strength of the ABCD coalition or, if that did not happen, Japan should try to divide the four nations. Some such thinking led to the initiation of diplomatic talks in Washington in the spring of 1941. On the American side, there was confidence that, given Japan's growing isolation, its leaders would recognize the crisis and decide to mend their ways. When, in April, two Maryknoll priests appeared in Washington purporting to speak for Japanese moderates who were interested in peace with America, it fitted into such an expectation. President Roosevelt, Secretary of State Hull, and others could reason that at least the Japanese leadership was split and that the moderates might be reasserting themselves. If so, the United States should do what it could to help their cause and bring Japan back to sanity. The fact that Admiral

Nomura Kichisaburō who, as foreign minister in 1939, had tried to improve Japanese–American relations, was sent as ambassador to the United States in early 1941, added to the sense of optimism. Hull agreed to initiate talks with Nomura and started by giving the Japanese ambassador a list of four principles as the foundation of a better relationship across the Pacific. These were territorial integrity, non-interference in internal affairs, equal commercial opportunity, and peaceful alteration of the status quo. This was a statement that the United States would expect all countries to accept, including its potential allies and adversaries. The four principles had traditionally defined American foreign policy and underlain its internationalist vision. Hull's reiteration of them indicated that the United States government believed it was possible to reconstruct world order once again on the basis of liberal internationalism. Japan would be given a choice of either joining such an order, or alienating itself from all the others.

That was not what the Japanese expected to find in Washington. Their main concern was with having the United States recognize the *fait accompli* in Asia, thus acquiescing in Japan's control over China and possibly South-East Asia. By doing so, America would in effect be weakening, if not nullifying, the ABCD *entente*. As Matsuoka told Nomura, the United States must stop trying to act as the world's policeman and refrain from intervening in other countries' 'spheres of living'. As can be seen in such a statement, there was growing desperation among Japanese officials that the United States was being successful in establishing a global alliance of forces that would challenge the efforts by the Axis powers to establish new regional orders. One way of frustrating the American scheme, Matsuoka reasoned, would be to seek an understanding on the basis of the given *faits accomplis* in Asia and the Pacific. On that basis, war could be avoided and the two powers bring 'peace and prosperity in the Pacific'.[27]

Japan was clearly put on the defensive, and American officials knew it. Talks in Washington dragged on inconclusively, their only rationale from the American standpoint being the time they enabled the United States to gain for preparedness. Military strategists advised Roosevelt that they would need more time, perhaps till mid-1942, before the United States would be ready to risk war with the Axis. In the meantime, it would continue to assist Britain and China to enable them to continue to resist Germany and Japan, respectively. In such a context, diplomatic conversations with Japan were purely a tactical manoeuvre. There was only a slight chance that they would yield significant results, involving Japanese acceptance of Hull's principles.

It will be neither necessary nor useful to chronicle in detail the course of the Washington conversations. Suffice it to stress that the talks further strengthened the ABCD coalition and weakened the Axis alliance. Hull specifically aimed at helping China by insisting that all

Japanese troops be withdrawn from China proper, if not from Manchuria. He was at least willing to let the Japanese stay in Manchuria, more or less re-creating the situation prior to 1937, but they would have to get out of the rest of the country. Obviously, such insistence was designed to strengthen the American–Chinese coalition. Any concession the United States made on this point would be taken by the Chinese as a betrayal, counter to the emerging alliance between the two nations. It is no accident that President Roosevelt chose this time to send a special emissary, Owen Lattimore, to Chungking. The Johns Hopkins scholar had been preceded by others such as Lauchlin Currie, the president's special adviser, but the Lattimore mission was significant since it was specifically designed to establish a direct channel of communication between the two heads of government. Lattimore left for China in June, and as soon as he reached Chungking he began energetically impressing upon Chinese leaders Roosevelt's determination to stand by their country till Japan was finally repulsed.

The Chinese at that time may have needed such strong assurances in view of the signing of the Japanese–Soviet pact. The neutrality treaty shocked Chinese of all persuasions, who inevitably saw it as a betrayal of the anti-Fascist coalition they had helped establish. The Nationalists feared the stoppage of Soviet shipments of arms across the north-west frontier and were chagrined at Moscow's pledge of non-interference in Manchukuo, implying recognition of the puppet regime. Such a step would, it was feared, enable the Japanese to shift some of their forces out of Manchuria to other parts of China. The Chinese Communists, on their part, were in a quandary. They could not openly criticize the Soviet Union for the neutrality pact with Japan, and they even went so far as to declare that the treaty would 'benefit the peace-loving persons and oppressed peoples of the world'. But clearly, the Communists could not swallow the Soviet comrades' apparent sell-out of Manchuria, and the neutrality treaty would long be remembered as an instance of Soviet opportunism.[28]

In such a situation, for both Nationalists and Communists it was more than ever imperative to count on the support of the United States. The latter would have to demonstrate that the Japanese–Soviet pact would not weaken America's resolve to strengthen the anti-Japanese coalition. The Washington conversations could, of course, give rise to suspicion that America and Japan were about to enter into a deal at China's expense. It was imperative to dispel such fears, and the best way of doing so was to reassert again and again America's commitment to China's integrity, precisely what Hull and Lattimore were doing.

Britain, too, was not idle. Soon after the signing of the Japanese–Soviet pact, the British embassy in Chungking reported to London that there was an increasing tendency in China 'to regard the United States as China's only friend', a tendency that appeared to be strengthened by Britain's refusal to respond to Chungking's request at this time that if

The failure of an alliance

Japan should attack Yunan Province from Indo-China, Britain would help China by using aircraft manned by volunteer pilots. In order to assure the Chinese that there was no change in Britain's determination to support them, Foreign Secretary Anthony Eden instructed Ambassador Clark Kerr in Chungking to tell Chiang Kai-shek, 'We have made no compromise with Japan and we shall make none. Our wholehearted sympathy remains with China in her fight for freedom and independence.' The Chinese leader thanked him for such assurances, conveying a message to Prime Minister Churchill that 'I am gladly ready to follow in your footsteps, and to go with you towards our common goal of victory and peace. To this end we should co-operate still more closely to render to each other all help in our power.' Even if abstract, such statements reaffirmed the ABCD *entente*. Certainly, there was nothing comparable to such expressions of solidarity between the Japanese and the Germans, or between the former and the Russians.[29]

The Axis pact, in fact, was being weakened even as the ABCD coalition was being solidified. The Washington conversations aroused suspicions in Berlin that the Japanese were seeking an understanding with the United States at Germany's expense. Tokyo's continued refusal to commit itself to attacking Singapore, coupled with the Washington talks, exasperated the Germans. As Ambassador Ōshima reported from Berlin, German leaders were gravely concerned over these moves which could undermine the Axis alliance. Should Japan persist in seeking accommodation with the United States, Ōshima warned, Germany might be compelled to do likewise, nullifying the framework of Japanese foreign policy that had been painstakingly built up. While that was an extreme view, the conversations in Washington did indeed contribute to undermining the Japanese–German alliance. Not that Hull was entirely successful in weaning Japan away from the alliance. With Matsuoka exercising remote control over Nomura, the latter could not, even if he wanted to, openly proclaim Japan's disassociation from Germany. But Nomura tried to convey the message that Japan would not be obligated to go to war on the side of Germany against the United States unless the latter attacked first. Such assurances were not sufficient from the American point of view, but at least they diluted the symbolic significance of the Axis pact. Since the United States was not likely to attack Germany first, for all intents and purposes Japan would not be bound to enter into an American–German war. In other words, there would be little significance to the Japanese–German alliance, in sharp contrast to the ABCD coalition that continued to be solidified.[30]

The Japanese government was put on the defensive. Clearly, the nation was being isolated, with the favourite scheme for a Japanese–German–Soviet *entente* more impressive on paper than in actuality. The Washington conversations were carried out at that psychological moment and gave some officials in Tokyo momentary confidence that Japan could now come to an understanding with America. But they were mistaken in thinking that such an understanding would mean American recognition of Japan's new Asian order. That they should have indulged in such wishful thinking revealed their sense of desperation. They somehow thought Japan could undermine the ABCD *entente* and have the United States recognize the Asian-Pacific new order – the very thing that the ABCD partners were trying to frustrate. The only solid agreement between Japan and the United States would have had to be built on the annihilation of both the Axis pact and the ABCD coalition, implying a return to the Washington Conference structure of close Anglo-American–Japanese co-operation. Few Japanese leaders were willing to go that far, least of all Foreign Minister Matsuoka. He was chagrined that the talks in Washington had been carried on while he was in Europe and charged insubordination on the part of other officials. This displeasure would ultimately lead to his resignation. There is no evidence, however, that he would have been more successful in negotiating with the United States. He was so self-confident that he believed he could himself go to Washington and come to a deal with President Roosevelt, just as he had done with Hitler and Stalin. But he would have brought to Washington the same ideas that Nomura was already conveying to Hull; he could never have accepted Hull's basic principles and could instead have insisted on America's recognition of the *fait accompli* in Asia. Moreover, Matsuoka would never have consented to nullifying the German alliance. In short, even if he had had a direct hand in the Washington negotiations, the outcome would have been the same: disappointment and desperation that Japan was not getting anywhere.

In the spring of 1941, tnen, circumstances were such that Japan's top military and civilian leaders were coming to the realization that if the nation were to persist in its Asian policy it would have to do so more or less alone, not counting on the help of other powers. How to put it into practice was a question to preoccupy them throughout the rest of the year.

REFERENCES AND NOTES

1. *Matsuoka Yōsuke* (Tokyo 1974), pp. 768–9.
2. Ibid., pp. 772–4. See also Theo Sommer, *Deutschland und Japan zwischen den Mächten, 1935–1940* (Tübingen 1962), Ch. 4.
3. *Matsuoka*, pp. 779, 787–8.
4. Jonathan G. Utley, *Going to War with Japan, 1937–1941* (Knoxville 1985), p. 109.
5. Defence Agency, War History Division (ed.), *Daihonei rikugunbu* (The army supreme command; Tokyo 1968), 2: 91. See also Murakami Sachiko, *Futsuin shinchū* (Japan's thrust into French Indo-China; n.p. 1984); Ch. 6.

6. Irvine Anderson, *The Standard-Vacuum Oil Company and United States East Asian Policy, 1933-41* (Princeton 1975), p. 154.
7. *Foreign Relations of the United States: 1940* (Washington 1955), 4: 424.
8. *Chung-hua Min-kuo chung-yao chih-liao ch'u-pien: tui-Ju kang-chan shih-chi* (Important historical documents of the Chinese republic: the period of the anti-Japanese war; Taipei n.d.), 6.3: 418.
9. Ibid., 6.3: 431.
10. James R. Leutze, *Bargaining for Supremacy: Anglo-American Naval Collaboration, 1937-1941* (Chapel Hill 1977), p. 165.
11. Robert Dallek, *Franklin D. Roosevelt and American Foreign Policy, 1932-1945* (New York 1979), pp. 252-7.
12. John Hunter Boyle, *China and Japan at War, 1937-1945: The Politics of Collaboration* (Stanford 1972) p. 304.
13. Leutze, *Bargaining*, p. 176; David Reynolds, *The Creation of the Anglo-American Alliance, 1937-41* (Chapel Hill 1981), pp. 182-5.
14. *Daihonei rikugunbu*, 2: 128-9.
15. Ibid., 2: 132.
16. Boyle, *China and Japan*, p. 303; *Matsuoka*, pp. 834-42.
17. *Chung-hua Min-kuo*, pp. 193-215.
18. *Daihonei rikugunbu*, 2: 138.
19. Ibid., 2: 140-6; Tanemura Sakō, *Daihonei kimitsu nisshi* (A secret diary of the supreme headquarters; Tokyo 1952), pp. 38-9.
20. *Daihonei rikugunbu*, 2: 175-6.
21. Ibid., 2: 204.
22. *Matsuoka*, p. 846; Japan Association of International Affairs (ed.), *Taiheiyō sensō e no michi* (The road to the Pacific war; Tokyo 1962-1963), 5: 265-7.
23. Tanemura, *Daihonei kimitsu nisshi*, pp. 49-50.
24. *Daihonei rikugunbu*, 2: 184.
25. *Matsuoka*, pp. 849-57.
26. Leutze, *Bargaining*, Ch. 15.
27. *Matsuoka*, p. 916.
28. Tang Tsou, *America's Failure in China, 1941-50* (Chicago 1963), pp. 212-13.
29. FO 3017/60/10, FO 3796/60/10, J 4276/60/10, Foreign Office archives, Public Record Office.
30. Akira Iriye, *Power and Culture: The Japanese-American War, 1941-45* (Cambridge, Mass. 1981), p. 14.

Chapter 5

THE ROAD TO WAR

War across the Pacific was not inevitable. At least as of June 1941, both Tokyo and Washington were intent upon avoiding such an eventuality. But whereas the Japanese thought war could be avoided if only the United States desisted from assisting Britain against Germany and intervening in Asia, American officials were fast establishing a global system of collective security to push back Germany and Japan to earlier positions. Given the success of American strategy, Japan's only hope, if it were to persist in its Asian scheme, lay in establishing an impregnable empire so as to withstand the pressures of the United States and its allies.

Developments in the summer of 1941 confirmed these two trends. On one hand, the German invasion of the Soviet Union, commenced on 22 June, had the effect of adding the latter to the global American-led coalition. On the other, Japan's decision to take advantage of the German–Russian War by invading southern Indo-China was designed to prepare the nation for an ultimate confrontation with the ABCD powers. Under these circumstances, only a break-up of that partnership or Japan's reversal of southern expansionism could have prevented a Pacific war.

THE GERMAN–SOVIET WAR

Hitler's decision to nullify the Soviet non-aggression pact and invade Russian territory at once weakened Japan's and strengthened America's respective positions. It signalled the bankruptcy of Tokyo's grand strategy, coalescing Japan, Germany, Italy, and the Soviet Union as revisionist powers against the Anglo-American nations. Overnight the scheme broke into pieces, forcing the Japanese leadership to consider alternatives. Prime Minister Konoe understood that Germany's invasion of the Soviet Union would push the latter to seek the assistance of Britain and the United States, thus in effect adding the country to the Anglo-American coalition. As he wrote, the Soviet Union had been 'driven to the Anglo-American camp'. That would further isolate Japan and might even involve it in a war against all these countries.[1]

The question, of course, was what was to be done. One drastic alternative would have been for Japan to recognize frankly the failure of its pro-German policy and, as Konoe said, reorient Japanese policy to effect a *rapprochement* with the United States. He reasoned that the Axis pact had outlived its usefulness; now that it had revealed its utter bankruptcy, Japan should release itself from it and seek an accommodation with the United States. As the prime minister wrote to Matsuoka in early July, Japan could never afford to go to war with both America and the Soviet Union; the two powers must be prevented from establishing a close relationship, and in the meantime Japan must have a continued supply of raw materials. All such aims necessitated a readjustment of Japanese relations with America. That would require that Japan make concessions in China and South-East Asia, but Konoe believed such concessions would be worth an improved relationship with the United States. In essence he was arguing for a return to an earlier pattern of Japanese foreign policy in which economic and political ties to America had been of fundamental importance.[2]

It is not certain that such reorientation, even if it had been implemented, would have prevented the American–Soviet *rapprochement*, or weakened the ABCD coalition. But at least it would have undermined the rationale for such a coalition, and the United States, Britain, and the Soviet Union would have focused their efforts on the Atlantic and Europe. Japan might have maintained itself as the key Asian power but would no longer have been ostracized. The question of China would have remained, but there might have developed some understanding with the Nationalists. (Konoe believed a peace with Chungking would be an important part of the Japanese–American *rapprochement*.)

This was too drastic a scheme to be acceptable to Japan's military, or to Matsuoka. For them, to go back to the framework of co-operation with the United States would be incompatible with the Axis alliance and entail giving up the scheme for establishing an Asian co-prosperity sphere. They were right, of course, and Konoe was asking them to reorient their thinking so as to accommodate the drastic turn of events overseas. From the military's point of view, however, such reorientation was tantamount to yielding to American pressure and giving up the war in China as hopeless. They could not do so without risking loss of prestige and their privileged position in domestic affairs. Some army strategists, moreover, judged that the world was finally becoming divided into two fighting camps, with Japan, Germany, and Italy on one side and the United States, Britain, the Soviet Union, and China on the other. In such a situation, it was too late for Japan to change sides, it was argued; what the nation must do was to consider the most appropriate strategy for the impending global war. Here, however, no consensus emerged for a speedy response. Some argued for joining forces with Germany to attack the Soviet Union, to destroy one corner of the emerging anti-Axis alliance. But most strategists urged caution, fearing that too precipitous a move in the north would drain resources away from China and South-East Asia. In fact, a prolonged war with the Soviet Union would itself necessitate an enlarged southern empire so as to secure continued supply of raw materials needed for the prosecution of the war. The best strategy, then, would be for Japan to be in a state of preparedness against the Soviet Union without actually going to war until the course of the German–Russian conflict became clearer. This was a strategy of opportunism – to wait till 'the persimmon ripened', as they said. The navy, on its part, was reluctant to go to war in the north right away. It retained its preoccupation with southern expansion as the first priority, and would agree only to preparedness against the Soviet Union. Here again, the basic factor that had to be taken into consideration was the possibility of a global war. As the navy minister pointed out, the imperial navy could possibly manage a war with the Anglo-American powers, but not against the combination of America, Britain, and the Soviet Union. Therefore, it was best not to provoke the latter and bring into being a *de facto* alliance between the Soviet Union and the United States.

Foreign Minister Matsuoka, in contrast, insisted on quickly turning north, abrogating the two-month-old neutrality pact which he himself had negotiated with the Soviet Union. The German–Soviet War clearly meant the failure of his grand design, but far from being discouraged, he reasoned that the Axis alliance must take precedence over the Russian treaty. He went further than the army in advocating an immediate declaration of war against the Soviet Union. He was convinced that Germany would soon defeat the nation, and that by the end of the year it would also have brought Britain to its knees, before American intervention. Japan, therefore, should seize the opportunity to attack the Soviet Union. That entailed no risk of American intervention, whereas southern expansion would. If Japan waited too long, an Anglo-American–Soviet alliance would be perfected, and the nation would become even more isolated. The thing to do, then, was to act before such an alliance became firmly established. Matsuoka was correct in foreseeing that Japan's move southward would eventually lead to a war against the three powers. Instead of stopping there, however, he reasoned that the nation must therefore turn north. To do nothing would solve nothing and would do irreparable damage to the Axis alliance.[3]

There was thus some logic to the views of the army, the navy, and the foreign minister. Their endless discussions in the last week of June were, in retrospect, the high point of prewar Japanese strategy. Earnest and serious discussion among the military, and at the highest echelons of the government, all reflected the sense of urgency. Japan's top leaders realized that the world was at a crucial turning-point, and that its decisions would have fateful consequences for the course of the European and Asian wars. Between 26 June and 2 July, they continued to debate on the next steps Japan was to take, and the result of their deliberations was the crucial policy document ('Outlines of fundamental national policy') adopted at a meeting in the presence of the emperor, held on 2 July. According to the memorandum, Japan was to 'construct the Great East Asian Co-prosperity Sphere regardless of the changes in the world situation'. More specifically, Japan would concentrate on the settlement of the Chinese war, prepare for southern expansion, and try to solve the 'northern problem'. In other words, both southern and northern strategies were to be pursued simultaneously; which came first would depend on circumstances, particularly the course of the European war. However, greater specificity was given to southern advance when the document referred to a 25 June decision by the liaison conference that had called for the stationing of Japanese troops in southern Indo-China. The 2 July memorandum stated that such action was part of the preparedness against the United States and Britain.[4]

In other words, the policy that emerged from the deliberations of late June and early July combined a determination to extend Japanese control to southern Indo-China with, at the same time, preparing for war against the United States, Britain, and the Soviet Union. Since Japan was already fighting a war with China, what was visualized was the possibility of a war with four powers, plus probably Indo-China and the Dutch East Indies. This sort of development was the very thing the Japanese had sought to avoid, and apparently they still believed it could be prevented by acting with lightning speed to entrench Japanese power in southern Indo-China. If that could be carried out without incurring foreign intervention, then Japan would have successfully enlarged its empire and be in a better position to fight an all-front war, should it become necessary.

In retrospect, there was faulty logic behind such a decision. Since all parties in Japan were agreed on the imperative of preventing a war against the combined force of its potential enemies, in particular America, Britain, and the Soviet Union, every effort should have been made to establish clear-cut priorities and concentrate on preparedness against one enemy at a time. Matsuoka saw this clearly, and he sought in vain to persuade his military colleagues to reverse themselves about the planned invasion of southern Indo-China which, he predicted accurately, would ultimately lead to war with the Anglo-American powers. Instead, he thought the logic of the German alliance dictated that Japan first concentrate on a war against the Soviet Union. If Japan did so, and postponed its advance into southern Indo-China for six months, the nation would be in a far better position strategically. The supreme command, however, was all set to undertake the Indo-China invasion, and it was too late to reverse that decision. At the 2 July meeting in the presence of the emperor, the army chief of staff, General Sugiyama Gen, explained that an advance to southern Indo-China would serve to sever links between Chungking and the Anglo-American powers. Should the United States, Britain, and the Dutch East Indies retaliate by an embargo, Japan could respond by formally declaring war on China and take over these Western countries' concessions and settlements in that country. In the meantime, Japan would continue to prepare itself for a possible war with the Soviet Union. But, Sugiyama noted, it would be best not to become involved in such a conflict while Japan undertook to expand southward and bring the Chinese war to conclusion. The chief of naval operations, Admiral Nagano Osami, added that southern expansion was necessary to prepare the nation for a possible war with the Anglo-American–Dutch forces. Hara Yoshimichi, president of the Privy Council, reverted to Matsuoka's argument and asserted that Japan should avoid war with the United States and instead go to war against the Soviet Union. That was because sooner or later it would be necessary to combat the communist policy the Soviet Union was pursuing throughout the world, whereas there was no good reason for going to war against the Anglo-American nations. Despite such strong opinions, the conferees let stand the basic document, oriented both to southern expansion and preparedness against the Soviet Union.

Regarding the latter, the supreme command put into effect a plan of mobilization, to concentrate as many as sixteen divisions (about 850,000 men) in Manchuria to keep them in a state of readiness for a Russian war which was expected to come around 1 September. That assumed that at least one-half of Soviet forces in Siberia would be shifted to the German front, leaving roughly fifteen divisions to face Japan. The Japanese soon noted, however, that many more troops than anticipated were still remaining in eastern Siberia, so that Japan's force level would also have to be augmented accordingly. All that would take time, and already in mid-July the General Staff was worrying that an offensive against the Soviet Union might not materialize till after winter. There appeared to be no imminent collapse of the Soviet government or a rout of Russian by German forces, so that if war should come soon, Japan would have to confront a Soviet force that had not been significantly depleted. In any event, the army high command assumed that Japan would have to step up its preparedness against the Soviet Union.[5]

Given such developments, the Japanese leaders might have postponed the invasion of southern Indo-China for fear that it might incur Anglo-American retaliation and enhance risks of war with them. Nevertheless, on 3 July, the day after the crucial policy guidelines had been approved, the army issued an operational order for the stationing of Japanese forces in southern Indo-China. The invasion was to proceed 'peace-fully', that is, through agreement with French authorities; but if they refused, it would take the form of military action. In either case, the occupation of southern Indo-China was to take place around 24 July.

Little thought was given to possible Anglo-American intervention. As General Sugiyama told the emperor, the army did not expect British intervention; if there was to be bloodshed, that would involve fighting with French troops. As for the United States, no intervention was envisaged unless Britain became involved, which was considered highly unlikely, so long as Japan confined its operations to Indo-China, or at most to Thailand and Burma.

In other words, Japan was pursuing a two-front approach, even while its strategists recognized that it would be impossible to go to war against the combined forces of the Soviet Union, China, the United States, and Britain. This lack of consistency can be explained only by noting that neither preparedness against the Soviet Union nor expansion into Indo-China was believed to enhance the risk of war. In all likelihood, the supreme command thought that in the immediate future the German–Russian War would be the principal fighting in the world, and that its outcome would determine whether or not Japan, the United States, and Britain would become involved in an Asian conflict. Even if sooner or later war with the latter nations should occur, Japan would be in a more advantageous position for having incorporated Indo-China into its empire. The fact remains that little was done to keep the Soviet Union and the Anglo-American powers separated. That would have entailed making concessions to one or the other, but given the 2 July decision, it would now be extremely difficult to do so.

The only Japanese initiative *vis-à-vis* the United States at this time was the resignation of Foreign Minister Matsuoka and the formation of a new Konoe cabinet, established on 18 July. From Prime Minister Konoe's point of view, the cabinet reshuffling, in particular the replacement of Matsuoka by Admiral Toyoda Teijirō, was meant as a signal to the United States. As noted above, Konoe had wanted to reorient Japanese policy after the German invasion of the Soviet Union but had been powerless to do so, and had accepted the 2 July decision. Even so, he was still hopeful of preventing a combination of America and the Soviet Union so that Japan could concentrate on a Russian war. To that extent his and Matsuoka's views coincided; both preferred postponement of the invasion of southern Indo-China. Nevertheless, they were equally powerless to stem the tide once the momentum had set in. Under the circumstances, Konoe believed the best way of avoiding a crisis with the United States was to resume the conversations in Washington to indicate Japan's sincere desire for an understanding with America. It was in that context that Konoe sought Matsuoka's resignation, as the latter had come to symbolize Japan's commitment to the Axis pact and an obstacle in the way of Japanese–American negotiations. To spare Matsuoka embarrassment, the Konoe cabinet resigned as a group on 16 July, and then two days later the third Konoe cabinet was established.

In retrospect, it is not easy to see if Matsuoka should have been singled out for the failure to accommodate the United States. After all, he had begun strongly to urge postponement of the southern strategy, and he remained hopeful that somehow Japan and the United States would be able to live in peace in the Pacific. Nevertheless, he was the architect of the Axis pact, and was extremely suspect in Washington. Moreover, even talk of a possible war with the Soviet Union did not mollify American officials. On the contrary, they conveyed their strong concern for such an eventuality; obviously, a Japanese attack on Soviet territory would compel the latter to fight a two-front war and might lead to German victory. For all these reasons Matsuoka was an unpopular figure in Washington, and Konoe sensed it. By organizing a new cabinet, he hoped negotiations with America could be renewed and lead to a better relationship across the Pacific. The idea was that Washington would see Matsuoka's resignation as a gesture of goodwill on Konoe's part towards the United States and be interested in reciprocating his overtures.

Unfortunately, the tactic did not work. Within three days after the formation of the new cabinet – which retained all but four of the preceding cabinet ministers – the supreme command presented Konoe with a list of three demands: adherence to the 2 July decisions, the implementation of the southern and northern policies without delay, and observance of the spirit of the Axis alliance. The demands amounted to asking Konoe to confirm the twin policies of undertaking the invasion of southern Indo-China while at the same time mobilizing forces for war with the Soviet Union. The prime minister meekly acceded to the demands, thus from the outset nullifying his efforts for a *rapprochement* with the United States. He and his defenders would subsequently justify his action by saying that he had hoped to delay war with the Soviet Union by shifting the military's attention southward through a promise of Indo-China invasion, while at the same time resuming talks in Washington so that the southern strategy could also be forestalled. If so, he was too naïve, trusting in the good sense of the military as well as in America's flexibility. In the event, the occupation of Indo-China would be carried out as planned, and the United States would retaliate immediately.[6]

THE POINT OF NO RETURN

The last ten days of July were crucial in determining the future of Japanese–American relations. Already on 21 July, Under-Secretary of State Sumner Welles warned the Japanese that their occupation of Indo-China would be incompatible with the negotiations going on between the two countries. Through 'Magic', the code-breaking device that had now become operational, American officials had known of

Japan's intention to occupy southern Indo-China, an action which they believed would seriously affect the situation in South-East Asia and must be resisted. American policy after the German invasion of the Soviet Union a month earlier had been quite forceful and clear-cut. The United States welcomed the new development, Roosevelt agreeing with Churchill that, in the latter's words, 'Any man or state who fights on against Nazidom will have our aid'.[7] The government in Washington immediately started planning for extending lend-lease aid to the Soviet Union, and in the meantime Roosevelt released part of the latter's assets, frozen after the Soviet invasion of Finland in late 1939. 'If the Russians could hold the Germans until October 1', he said, 'that would be of great value in defeating Hitler'. In that connection, the president wanted to discourage any Japanese attack on the Soviet Union, warning Prime Minister Konoe in a personal message on 4 July that any such action would jeopardize the negotiations in Washington and undermine the peace in the Pacific.[8]

The United States, in short, was already seeing itself as being tied to the Soviet Union in the European war. It could help the latter by shipping aid goods and by frustrating Japanese attempts to take advantage of the German assault to attack the Soviet Union from the rear. In that connection, Japan's southern advance would be welcome inasmuch as it might divert resources from the north and make less likely an impending Japanese war with the Soviet Union. Instead of acquiescing in Japanese occupation of Indo-China, however, the Roosevelt administration decided to throw obstacles in its way, thus in effect choking off Japan from both northern and southern options. The main instrument was to be economic, in particular the freezing of Japanese assets in the United States. Just as the United States was unfreezing Soviet assets to enable the latter to fight Germany, it would make it impossible for Japan to obtain funds with which to purchase goods in America, especially much-needed oil. A total cessation of exports to Japan was not visualized, however. What Roosevelt, Hull, Welles, and others had in mind was that henceforth Japan would require an export licence whenever it wanted to buy American commodities. Moreover, some small quantities of low-octane gasoline could still be sold to Japan so as not to provide the latter with an excuse for going into the Dutch East Indies. Nevertheless, the intent of such measures was unmistakable.[9] The United States would take steps to deter Japan both from attacking the Soviet Union and occupying Indo-China. Such warning was explicitly communicated to Tokyo so as to leave little room for doubt about America's serious intentions. If additional evidence was needed, the 7 July agreement between the United States and Iceland provided it; it gave American forces the right to occupy Icelandic territory, which action was carried out on the same day. It brought American military intervention in the European war a step closer to realization. Thus it was clear that the United States was acting as a *de facto* ally of both Britain and the Soviet Union, and as a *de facto* foe of Germany. It was presenting Japan with a choice of either being included in a list of its foes or of returning to the negotiating table so as to redeem itself and gain American goodwill and trade.

Konoe should have taken such warning seriously, but he was too weak to stop the momentum. On 14 July Japan had presented a note to the Vichy regime, demanding the right to station troops in southern Indo-China, and five days later the new foreign minister, Toyoda, gave Vichy the deadline of 23 July. Regardless of Vichy's response, the supreme command was determined to carry out the invasion, and plans were completed for the dispatch of necessary troops on 24 July. Vichy's acceptance came on the 23rd, and thus a 'peaceful' landing on the Indo-China coast was accomplished between 28 and 30 July. In retaliation, on 25 July the United States ordered the freezing of Japanese assets. The following day, Britain and the Philippines followed suit, and on 27 July New Zealand and the Netherlands did likewise. The ABCD encirclement of Japan was virtually complete.

Why did the Japanese leadership fail to foresee this? The United States had given ample and explicit warning to Tokyo to desist from occupying Indo-China, and yet neither the civilian government nor the military took it seriously. Foreign Minister Toyoda asserted on 24 July that he thought the United States would not impose a total embargo on oil even after the freezing of Japanese assets, and that in any event he hoped the United States would be interested in resuming talks in Washington for adjustment of diplomatic relations. The military, on their part, appear to have reasoned that the occupation of Indo-China would not present a *casus belli* to America so long as Japan stopped there; it was not yet intending to invade Singapore, the Dutch East Indies, or the Philippines, and so the United States and Britain would not take drastic action that could further escalate the crisis. Such complacency, of course, was treated to a rude shock through a series of counter-measures adopted by the ABD powers. In addition, steps were being taken to consolidate further American support of China; since Japanese control over the whole Indo-China peninsula was designed to cut off one vital link between Chungking and the outside world, the United States would retaliate by establishing a military advisory corps in Chungking. The decision to do so had been made on 3 July, but initially it was intended for overseeing the implementation of the lend-lease programme. Now, however, it came to have more military significance. In addition, on 23 July the president authorized the stationing of volunteer airmen in China, consisting of some 100 pilots under the command of Claire Chennault, who would fly 500 aircraft for the Chinese air force. Also at this time, Roosevelt decided to call the Philippine army into federal service and to create a new Far Eastern command for the defence of the islands.[10]

Given such decisive steps, the conclusion is inescapable that the

Japanese leaders seriously misjudged American determination to resist any further change in the status quo. By their complacency, they further solidified the ABCD coalition, to which the Soviet Union was now being added. From this time on, the confrontation between Japan on one hand and the ABCD powers on the other became even more pronounced than earlier, so that if war were to be avoided it would be incumbent upon Japan to try to break up that coalition, or otherwise to join it. It did neither.

America's stiff measures had at least one effect on Japanese policy. The supreme command in Tokyo became less and less sanguine about the prospect of waging a successful campaign against the Soviet Union. Given the deteriorating condition of Japanese–American relations, the nation would have to be prepared for a grave crisis in South-East Asia which could lead to war against the ABCD powers. Under the circumstances, even the die-hard exponents of the northern strategy began showing signs of hesitancy, the more so as the German assault on the Soviet Union was not proceeding as smoothly as had at first been anticipated. Despite such misgivings, the General Staff went ahead with the planned deployment of sixteen divisions in Manchuria, concentrating on the Siberian border. They were, however, to avoid provocative action that could cause Soviet retaliation and lead to war. Since earlier a possible attack on the Soviet Union had been planned for early August, such caution, coming on the heels of America's economic sanctions, meant there would be no chance for undertaking the northern strategy. On 9 August, the army supreme command formally accepted the inevitable, concluding that it was impossible to go to war against the Soviet Union in the near future. As the General Staff reasoned, there was little chance that Germany would be able to defeat that country by the end of the year, and in the meantime the situation *vis-à-vis* the United States was growing more and more serious. International conditions, in other words, had changed since 2 July, and therefore the guidelines adopted that day would no longer be adequate.[11]

Between 2 July and 9 August, then, a crucial reversal of Japanese strategy had taken place. From preparedness for an impending offensive against the Soviet Union, the supreme command reverted to a more passive stance in the north. Sixteen divisions would still be mobilized, but they would not be engaged in any action for the time being. Henceforth, Japanese strategy would focus on a possible conflict with the ABCD powers. In this sense, 9 August may be taken as the point of no return as far as Japanese–American relations were concerned.

The United States contributed to that turn of events by instituting a *de facto* embargo on oil. The freezing of Japanese assets, announced on 25 July, had been followed by a week of intensive work by State department, Treasury, and other officials to set up a machinery for implementing the order. The idea, which Roosevelt approved, was to let the Japanese apply for export licences which would then be examined on a case-by-case basis and necessary funds released from blocked Japanese monies to purchase the goods. Oil, too, would be dealt with in this fashion. But the processing of applications for licences and release of funds took time, and the matter was overseen by Dean Acheson, assistant secretary of state, who refused to release funds, intent upon punishing Japan for its southern expansionism.[12] The result was that Japan never got any oil after 25 July, a fact that even Roosevelt did not find out till early September. But the Japanese were under no illusion about the matter. They now realized that a total oil embargo was being put into effect. Japanese strategy would now have to take that development into consideration.

The feeling of a fatal clash with the United States mounted in the first week of August. Officers of the General Staff began talking of an impending war against the Anglo-American powers, and Prime Minister Konoe himself told the war and navy ministers that matters stood 'only a step this side of entering into a major war'.[13] They reasoned that the American oil embargo would force the nation to look for alternative sources of supply in South-East Asia, which would necessitate military action to incorporate the region into the empire. But such action would inevitably draw the United States, Britain, and the Dutch into war. Thus, Japan must be prepared to fight against the ABD powers. The oil embargo was seen as tantamount to an act of war, and Japan would respond by its own military action.

At least the Japanese were careful to avoid a two-front war; they would not provoke the Soviet Union while they prepared for a new war with the ABD powers. But they recognized the futility of separating these latter nations. They were seen as a united coalition, so that Japanese strategy would have to envisage a war against them all. The war was expected to come in late November or early December. This was because the total oil embargo by the United States made it imperative to act before the navy's oil reserve was depleted. In other words, Japan's strategists had at most four months to devise a plan of attack.

This was not an easy task, given the abrupt decision not to go through with the Soviet strategy and the suddenness with which the United States confronted Japan with its economic sanctions. Although war with the combined ABCD powers had been envisaged for some time, as of early August there had been no comprehensive master plan, integrating army and navy thinking. Each service had worked out its own blueprint, but no agreement had been reached between the two. The sudden crisis of late July forced the services to change their ideas seriously so as to develop a detailed, comprehensive plan of attack. It was not till 6 September, however, that such a plan was adopted by the top leaders.

It will be unnecessary to trace here changing army and navy strategic concepts in detail. The important point is that by August 1941, both services foresaw a 'southern strategy' involving the whole region of

South-East Asia: the Philippines, the Dutch East Indies, Indo-China, Thailand, Malaya, Singapore, and Burma. The army was primarily interested in first assaulting Malaya as a stepping-stone to the Indies, whereas the navy preferred attacking the Philippines on the way to the Dutch empire. In both instances, the resource-rich Dutch East Indies was an ultimate goal, but the army was convinced that military action in Burma and Malaya would have a vital effect on the course of the Chinese war, whereas the navy's primary focus was on the United States and for that reason an attack on the Philippines was considered of primary importance. The disparity in army–navy thinking reflected the former's continued preoccupation with the war in China and the latter's concern with the American war. In either case, however, what was being developed was a comprehensive anti-ABCD strategy.

It was in this context that the navy broached the possibility of an air attack on the United States fleet in Hawaii. Both the army and the navy agreed that an American war would involve air and naval power to a far greater extent than a war against Chinese, British, or Dutch forces, and they recognized America's intrinsic superiority in this regard, which could force a long, drawn-out conflict in the western Pacific even as Japanese forces were engaged in the conquest of South-East Asia. For this reason some, particularly those around Admiral Yamamoto Isoroku, commander-in-chief of the combined fleet, had studied the possibility of attacking the naval base at Pearl Harbor, with the aim of destroying the fleet stationed there. He shared with his colleagues, both in the navy and the army, their view that Japan had no chance to win a prolonged conflict with the United States and its allies. Of course, some talked of a 'hundred years war' with the West, but that was not to be taken literally. Even those who were convinced of a long-term struggle recognized that what Japan must do was to take advantage of the European situation and to make the most efficient use of its limited resources, especially oil. Yamamoto's idea was to gamble on a quick assault on the United States fleet in Hawaii to obtain a temporary tactical advantage, and then to use the time thus gained to build up a more secure empire in the western and southern Pacific. The Pearl Harbor strategy was presented by navy strategists to their army counterparts on 22 August, and the latter accepted it, in their turn finalizing detailed plans for the mobilization of forces for action in Malaya, the Philippines, and the Indies.[14]

Even at this late hour, however, it appears that there was disagreement between the army and navy regarding the Japanese–American crisis. While the navy now had a concrete plan of attack on Pearl Harbor, it refused to commit itself totally to a war with the United States. Its attitude was that if war should become inevitable, then the best strategy was to attack the United States fleet first, but that war was by no means inevitable yet. Much depended on the course of the European conflict and on diplomatic talks in Washington. The army, on the other hand, had come to the conclusion that diplomacy was hopeless, and that war should be faced as an immediate prospect. Mobilization would take time, at least a month, and once it was started it would be extremely difficult to turn back the clock. The army, therefore, wanted an explicit policy from the government for going to war against the ABD powers by a certain date. Clearly, there were important differences concerning a possible compromise with the United States. The navy on the whole stressed the resumption of oil shipments, so that if Washington should agree to it, the main *casus belli* would have disappeared. For the army, however, it was not enough to obtain oil once again. Far more at stake was Japan's control over China and South-East Asia, that is, the new order in East Asia. Since it was very unlikely that the United States would ever reverse its support of China or its ABCD alliance, Japan would have to go to war if it meant to persist in its scheme for the Asian order.

As if to confirm the consolidation of the alliance, Roosevelt and Churchill conferred in person off Newfoundland during 9–14 August. The Atlantic Conference cemented the two powers' strategic ties, although the only published product of the meeting was the Atlantic Charter. President Roosevelt was reluctant to declare war on Germany, as Churchill wished, for fear of dividing domestic opinion; but otherwise he frankly discussed how the United States could best help Britain defeat Germany and prevent Japanese intervention. On this second point Churchill proposed that the United States, Britain, and the Dutch East Indies issue parallel warnings to Japan to the effect that further Japanese encroachment on the south-western Pacific would bring about their counter-measures. Such warnings would formalize the ABD *entente* and confront Japan with a stark choice of either holding the line or risking war with all three powers. While Japan's holding the line would still mean its presence in China and Indo-China, at least it would enable the Western powers to concentrate on the Atlantic theatre of war. The United States delegation, headed by Roosevelt and including Under-Secretary Welles, agreed with the idea in principle but believed the time was not quite propitious for a final showdown with Japan. American strategy was to avoid war with Japan by maintaining a firm stand, but not to precipitate a crisis that could lead to war in the immediate future. This was a very fine line to draw, but Roosevelt and Welles believed the stringent economic sanctions, plus the very fact of the Atlantic meeting, would deter the Japanese from rash action.

In the end the American and British delegations agreed on a statement that President Roosevelt would communicate to Ambassador Nomura, warning that 'various steps would have to be taken by the United States' in retaliation against further Japanese military action, 'notwithstanding the President's realization that the taking of such further measures might result in war between the United States and Japan'. This rather clumsily phrased statement did not explicitly commit the United

States to enter into war if Japan should invade British or Dutch possessions in Asia, but it indicated additional sanctions against such aggression. The content of the warning was less important than that it was to constitute part of a parallel action by the three governments. The British and Dutch governments would issue similar warnings, so that the Japanese would be under no illusion about the solidarity of the tripartite *entente*. This point was underscored when the Atlantic Charter was issued after the end of the conference. As Alexander Cadogan, Britain's under-secretary of foreign affairs, noted, warnings to Japan 'must be read in conjunction with the Joint Declaration, which will give the Japanese a jar'.[15] This was because the Atlantic Charter constituted a statement of principles the two powers shared – principles which they implied would also be supported by those struggling against the Axis powers.

In view of its symbolic and strategic significance, it will be well to examine the Charter in some detail. It consisted of eight 'common principles in the national policies' of the two countries 'on which they base their hopes for a better future for the world'. First, 'their countries seek no aggrandizement, territorial or other'. Seemingly a simple statement, it not only sought to contrast the Anglo-American nations' peaceful and purely defensive intentions in the war in sharp contrast to the Axis powers' aggressive acts, but would also be a signal to other belligerents, in particular the Soviet Union, that they should likewise refrain from seeking territorial aggrandizement as a result of the war. This point was further emphasized in the second article, which asserted that 'no territorial changes' should be made 'that do not accord with the freely expressed wishes of the people concerned'. This principle would nullify the territorial changes Germany, Italy and Japan had imposed on their neighbouring peoples, but could be potentially troublesome in that the Soviet Union could be expected to seek changes in Europe and Asia to enhance its security. Third, the Anglo-American powers 'respect the right of all peoples to choose the form of government under which they will live; and they wish to see Sovereign rights and self-government restored to those who have been forcibly deprived of them'. This was the familiar self-determination principle, to be applied for the time being to those 'who have been forcibly deprived of' these rights. It was meant to refer to peoples in Europe and Asia occupied by Axis forces, but it could also be relevant to such lands as Taiwan and Korea where, it could be argued, the indigenous populations had been 'forcibly' subjected to Japanese rule. Of course, the Japanese could use the same principle to argue, as they would during the war, that the ABD powers themselves, if they were to be true to the principle, would have to restore sovereign rights to their colonies. In the immediate circumstances of 1941, however, the third article was intended to assure people in occupied territory that their rights were uppermost in the minds of the leaders of the democracies.

The fourth principle was in many ways the most important: 'they will endeavour, with due respect for their existing obligations, to further the enjoyment by all States, great or small, victor or vanquished, of access, on equal terms, to the trade and to the raw materials of the world which are needed for their economic prosperity'. An amazing statement of economic internationalism, this article indicated that 'economic prosperity' was a goal common to all countries, and that the attainment of this objective required the opening up of the entire world's resources and markets for their access. The statement was a ringing reaffirmation of those principles that had been subverted, distorted, or abandoned by various countries throughout the 1930s. The United States and Britain themselves had not been blameless in this regard, so that the two leaders' endorsement of this article meant that their governments were willing to take the initiative to bring the world economy back to the more open conditions prevailing before the Depression. The British government was reluctant to commit itself to a wholesale reversion to internationalism; the 1932 Ottawa agreement on imperial preferences was still the framework envisaged for the foreseeable future to protect the economy after the devastations of war. The clause 'with due respect for their existing obligations' was inserted to take account of this. Nevertheless, the article on the whole clearly indicated that the renewed American stress on the Open Door would emerge once again as a guiding principle in the postwar world. Equally important, the statement assured that even the Axis nations need not worry about their impoverishment or exclusion from economic opportunities after the war. Because Germany and Japan had rationalized their aggression by identifying themselves as 'have not' nations, the Atlantic Charter sought to reassure them that they would enjoy access to trade and raw materials after the war on an equal basis. To Japan in particular, the principle was addressed as a way of promising that it could obtain all the oil, iron, and other materials it needed if it stopped its aggressive behaviour and its scheme for an exclusive Asian empire.

The next item on the Charter continued the fourth article's economic theme and asserted the two countries' commitment to 'the fullest collaboration between all nations in the economic field, with the objective of securing for all improved labour standards, economic advancement, and social security'. This was an interesting statement in that it reasserted traditional liberal principles, but in a form modified because of the crisis of capitalism during the Depression. The idea that governments must concern themselves with labour standards and social security was relatively new and was not an intrinsic part of classical liberalism. Both in the United States and Britain, however, the disastrous consequences of the economic crisis had produced the recognition that the state must aim at improving working conditions and caring for the welfare of all people. In a sense this commitment was reinforced as non-liberal states such as Germany, Japan, and the Soviet

Union were seen to be pursuing such objectives in a non-democratic framework. These totalitarian nations appeared to be successful in obtaining the support of the masses through social welfare programmes, and if the democracies were to meet their challenge, they too would have to implement similar programmes.

The sixth, seventh, and eighth articles sought to give specificity to the shape of a 'future peace' that would come 'after the final destruction of the Nazi tyranny'. Although Japan was not mentioned, clearly there would be no peace until after its imperialism, too, was destroyed. The peace that would follow the Axis defeat, Roosevelt and Churchill declared, must be such as to 'afford to all nations the means of dwelling in safety within their own boundaries', to ensure that 'all the men in all the lands may live out their lives in freedom from fear and want', to enable 'all men to traverse the high seas and oceans without hindrance', and to 'lighten for peace-loving peoples the crushing burden of armaments'. This was a sweeping enunciation of the principle of collective security that would rule the world after the war. Like the post-First World War doctrine of collective security, the new vision emphasized the inviolability of national boundaries, arms control, and freedom of the seas. All such principles would be implemented and safeguarded through 'a wider and more permanent system of general security', the Atlantic Charter added. This was Wilsonianism pure and simple, in its stress on territorial integrity and on collective action to punish its violators. Coupled with the preceding articles that referred to economic principles, the last three summed up the internationalist aspirations of the two governments, as well as their determination that those aspirations should survive the disasters of the 1930s.

Because the Atlantic Charter was essentially a reaffirmation of Wilsonian internationalism, it is not surprising that contemporary observers found little new in it. Typical of American public reaction was an essay that appeared in the *New Republic* in late August. 'The peace aims announced by Messrs Churchill and Roosevelt', it stated, 'aroused little enthusiasm in either country. Their general tenor had long been taken for granted'. At the same time, however, the writer noted that other people around the world would be pleased with such a clear statement of war aims. 'Populations of the conquered countries certainly may be encouraged by the assurance of the two greatest democracies that they intend to disarm the aggressors and restore self-government'. The Japanese militarists, on their part, 'may find more difficulty in convincing the people that Britain and America are out for conquest and that Japan needs to fight for raw materials'.[16]

That was a correct reading of the Atlantic Charter, but it was not necessarily how it impressed the Japanese. A staff officer of the General Staff commented that the Atlantic Charter was tantamount to America's declaration of war, and that the eight articles signalled the Anglo-American powers' intention of world conquest through the maintenance of the status quo as defined by liberalism. Others particularly took note of the eighth article in which the two democratic leaders had asserted,'Since no future peace can be maintained if land, sea or air armaments continue to be employed by nations which threaten, or may threaten, aggression outside of their frontiers, they believe, pending the establishment of a wider and more permanent system of general security, that the disarmament of such nations is essential'. That sounded like a call for the disarmament of the Axis powers and the establishment of an Anglo-American police force to preserve peace. Thus, whether through liberalism or through military power, the United States and Britain would seek to continue to dominate the world. The leading Tokyo newspaper, *Asahi*, devoted considerable space to an analysis of the Atlantic Charter. The paper's New York correspondent asserted that unlike Wilson's Fourteen Points, the new declaration frankly aimed at disarming only the enemy nations, with the result that America and Britain would retain police power throughout the world. In other words, he said, the declaration was tantamount to clearly expressing the two nations' intention of 'world domination'. Regarding the Atlantic Charter's reference to equal economic opportunity to be provided victors and vanquished alike, the *Asahi* correspondent was adamant that it simply implied Anglo-American capital's control of world markets, since in a situation of open competition few doubted that the two countries would win. The Charter, then, was a *de facto* declaration of war which the United States and Britain clearly intended to win, as well as an assertion of postwar leadership in world economic and military affairs. Very similar views were expressed by the newspaper's London correspondent.[17]

Although extreme, such views served to define, for the Japanese, the growing crisis in which they found themselves. As a front-page news report of *Asahi* noted, the Atlantic Charter aimed at maintaining 'a system of world domination on the basis of Anglo-American world views'. In order to solidify such domination, the two democracies were trying to isolate Germany and Italy in Europe, whereas in Asia they were supporting China and the Dutch East Indies to keep them from accepting Japanese policy. Furthermore, the Anglo-American leaders appeared interested in dividing Japanese opinion so as to undermine Japan's war preparedness. Thus put, the document clarified the nature of the confrontation between the old order dominated by the Anglo-American powers and the forces that opposed it. If the Japanese did not wish to submit to a Pax Britannica or Pax Americana, the *Asahi* noted, then they must be willing to defend their nation even at the risk of war. On the other hand, if war were to be avoided, Japan would have to be prepared to accept the Anglo-American terms substantially if not totally. The logic was quite clear: the Japanese were being challenged by America and Britain to choose between going back to the earlier framework of co-operation with them, or refusing to do so and isolating themselves from the rest of the world except for the Axis partners.[18]

The Japanese army leaders were quite correct, then, in arguing throughout July and August that the nation faced the parting of ways, and that it must choose between war or accommodation with the United States. Since accommodation would be unacceptable, the army reasoned that the only alternative was war, and it grew progressively impatient both with the navy, which was making war plans without a definite commitment to implement them, and with the civilian leadership that appeared incapable of making up its mind regarding the question of war or compromise. Actually, at this time Prime Minister Konoe was toying with the idea of a personal meeting with President Roosevelt. He saw it as one last desperate effort to prevent war. In order to do so, Japan should be willing to offer some concessions regarding the East Asian order, presumably indicating a willingness to withdraw troops from Indo-China. If, after all such efforts, no compromise could be arrived at, then the Japanese would be able to persuade themselves and the world that they had done everything possible to avoid war but had failed.[19]

Konoe intimated this scheme shortly before the Roosevelt–Churchill meeting to Japan's military leaders. Navy Minister Oikawa endorsed it right away, whereas War Minister Tōjō reluctantly gave his support, saying the army would respect the prime minister's last-minute effort to avoid an American war, but that if nothing should come of it the nation must resolutely be prepared to go to war. A cable to Ambassador Nomura was sent on 7 August to seek a summit meeting. But since Roosevelt was about to attend his own summit conference, America's response was not forthcoming right away. Secretary Hull, who stayed behind in Washington, told Nomura that he saw no point in holding such a meeting between the president and the prime minister unless there were to be a drastic change in Japanese policy. When Roosevelt returned from Argentia Bay, he immediately transmitted to Nomura the warning that he had promised Churchill. The language was somewhat modified and did not include the crucial phrase 'notwithstanding the President's realization that the taking of such further measures might result in war between the United States and Japan'. Instead, Roosevelt warned that further aggressive acts by Japan would compel him to take measures 'toward insuring the safety and security' of the United States. The message was coupled with an expression of interest in meeting with Konoe if Japan were to suspend its 'expansionist activities' and agree to 'peaceful plans' for the Pacific on the basis of the principles for which the United States stood. Such plans and principles would be essentially those the president had just enunciated in the Atlantic Charter. In other words, Roosevelt would insist that Japan return to liberal inter-nationalism if it sincerely desired to restore a peaceful relationship with the United States.

Given such a stand on the part of Roosevelt, Konoe's scheme was doomed to failure from the beginning. And yet, during the second half of August, the two leaders continued to exchange messages, and there was much talk of a possible summit conference. This was because both sides, for different reasons, clearly wanted to avoid a showdown. The Japanese would not go so far as to embrace the entire principles of the Atlantic Charter, viewing them as a unilateral list of America's traditional beliefs with little regard for other countries' special needs. As the Japanese government noted in a message transmitted to Washington on 28 August, certain nations such as the United States that were endowed with superior economic and geographical advantages should be more understanding of other countries and co-operate with the latter in a more equitable distribution of material resources. Japan, in other words, was struggling for its needs and for security, an objective it was finding more and more difficult to accomplish because of the ABCD encirclement. Nevertheless, despite such differences, Konoe believed a compromise settlement was possible. Because of the lateness of the hour, he believed a personal meeting with Roosevelt alone would defuse the crisis atmosphere and might conceivably lead to a more stable relationship across the Pacific.

President Roosevelt, on his part, was interested in the idea of a summit meeting with Konoe, but not necessarily because he believed a long-lasting settlement of the crisis could be achieved. For him it would be unthinkable to give up the basic principles, but at least a meeting with Konoe would give time for the United States armed forces to be better prepared for a possible war. The president's enthusiasm, however, was not reciprocated by Hull, who believed no summit meeting would be useful until some fundamental issues had been discussed beforehand. Moreover, he was worried lest the meeting affect the solidarity of the ABCD *entente* and drive China out of desperation to the Japanese. If the Chinese should feel they were being betrayed by the Americans, such an outcome would not be unthinkable, Hull believed, and could even lead to releasing Japanese forces out of China for use southward.

At this time there would seem to have been some justification for such fears. When the Atlantic Charter was announced, Quo Tai-chi, the foreign minister, declared, 'China believes the final destruction of the forces of aggression can most swiftly be achieved by bringing about the defeat of Japan, first through a tightening of the encirclement of which Japan herself is the sole architect'. It was an excellent expression of the Chinese belief in the strategy of encirclement through the ABCD alliance. For that very reason, however, there was some unhappiness that the Americans and the British appeared to be carrying on a bilateral conversation without taking the Chinese into their confidence. As reported by British Ambassador Clark Kerr in Chungking, Chiang Kai-shek 'is feeling sore because the declaration [the Atlantic Charter] was followed by [a] joint message to Stalin while none was sent to

Chiang Kai-shek, who claims that China's defence against Japanese attack is just as important as Russia's against Nazi attack, and that he deserved special mention'. This sort of complaint was a perennial one, but the Chinese felt extremely uneasy when, upon returning from the Atlantic Conference, President Roosevelt was reported to be in constant contact with Japanese officials. The fear that the United States might 'sell China down the river' in order to buy a temporary peace in the Pacific was genuine, and at this time it fell to the British to assure the Chinese that no such possibility existed. As Richard Law, permanent under-secretary for foreign affairs, told Wellington Koo, the Chinese ambassador in London, at the end of August, it was 'inconceivable that the United States should have any idea of selling China down the river'. On the contrary, 'the Netherlands East Indies, Australia, the United States, and indeed China herself, were all engaged in fighting the same enemy even though there was no declared alliance .... We were all fighting the same war whether in Europe or the Pacific, and events in Europe would prove to be decisive in the Pacific as well as in Europe'.[20]

Given Chinese sensitivity about any sign of the weakening of the ABCD *entente*, the American government had to tread very cautiously in considering a summit meeting between Roosevelt and Konoe. Nevertheless, the United States might have gone through with the meeting if the Japanese side had been solidly behind Konoe and willing to modify significantly its policy in Asia. Such was not the case, and in the final analysis the aborting of the summit conference must be attributed to the unwillingness of Japan to change course.

JAPAN'S DECISION FOR WAR

For it was during the crucial weeks of late August and early September 1941 that the Japanese leadership finally decided on war. Even as Konoe and his supporters were trying desperately to avert a crisis with the United States through his meeting with President Roosevelt, the supreme command's army and navy sections began a series of intensive discussions to arrive at a consensual decision concerning the timing and scale of preparedness for war against the ABD powers. As noted above, the navy had believed that war preparedness could be undertaken without a national decision for war, whereas the army believed a definite commitment to go to war was needed before mobilization of necessary forces could be implemented. After daily meetings, the two sides finally reached a compromise at the beginning of September. It was to the effect that Japan should complete war preparedness by late October and decide on war against the ABD powers if no diplomatic settlement had been arrived at by the first part of the month. In other words, war preparedness would be followed by a decision for war, but in the meantime diplomatic efforts would be continued to see if war could be avoided. The army's and the navy's viewpoints were neatly balanced in the compromise. The formula was written into a document, 'Guidelines for implementing national policies', which was formally adopted at a leaders' conference in the presence of the emperor on 6 September.

That document may be regarded as a virtual declaration of war by Japan. It clearly implied that war would come unless a peaceful settlement could be worked out with the United States and Britain. In an appendix to the document the minimal terms acceptable to Japan were spelled out; if those terms were not met, then war would come. Japan would insist, first, that the Anglo-American powers desist from extending military and economic aid to the Chiang Kai-shek regime; second, that they refrain from establishing military facilities within Thailand, the Dutch East Indies, China, or the Far Eastern provinces of the Soviet Union and from augmenting their forces beyond their existing strength; and, third, that they provide Japan with resources needed for its existence by restoring trade relations and offering friendly co-operation with Japan as the latter undertook to collaborate economically with Thailand and the Dutch East Indies. In return for such concessions on the part of the United States and Britain, Japan would be willing to promise not to undertake further military expansion in Asia and to withdraw its troops from Indo-China 'upon the establishment of a just peace in East Asia'. Furthermore, it would be prepared to guarantee Philippine neutrality and refrain from hostile action against the Soviet Union so long as the latter observed the neutrality treaty.

The 6 September guidelines were interpreted by some, the emperor and the prime minister for example, as sanctioning one last effort to negotiate with the United States in order to avoid war. The emperor emphasized this point both at the meeting of the top leaders held on that day, and also at his prior conferences with Konoe, Sugiyama, and Nagano. The emperor's approval of the guidelines may, therefore, have been intended as a way to encourage further diplomatic endeavours. For the military, however, the decisions clearly signalled war. The best statement of the army's views is a document the General Staff prepared for the 6 September meeting. The war was defined as one against the United States, Britain, and the Netherlands, its purposes being 'expelling American, British, and Dutch influences from East Asia, consolidating Japan's sphere of autonomy and security, and constructing a new order in greater East Asia'. Japan intended to establish a close military, political, and economic relationship with other Asian countries, whereas the ABD powers sought to obstruct the attempt, the paper noted. They stood for the status quo in the name of the defence of democracy, in reality trying to prevent Japan's growth and development. If Japan should give in, America's military position would be further strengthened, and the nation would become even more subordinate to its influence. In such a situation, war was inevitable. The army document frankly recognized the difficulties Japan faced in going to war. The ABD powers had entered into a *de facto* military alliance with China, and moreover those four nations appeared eager to effect a similar *entente* with the Soviet Union. In other words, there was the likelihood of Japan's becoming engaged in war with five powers, in northern and southern Asia as well as on the China mainland. That was a formidable undertaking but, the army document noted, not entirely hopeless if Japan should be able to occupy quickly important strategic locations in the south, develop their rich natural resources, create a region of long-term self-sufficiency, and continue to co-operate with Germany and Italy, for these steps could conceivably lead to British defeat and the break-up of the Anglo-American alliance. That was conceded to be a remote possibility at best, but the alternative would be to persist in a state of uncertainty in which Japan's oil reserves continued to dwindle while American naval strength would come to exceed Japanese. Thus, Japan would come under greater Anglo-American control even without a fight. For all these reasons, war was a gamble that had to be taken.[21]

The navy, too, was in essential agreement with the army viewpoint. As Nagano explained to the emperor, Japan had the choice of doing nothing, which would lead to its collapse within a few years, or going to war while there was at least a 70 or 80 per cent chance of initial victory. A diplomatic settlement with the United States that merely bought a temporary peace for one or two years was unacceptable; therefore, to build for a longer-term peace, the nation must resolve to go to war. Should war come, Nagano explained at the 6 September meeting, Japan should quickly occupy strategically important and resource-rich areas so as to establish a firm zone of power as a base for engaging in a long, drawn-out war. In other words, initial successes would not be enough to cripple the enemy's will, but they were imperative to enable the nation to prepare for a long war. In order to achieve a quick initial victory, war should be declared as soon as possible.

Given such discussions and the final decision taken in the presence of the emperor, there was little chance that Konoe's meeting with Roosevelt, even if it should materialize, would be successful. He would have to come back with substantial American concessions to satisfy the army and navy supreme command, and he would have to do so by early October. The conferees at the 6 September meeting agreed that in order to facilitate Konoe's last-minute efforts, military preparedness till early October would be undertaken discreetly so as not to provoke the United States, but that after that time plans must be put into effect to go to war by early November. Everything, then, would depend on what happened in the month following 6 September. On that very day, Konoe conferred in secret with Ambassador Grew and urged on the latter the importance of meeting with Roosevelt as soon as possible. The American ambassador agreed and sent an urgent cable to Washington to transmit Konoe's sincere wishes for peace. But the Japanese military remained sceptical. On 7 September War Minister Tōjō privately expressed his view that the United States would insist on Japan's denouncing the Axis pact, withdrawing from China and Indo-China, and observing the principles of the Open Door and equal opportunity in China. Those terms were unacceptable to the army, and even if Japan were to grant them so as to purchase peace, it would not last long, for the United States would take advantage of it to strengthen itself and assault Japan. Given such thinking, even Konoe began to grow pessimistic about the chances of a fruitful meeting with Roosevelt.[22]

War with the ABCD powers, then, was daily becoming a reality. Both the army and the navy began their specific preparations for mobilizing their forces, with a focus at this time on a southern strategy: a simultaneous attack on Hong Kong, Malaya, the Philippines, Guam, and the Dutch East Indies. The navy, of course, was also finalizing its strategy for attacking the United States fleet in Hawaii. These offensive assaults in combination were expected to 'cripple the main bases of Britain and America in East Asia' while at the same time establishing a condition of 'autonomy and security', which in turn would enable Japan to 'subjugate China'. In carrying out its southern attack, the army supreme command pointed out, Japan was at an advantage in that the indigenous populations had long been suppressed by whites and had therefore developed a friendly attitude towards it. The ABD powers, therefore, would find it difficult to resist the Japanese offensive. The former, on the other hand, could try to divide Japanese forces by encouraging Soviet moves in the north, a possibility that could be prevented if Japan struck in the south for a quick victory in the coming winter, since during the cold months no large-scale military action could take place in the north. The strategy, then, was to act speedily in South-East Asia by diverting some of the forces and resources from China, while keeping open the possibility of a northern campaign in the following spring. It was hoped that the whole southern offensive would last for about five months, by which time Japanese troops would have completed the occupation of the Philippines, Malaya, the Dutch East Indies, British Borneo, Guam, and Hong Kong.[23]

It was around this time that the supreme command began in earnest a study of the administration of occupied territory. It was realized that the occupation of South-East Asia would present problems different from that of China, and staff officers had been dispatched to the region to observe local conditions at first hand. Officials of the Planning Board had for some time been collecting data in preparation for economic planning for the area, and they were becoming increasingly insistent on an early decision for war in view of the rapid depletion of mineral supplies in the wake of the American embargo.

War, then, would mean fighting against the ABD nations in addition to China. It could be avoided only if Japan and the United States came to some agreement, but such agreement would no longer be a bilateral arrangement, for the United States was more firmly than ever committed to an *entente* with the anti-Axis powers so that its negotiating stand would have to embrace positions acceptable to the British, Dutch, and Chinese, as well as to Americans. It was thus inevitable that China should continue to be a key to Japanese–American differences.

From the American perspective, there was little point in coming to any understanding with Japan that did not include the latter's commitment to withdraw from China. As seen above, the State Department's negative response to the idea of a meeting between Konoe and Roosevelt was based on the fear that it could drive China out of the ABCD *entente*. Roosevelt reiterated to Ambassador Nomura that any agreement with Japan would have to be endorsed by Britain, China, and the Dutch. And it was extremely unlikely that the Chinese would accept anything less than Japan's evacuation of China and observance of Hull's four principles. Throughout the crucial month of September, both Roosevelt and Hull made it abundantly clear to the Japanese that the United States would not budge from this position. Nomura clearly understood this; as he cabled Tokyo on 12 September, the main difficulty in Japanese–American negotiations lay in the latter's emphasis on withdrawing Japanese troops from China, a matter on which both American public opinion and the Chinese government insisted. The ambassador suggested that the only way to come to terms with America would be through an explicit promise of withdrawing forces from China within two years. He correctly judged that the China question was the main obstacle. Both in order to assure the Chinese that there were no back-door negotiations between Tokyo and Washington at their expense, and in order to gain as much time as possible while American forces were being readied for military action, it was necessary for the United States to revert time and again to the issue of Japanese presence in China.[24]

The Japanese recognized this, and on 13 September the liaison conference discussed the minimally acceptable terms on China. They included continued stationing of Japanese troops in certain parts of Inner Mongolia and north China in order to effect 'co-operation' between the two countries for the maintenance of order and security against Communist and other subversive activities. Japan would be willing to evacuate its troops from the rest of China and support the merging of Chiang Kai-shek's and Wang Ching-wei's governments. Manchuria, of course, would remain independent. Economic co-operation for 'developing and utilizing resources necessary for national defence' would be effected. In other words, Japan would continue to retain its special position in China, which from the army's point of view could not be given up. If the United States should reject these terms, then Japan must be willing to go to war.[25]

By the same token, such terms were clearly unacceptable to America. Although the language was somewhat modified, the American side was unimpressed when they were transmitted on 23 September. At a meeting with Nomura on 2 October, Hull bluntly told the ambassador that he saw little point in holding a summit conference, and reiterated the four principles. Again, China was the crucial question. Without further concessions on Japan's part on this point, it was extremely unlikely that any agreement could be reached with the United States – a contingency that could only mean war. If war were to be avoided, therefore, the Konoe cabinet would have somehow to persuade the army to commit itself to withdrawing from China, an impossible demand at this late hour. Thus the Japanese army seized on Hull's 2 October message as a virtual rejection of the peace efforts and pressed Konoe to give up the idea of a summit conference. As the army leaders saw it, the United States was reiterating its basic principles merely in order to gain time, and for Japan to continue to negotiate would only play into its hands. At a meeting of 5 October, the top army leaders resolved that there was no point in further continuing talks with the United States, and that war should be decided upon. The next day, Tōjō and Sugiyama agreed that the crucial decision should be reached by 15 October.

With the army taking such a strong stand, Konoe's only hope in avoiding, or at least postponing, a fatal decision for war may have lain in the Japanese navy. If the navy could support his efforts for continued negotiation with America, he might be able to defuse the crisis. The navy, however, was internally divided. On one hand, Nagano was willing to go along with the army's bellicosity, saying at a liaison conference of 4 October that the time for discussion had passed. The next day, however, the top navy officials came to the conclusion that 'it would be the height of folly to fight with the United States on the issue of withdrawing troops from China'. From the navy's standpoint, the army was forcing a war which would have to be the navy's main responsibility, in order to retain its rights in China. Despite this scepticism, however, Nagano refused to speak resolutely against the army, fearing it would divide the services at a moment of national crisis. Navy Minister Oikawa, who shared his colleagues' lack of enthusiasm for an American war, was no match for Army Minister Tōjō's decisiveness when the two met on 7 October. The latter insisted that to accept Hull's four principles was tantamount to reverting to the Washington Conference system, in particular to the regime of the nine-power treaty. Why had Japan gone to war in Manchuria and China? Tōjō asked, and answered his own question by saying that it had been in order to destroy the regime. The basic premise for the establishment of the Great East Asian Co-prosperity Sphere lay in creating a system free from the treaty. This was another way of saying that Japan must persist in its anti-ABCD stand. Japan's military presence in parts of China was at the very core of the new order, without which the Co-prosperity Sphere could never be established. On this point Japan should never yield. Navy Minister Oikawa was taken aback by Tōjō's strong language, and tamely stated that the navy still stood behind the 6 September decision. Immediately following their meeting, they proceeded to attend a cabinet meeting where Tōjō reiterated his strong views. Other cabinet members indirectly criticized such a stand, expressing pessimism about the state of national preparedness, but no firm decision was made to avoid war with the United States. Konoe nevertheless continued to try to persuade the army to accept a compromise on the question of troop withdrawal, but the army remained adamant about the 15 October deadline. The navy opposed the imposition of such a deadline but hesitated to contradict the army in the open, preferring to leave crucial decisions to the prime minister. In this way, Konoe found himself isolated, feeling that he was not being supported in his efforts to avoid war.[26]

High-level meetings held between 12 and 16 October persuaded the Japanese leader that all his endeavours had ended in failure. At a meeting held on 12 October at Konoe's private residence, Foreign Minister Toyoda insisted that war could still be avoided through some compromise on the troop withdrawal question, but Tōjō reiterated his view that the time for talks had passed; there was no evidence that the United States was interested in a compromise with Japan. Navy Minister Oikawa said the decision for war or peace must be made by the prime minister, and that the navy would support diplomacy if that would work. Tōjō rejoined that even if the prime minister decided for diplomacy, the army could not blindly follow the decision. After all, he said, the supreme command was bound by the 6 September decision and preparations were proceeding for war. They could not be stopped unless there was ample assurance that negotiations with America would succeed – by 15 October. Foreign Minister Toyoda then said perhaps the 6 September decision had been premature, and Prime Minister Konoe added Japan could not possibly continue a war for more than a couple of years. He himself must persist in diplomacy, and if war should be the decision, then he would have to resign. Navy Minister Oikawa maintained his irresolute stance. Thus no clear-cut decision was arrived at. Then on 14 October, Tōjō made an impassioned speech at a cabinet meeting against making concessions on the troop withdrawal question. If Japan should submit to American pressure, he said, the fruits of the war with China would be nullified, the existence of Manchukuo jeopardized, and colonial control over Korea itself endangered. It would signal the nation's return to 'Little Japan before the Manchurian incident'. That was the crux of the matter. The army refused to return to the situation existing in the 1920s, something the United States was insisting upon. The question of Japanese troops in China had come to symbolize this conflict. There could be no compromise on that issue. Tōjō reminded the other cabinet members that the 6 September decisions still stood, and that according to them the nation was to have decided on war if no diplomatic settlement had been achieved by early October. Military mobilization had been going on in accordance with the guidelines, and it could not now be stopped unless agreement were reached with Washington concerning the troops question.[27]

Here, in stark simplicity, was the moment of decision forced upon the cabinet by the war minister. Tōjō was correct in saying that if war was not to be the decision, then the 6 September guidelines would have to be revised. Since the cabinet had been responsible for those guidelines, it was accountable for not having carried out those policies. Thus the only thing left was for the entire cabinet, including Konoe, to resign. The prime minister understood the logic. If war were to be avoided, then a new cabinet would have to start afresh, unencumbered by the 6 September decisions. Konoe, too, had his logic. For him, the most important thing was to avoid war with the United States, and all decisions, including those of 6 September, must be the means towards that end. He recognized that Japan had no chance of winning an American war and did not understand why the army insisted on it. He was acutely aware that no power, not even Germany, could be counted upon to come to Japan's aid in its struggle against the ABCD combination. There was no point in going into a war which the nation was bound to lose. But he, too, realized that if peace at any cost were to be sought, a new cabinet would have to be organized. All such developments led inevitably to the cabinet's resignation on 16 October. With it the idea of a conference with President Roosevelt, on the realization of which Konoe had pinned his hopes for peace, also evaporated.

Historians have debated whether the summit conference, had it materialized, would have achieved anything significant and prevented a Japanese–American war. It seems highly unlikely. On the American side, there would have been little cause for yielding to Japanese conditions for peace, particularly Japan's insistence on retaining troops in China. Such a concession would not have been popular at home and would have embittered the Chinese, undermining the solid *entente* among the ABCD nations. On the other hand, the United States was clearly interested in 'gaining useful time', as Roosevelt said, and therefore a summit meeting with Konoe might have served to postpone a final showdown.[28] The two leaders would certainly not have come to any tangible settlement, but some ambiguous agreement might have been made. It might have been unacceptable to the Japanese army, but Konoe, coming to recognize personally American resolve to stand by China, might have been emboldened to oppose the army more strongly. If Konoe had somehow been able to keep talking with the army leadership, winter might have arrived before Japanese forces were readied for action, and the supreme command might have decided to wait till spring. All this would have helped the United States in building up its armed strength for war. In other words, there might have been a way for the United States to keep encouraging Japanese hopes for some compromise without alienating the Chinese or actually giving in to Japanese demands at China's expense. In this sense there may have been a tactical blunder on the American side.

REFERENCES AND NOTES

1. Yabe Teiji, *Konoe Fumimaro* (Tokyo 1952), 2: 299.
2. Ibid., 2: 308.
3. *Matsuoka, Yōsuke* (Tokyo 1974), pp. 1020–7.
4. Defence Agency, War History Division (ed.), *Daihonei rikugunbu* (The army supreme command; Tokyo 1968), 2: 305, 309–18.
5. Ibid., 2: 338, 353–4.
6. Yabe, *Konoe*, 2: 326.
7. Robert Dallek, *Franklin D. Roosevelt and American Foreign Policy, 1932–1945* (New York 1979), p. 268.
8. Ibid., p. 278–9; Yabe, *Konoe*, 2: 308–9.
9. Dallek, *Roosevelt*, p. 274.
10. *Daihonei rikugunbu*, 2: 362–3, 398–9; Yabe, *Konoe*, 2: 329.
11. *Daihonei rikugunbu*, 2: 378.
12. Jonathan G. Utley, *Going to War with Japan, 1937–1941* (Knoxville 1985), pp. 154–5.
13. *Daihonei rikugunbu*, 2: 376.
14. Ibid., 2: 410, 418.
15. *The Diaries of Sir Alexander Cadogan, 1938–1945*, David Dilks (ed.) (New York 1972), p. 397.
16. *New Republic*, 105. 8: 239 (25 Aug. 1941).
17. *Asahi*, 11, 16, Aug. 1941.
18. Ibid., 16 Aug. (evening), 1941.
19. Yabe, *Konoe*, pp. 338–40.
20. Utley, *Going to War*, p. 159; F 10904/280/10, F 136/280/10, F 8496/60/10, Foreign Office Archives.
21. *Daihonei rikugunbu*, 2: 427–9.
22. Yabe, *Konoe*, p. 365.
23. *Daihonei rikugunbu*, 2: 447–54.
24. *Foreign Relations of the United States: Japan* (Washington 1943), 2: 571–2, 588–91.
25. *Daihonei rikugunbu*, 2: 462.
26. Ibid., 2: 504–12; Yabe, p. 378.
27. *Daihonei rikugunbu*, 2: 519–21.
28. Dallek, *Roosevelt*, p. 303.

Chapter 6
CONCLUSION

The fifty-two days between 17 October, when a new cabinet headed by General Tōjō was formed, and 8 December, when Japan launched a surprise attack on America, Britain, and the Dutch East Indies, held many possibilities. For Japan, the resignation of the Konoe cabinet meant that the crucial decisions of 6 September would be reconsidered, and therefore that war would not have to be decided upon by late October, as specified in those decisions. For the United States and its partners, Tōjō's premiership confirmed the ascendancy of the military in Japanese politics and indicated the possibility of war. But America's military advisers wanted to avoid a premature confrontation with Japan at that time, in order to focus first on the European war. Thus, with war a real possibility, there grew serious concern on the American part to avoid its immediate eruption, while on the Japanese side the new cabinet had a mandate to redefine the nation's overall policy and strategy. There was thus a chance that the two sides might come to terms, if only temporarily, at this late hour. In the meantime, Japanese and American strategists continued to mobilize their forces just in case war should become a reality. Britain, China, the Soviet Union, and other interested parties, on their part, were extremely concerned over any softening of the American stand as it would have serious repercussions elsewhere. All these moves and counter-moves created an extremely volatile situation in Asian-Pacific affairs. In the end, however, Japan struck because it saw no other way of weakening the ABCD coalition. That was its mistake; by striking at the coalition, it further strengthened it. The only way of overcoming the ABCD encirclement would have been for Japan itself to join these nations.

THE TŌJŌ CABINET

Tōjō was a typical bureaucrat. As a career army officer and as an official of the War Ministry up to his elevation to prime minister, he had loyally represented the interests and concerns of the Japanese army, often in violent opposition to the navy and to civilian agencies. He had adamantly insisted on the retention of Japanese troops in China even at the risk of bringing down the Konoe cabinet, since their presence on the continent symbolized the army's special position in national politics. This smallness of vision, however, was now to be tested as he was to represent not simply the army, but the entire country. It was characteristic of him that once he was appointed prime minister, he realized that he could no longer simply be a spokesman for his comrades-in-arms, but must carry out the will of the nation as expressed through the emperor. And the latter made it quite clear, at his first meeting with Tōjō, that he wanted him to abide by the constitution and to effect co-operation between army and navy. That was sufficient to define Tōjō's new role. He must now stop being preoccupied with the parochial concerns of the Japanese army and carry out the country's affairs in ways that would best serve the interests of all. He understood his mandate to mean that the government must try afresh to reach some settlement with the United States, regardless of the 6 September guidelines. The new cabinet would not be bound by them, but would 'return to white paper', in other words, scratch out earlier policy decisions and chart its own course in negotiating with the United States.

Tōjō's cabinet appointments, completed on 18 October, merely a day after his appointment as prime minister, reflected his recognition of the new responsibilities. He rejected the suggestion from his former colleagues in the War Ministry that he recall former Foreign Minister Matsuoka Yōsuke from retirement and reappoint him. Instead, he turned to the veteran diplomat Tōgō Shigenori for the post. Tōgō had served in Berlin and Moscow as ambassador before he was 'purged' by Matsuoka in favour of 'radicals' more in sympathy with Japan's pro-Axis diplomacy. Tōjō's selection of him over Matsuoka was thus a slap in the face of those associated with anti-Anglo-American factions. Tōgō was surprised by the nomination and told Tōjō he would accept only if the new cabinet were committed to working hard to bring negotiations with the United States to success. The prime minister assured him that indeed this was his intention. Tōjō, moreover, appointed himself war minister and, for the time being, home affairs minister. The first reflected his view that only by heading the War Ministry himself would he be able to control army opposition to the new cabinet's foreign policy. (The army had wanted someone else to be named to the post.) Equally important, he wanted to assume control over police functions by becoming home affairs minister in order to deal sternly with demonstrations and violent outbursts in the event that Japan should accept American conditions for peace. Although it is unlikely that Tōjō at that time was thinking of swallowing Hull's four principles and other terms, at least he was anticipating an emergency that would be created if Japan should reach settlement with the United States on the latter's

169

terms in order to avoid war. Such a settlement would, he confided to his secretary, be likely to create a crisis like that of February 1936 which resulted in assassinations and an attempted army takeover of the government. In order to prepare for such an emergency, Tōjō sought dictatorial powers by appointing himself concurrently war minister and home affairs minister.[1]

Even such desperate resolution, however, was not enough to prevent war. For one thing, Japan's military planning proceeded on its own momentum despite the cabinet change. Tōjō could do little but retain the two chiefs of staff, General Sugiyama Gen and Admiral Nagano Osami, appointments that were not his to make in any event. Although the supreme command reluctantly recognized that the 6 September decision for completing preparedness for war by the end of October was no longer valid, its strategists remained adamant that war, if it were to come, should commence as early as possible. Between 18 October and the crucial 5 November meeting of the civilian and military leaders in the presence of the emperor, army and navy representatives of the supreme command met daily to work out a final strategy for what they called an 'American–British–Dutch war'. As such a term indicated, the coming war was still visualized as one against the three Western powers. The Chinese war, of course, would still be going on, and the Japanese military recognized that Chungking's position would harden as a consequence of the newer war, as it would be able to count on the ABCD solidarity to resist Japan. The supreme command was hopeful, on the other hand, that an open break with the Soviet Union could be avoided, at least for the time being. Thus, Japanese strategy continued to be defined in the framework of a war with the ABCD powers.

That strategy was now in its final stages of refinement. It consisted of several important components. First, there would be undertaken a simultaneous attack on Hawaii and South-East Asia (in particular, Singapore and the Philippines). The navy air force would strike at the United States fleet in Pearl Harbor, while at the same moment the army would bombard Malaya and the Philippines, to be followed a few hours later by the landing of troops on these latter areas. These initial assaults, followed by military action in the East Indies, were expected to establish Japan's initial supremacy in South-East Asia and the south-western Pacific within four to eight months. After the successful completion of the 'southern strategy', Japan would consolidate its initial gains, secure crucial strategic bases, obtain mineral resources, and prepare for a long-range conflict with the enemy. That was the second component of the emerging strategy. It was assumed that even though the British colonies and the Dutch East Indies might succumb to Japan, the United States never would, so that Japan would have to be prepared for a drawn-out conflict with America, primarily a naval confrontation in the Pacific. That confrontation would last for years, but it should be possible for Japan to maintain at least a status quo in the western Pacific once it established its supremacy in South-East Asia and the south-western Pacific. Third, the war in China would continue, but if Japan should successfully occupy and control Singapore, Hong Kong, Burma, and other areas adjoining China, the latter would find it progressively more difficult to obtain outside assistance. Fourth, although not much could be expected from the German ally, Japan should obtain the latter's co-operation in the war; presumably, Germany as well as Italy would declare war against the United States, and could possibly assist in disrupting the flow of American merchant shipping. But more crucial would be German military successes against Britain and, it was hoped, against the Soviet Union. Japan would have to make sure that Germany would not enter into a separate peace with Britain, which would enable the latter to concentrate on the Asian situation.[2]

These aspects of the emerging strategy were fully discussed by top army and navy officers in the last days of October and early November, and they in fact approximated what was actually to take place in the early stages of the Pacific war. It may be noted that the idea of a quick simultaneous assault on Hawaii and South-East Asia was to be carried out almost to the letter, and quite successfully. But the Japanese planners erred in expecting that the quick initial victory would be enough to give them command of the western Pacific and enable them to establish a position of 'self-sufficiency and economic invincibility', as a General Staff study put it. They recognized that because it would take time to develop the resources of the areas to be seized from the enemy and to produce large quantities of oil, rubber, tungsten, and other materials, the nation would suffer a temporary shortage of material and equipment during 1942 and 1943. But after 1944, it was hoped, with increased production and consolidation of the new empire, things should improve and Japan's military capabilities, too, would be strengthened. Strategically, by 'seizing all military bases in East Asia', Japan would be able to cut off communication between Britain and the Commonwealth countries as well as between the United States and the south-western Pacific. These developments should serve to isolate China, so that it should be possible to intensify Japan's pressure on the Chiang Kai-shek regime, and if necessary divert some of the forces to the north in preparation for a possible conflict with the Soviet Union.[3]

Such optimism doomed the Japanese strategy at its inception. It was flawed in two critical areas. One, it underestimated the capacity and determination of the United States and Britain to launch a speedy counter-attack after the expected initial disasters. Second, it over-estimated German power, assuming that Germany could continue to immobilize Britain in Europe and might even crush the Soviet Union. Most fundamental was Japan's lack of experience in fighting a multinational war. The First World War had not really been its war, and its participation had been actually limited to seizing German spheres of influence in China and the Pacific; it had essentially been a bilateral war, just like the first Sino-Japanese War and the Russo-Japanese War. Now, for the first time, the nation was having to face a conflict with a multiple number of enemy countries. For that reason alone, it would have been extremely important to develop a comprehensive strategy. In reality, however, as the above outline suggests, the Japanese army and navy were never able to integrate their ideas fully. To be sure they both accepted the idea of an ABCD war, but the army held to its primary concern with China and the Soviet Union, viewing the 'southern strategy' as a means for the objective of bringing the Chinese war to a satisfactory conclusion and preparing for a possible clash with the latter. In this regard, an overestimation of German strength played havoc with army thinking; it was optimistically believed that as Germany tied down, if not defeated, Britain and the Soviet Union, it should be possible for Japan to consolidate the gains in the south and 'solve' the 'northern' problems (China and the Soviet Union). The navy, on its part, focused its attention on the ABD part of the war, which was seen as a means for establishing a southern empire. It was supposed that after the initial surprise assault, the navy would be in charge of meeting the enemy's sporadic attempts to breach the empire, but neither the navy nor the army realized the need to develop an overall, comprehensive plan to cope with a massive counter-attack within months after the opening of hostilities.[4]

In other words, the relationship between the ABD war and the Chinese war, and between these two and a hypothetical war with the Soviet Union, was never clear. A telling document to reveal this deficiency was a memorandum written by a high officer of the General Staff at the end of October, in which he noted that there were three possible developments after the initial hostilities: (1) stalemate in the south and in China, uncertainty in the north (the Soviet Union); (2) settlement of the first two wars, and uncertainty in the north; (3) settlement of all three wars. How these three theatres of war were related was not clear.[5] And it was never spelled out how all of this was to be linked to the overall Axis strategy. Germany would somehow fight on in Europe, tying Britain and the Soviet Union down; but there was no discussion between Berlin and Tokyo about co-ordinating their respective strategies. Japan, in the meantime, would launch an attack on the ABD powers, but no systematic thought had been given to the connection between it and the future of Japanese strategy towards China and the Soviet Union.

Given such a state of confusion, the top military leaders might have counselled caution as the Tōjō cabinet proceeded to reformulate the fundamentals of national policy. The new prime minister understood that his mission, and the charge he received from the emperor, was to re-examine the 6 September decisions in view of the developments since that time, especially the lack of progress in the negotiations with the United States. He would be willing to reopen the whole question of war or peace. As he remarked at a meeting of the liaison conference on 30 October, there were three alternatives open: 'perseverance and patience' without war; an immediate decision for war; and a combination of negotiation with preparations for war. Tōjō himself preferred the third alternative.

As he told General Sugiyama on 1 November, the emperor was opposed to the second alternative, whereas the first, namely to desist from warlike action and even to consider accepting the American terms for a temporary understanding, would be unacceptable to the military. The third alternative was in essence the same as the 6 September decision, but the latter had specified a deadline – early October – for concluding talks with Washington, after which war was to be decided upon. Therefore, to adopt the third alternative was tantamount to postponing the deadline and to continuing negotiations with the United States. Sugiyama argued, therefore, that the time for negotiation had passed, and that by letting the earlier deadline lapse without action, the nation was in a worse position *vis-à-vis* the United States. The army, then, would have to insist on the second alternative. Specifically, preparations should be completed for war by early December.[6]

This meeting was followed by a sixteen-hour session of the liaison conference, held during 1–2 November. Those present realized that this was to be the last chance to determine the course of the nation's destiny, and deliberated in great detail pros and cons of the three alternatives. The first, namely the policy of 'perseverance and patience', was supported only by Foreign Minister Tōgō, who argued that since there was no apparent chance of winning a war against the combined ABCD forces, Japan must not go to war. There was little likelihood, he asserted, that Germany could conquer Britain. The United States, in the meantime, would concentrate on the defeat of Germany so that it would not start a war with Japan. The latter, therefore, should for the time being do nothing, watching the course of events in Europe. Finance Minister Kaya Okinori generally agreed with Tōgō that if Japan could not win a war, there was little point in going into it. Such logic, however, was unacceptable to the military, Admiral Nagano insisting that while Japan persisted in passivity, the United States would step up its assistance to China and the Soviet Union, so that the encirclement of Japan would be even further strengthened. Japan would continue to use up its precious petroleum, and the relative superiority of American power would increase. Although there was little chance of victory in a long, drawn-out war, at least for the first two years there would be sufficient military gains to enable the nation to prepare for the long haul. General Sugiyama reiterated the army's view that the southern strategy would serve to cut off the connection between China and the outside, inducing the former to give up.

Given the military's adamant opposition, the first alternative was abandoned. It would seem that both opponents and exponents of war with the ABCD powers had logic to support them. The former correctly argued that since even the military were agreed about the little possibility of success in a long war, and since there was no chance that the war could be ended speedily, Japan should never attempt it, for economic and strategic costs would outweigh temporary inconveniences suffered through the policy of passivity. The military, on their part, reasoned that anything could happen in the long run; the situation in Europe could improve, or China might drop out of the war. What Japan should do in the immediate future was to break the impasse imposed by the ABCD encirclement. Since they were confident of a quick initial success, but since such a success would become less and less obtainable the longer the nation waited, the supreme command and its supporters argued for gambling on an early war. From their point of view, the earlier the war came the more improved would be the chances for victory in the short run. To do nothing in the face of the ABCD encirclement and the American embargo was tantamount to losing without a fight, an unbearable alternative for the military. Even if there were no war with the ABD powers, the one with China would go on, and the army was convinced that there would be less chance of crushing the Chiang Kai-shek resistance if there were no war with the three powers. This was because the latter, in particular the United States, would further consolidate their ties to China. Only by attacking the ABD powers would Japan be able to sever those ties and bring China to its knees.

In the end, the conferees decided to scrap the first alternative because they shared the sense that the nation could not exist in a state of uncertainty much longer. Either war was going to be declared soon, or some dramatic diplomatic attempt should be undertaken to put an end to the state of uncertainty. That state was bad for the morale not only of the armed forces but of the people. They could not be expected to persevere much longer.

That left the second and third alternatives, namely, a definite decision for war on one hand, and continuation of diplomatic efforts on the other. Foreign Minister Tōgō and Finance Minister Kaya spoke strongly for continued negotiation, while General Sugiyama and Admiral Nagano insisted that war must be decided upon right away. At the very most they would give the civilian leadership till 13 November to conduct diplomacy, but if it failed, armed forces must be readied for action at the beginning of December. In the end, in response to a strong intercession by Prime Minister Tōjō, the military leaders backed down and accepted the deadline of midnight 30 November. If no successful conclusion had been arrived at in the Washington talks, then war would follow shortly after 1 December. Much, then, would depend on the course of negotiations with the United States. Although little had come of the preceding talks that had lasted intermittently for over six months, Tōjō and Tōgō were determined to make one final effort. If that should fail, they would be able to persuade themselves, the emperor, and the people that they had done all they could to avoid the war, and failed.

What should be the absolute minimal conditions Japan could accept to maintain a peace with the United States? Much time was spent on defining those terms. Here Tōgō came up with a two-pronged approach. The first (Plan A) was to arrive at a comprehensive settlement of the major issues with the United States. Japan, according to the policy approved by the liaison conference on 1 November, would agree to withdraw its forces from most areas of China within two years of the establishment of a truce, concentrating them in certain parts of north China, Mongolia, Sinkiang, and Hainan Island. They would stay in those areas for up to twenty-five years. Once the war with China was settled, all Japanese troops would be withdrawn from Indo-China. Japan would also accept the principle of non-discrimination in trade in the Pacific and in China if the same principle were applied throughout the world. This was in response to Hull's fundamental principles; the Japanese were in effect saying that the problem of commercial opportunity in China should not be treated in isolation from the rest of the world. It was a rather tame response and reflected a reluctance to make a firm commitment on China before the settlement of the war. As for the Axis alliance, Japan would act 'in accordance with its own decisions' – an indirect way of saying that the German pact would not be applicable to the United States unless the latter attacked Germany first.

These terms still indicated a determination to retain Japan's special position in China and the rest of Asia that it had sought to establish by force. As Prime Minister Tōjō explained at the crucial 5 November meeting of the Japanese leaders in the presence of the emperor, Japan could never go back to the 'constraints' of the nine-power treaty, which was what Hull's four principles signified. Since the nation had tried to free itself from these constraints by going to war in Manchuria and China, it made no sense to return to the situation existing before 1931. Because the United States appeared adamant on this point, there was little expectation in Tokyo that an agreement could be reached under Plan A. As Foreign Minister Tōgō stated frankly, there was too little time to negotiate a basic understanding on China. Since, however, every effort must be maintained to avoid war if at all possible, Japan was to present a second set of conditions (Plan B) to the United States as the absolute minimum acceptable terms. They would not try for a comprehensive agreement on China, and instead seek to prevent further deterioration of Japanese–American relations. Specifically, Japan would pledge not to advance militarily beyond French Indo-China; the two nations would co-operate in the Dutch East Indies so as to procure the resources they needed; the United States would restore its trade with Japan by lifting the freezing of Japanese assets and providing Japan with the oil it required; and the United States would not obstruct the attempts by Japan and China for peace. If an agreement could be reached on the basis of these terms, Japan would be willing to evacuate southern Indo-China and ultimately the entire peninsula.

These minimal terms were clearly understood to be the irreducible conditions. Barring their acceptance by the United States, Japan would go to war against the ABCD powers. Plan B was an attempt to detach America from China and the Dutch East Indies, in other words, to break up the ABCD alliance. Japan had tried to do so but had failed. Now, at the last moment, the Japanese leaders were counting on the possibility that their American counterparts would not want a Pacific war at that moment. By showing Japanese determination to go to war unless these minimum terms were accepted, Japan would put the American government on the spot and compel it to respond either affirmatively or negatively. If the latter, then it was believed the Japanese would have a justifiable cause for going to war against the ABCD alliance. If the former, it would serve to underscore Japanese–American understanding on South-East Asia. While the two nations' disagreement on China would remain, the United States would not be in as good a position as earlier to intervene in Chinese affairs. Thus at least the situation would revert to what had obtained on the eve of the freezing of the Japanese assets. But the most crucial outcome would be the weakening of the ABCD encirclement.

The Japanese recognized that despite such hopes, there really was little chance that the United States would give up its support of China or agree to the loosening of the ABCD *entente*. Thus virtually all who participated in the 5 November conference resigned themselves to the possibility of war against the ABCD powers. But they also realized that such a war would be an extemely difficult one to wage. Prior to meeting on 5 November, the top military leaders had conferred with the emperor on a number of occasions to apprise him of the crucial decisions that were being made. They all assumed that war would come in early December. Admiral Nagano expressed confidence that through a lightning attack on the enemy, Japan would be able to score initial victories and establish strategic bases in the south-western Pacific; however, he reiterated his earlier scepticism about Japan's chances in a prolonged war. Much would depend on the state of national mobilization as well as world conditions, he said. Japan's only hope, he went on, would lie in the possibility of British defeat through the severing of its oceanic routes by Japan and the landing of German troops on the home isles. Even so, Japan was disadvantaged in that it would never be possible to attack the United States at its source. General Sugiyama was more optimistic; he asserted that the initial southern strategy should enable the nation to establish a position of impregnability, from which to continue the war against American and British forces. At the same time, he cautioned that the United States would force the Soviet Union to offer its Asian territory for use as airfields and submarine bases, and the latter would find it impossible to resist the pressure. Thus, Sugiyama said, there was a possibility that the Soviet Union too might enter the war, especially if it became prolonged. Given such realistic estimates, why should Japan decide on war? Prime Minister Tōjō concluded that it was now the only alternative. If the nation should simply persevere, within two years America's position would become even more strengthened as it would have extended its air power to the Pacific, whereas Japan would have exhausted its oil stock. It would then be too late to undertake a southern strategy to obtain petroleum. In China, in the meantime, American-supported movements against the Japanese forces of occupation would intensify, and even the Soviet Union might be emboldened to help China. In other words, inaction would make matters worse in two years, whereas the military were saying that at least for that duration the war would go well for the nation. Japan would have a southern empire for two years, and although the China war might still not be settled within the time span, the situation could not be worse than the certain deterioration caused by passivity. It was some such thinking that persuaded Japan's top leaders to make the fatal decision for war, on 5 November 1941.

What the discussion revealed was lack of a long-range vision. Nobody knew how the war would go after the initial successes, still less how the ABCD nations would act in two years' time. But all agreed that the continuation of the existing situation was intolerable. It would, as Tōjō declared, relegate Japan to the status of a third-rate nation, since the nation would become more and more subject to American power and will. It would be better to resist this power as much as possible and see how things developed. It was believed that Japan would suffer in a United States-dominated world order, whereas if it challenged that order, the way might be opened for an alternative arrangement of international affairs.

The lack of a long-range vision was manifested in the fact that even as late as November, the Japanese leadership had not defined the aims and goals of the impending war. Tōjō assured those attending the crucial meetings that he would try to look for some justification for war; but for the time being the best he could come up with was the idea that the nation was going to war for its survival. That reflected the sense of desperation; to submit to American pressure appeared to threaten the country's very existence, for it would mean incorporation into an American-defined and dominated international system.[7] That, it would appear in retrospect, was the crux of the whole matter. Japan, it was believed, was surrounded by an ABCD coalition which might be joined by the Soviet Union as well. The only alternatives available would be submission to the coalition or resistance to it. Both would entail costs and risks, but resistance would at least safeguard the nation's honour, whereas submission would mean nullifying the achievements of the past ten years, to go back to the 1920s which had been defined by an American-led world order. An American-imposed peace. in other words, was considered less desirable and honourable than a Japanese-initiated war.

ABCD PREPAREDNESS

That was not too far from American thinking. In Washington, too, there was realization that the United States and Japan were facing a fatal choice. Top officials in Washington were able to discern trends in Japanese policy through talks with Ambassador Nomura and through 'Magic' intercepts, and there was no misunderstanding of Japan's position, or of the Japanese leaders' sense of desperation. The only variable, then, was the degree to which the United States would be willing to postpone a showdown with Japan through some compromise. If no compromise could be arrived at, American leaders knew war would be a distinct possibility.

At this late hour, however, it was not possible to agree on whether such compromise should be attempted, or, if that were to be the case, what the compromise should consist of. President Roosevelt toyed with the idea of a six-month freeze on the movement of armaments on either side, while State Department officials, led by Joseph Ballantine, a Japan specialist, suggested an armistice in China which would lead to peace talks between those two countries, during which the United States would not assist China and Japan would not move in Indo-China. These suggestions might have provided a plausible starting-point for negotiations with Japan; the latter's Plan A might then have been considered in earnest, for both it and some of the tentative American proposals focused on China. For that very reason, however, nothing came of any of these ideas, since they all implied a change in American policy towards China. An understanding with Japan for freezing the status quo, or American non-intervention on behalf of China as the latter discussed a possible peace with Japan, would clearly weaken the ABCD alliance. That possibility had earlier prevented the United States from being more receptive to Konoe's overtures for an understanding, and now more than ever it would be undesirable to break up the *entente*. Any weakening of American support for China would be taken by Britain and the Dutch as a sign of a corresponding change in American policy, a change that would damage an alliance which had been very effective in checking Japan.

Some observers then, and historians since, have wondered whether such a rigid stand was prudent; they have argued that America's reluctance to alter its policy in China doomed the peace with Japan, and that it made little sense to bring about a war with Japan over China, since America's essential interests lay in the Pacific, not on the Asian continent. In the aftermath of the war, when the erstwhile allies became fierce antagonists, many asserted that the policy of giving aid to China had been a mistake, for it only brought about war with Japan, resulting in the latter's withdrawal from the continent, which in turn meant an expansion of Soviet (and subsequently Chinese Communist) power. All such ideas miss the essential point, that China was no longer an isolated object of policy but an integral part of America's Asian-Pacific strategy. To forsake China at that late hour was tantamount to questioning the basis of the ABCD alliance, something that could not be undertaken lightly, for no alternative had been envisaged as a way of protecting American interests and Asian security. To come to some compromise settlement with Japan at the expense of the ABCD alliance was unthinkable, for it could not be imagined what would follow such a development. Japan, after all, was still tied to Germany and Italy, and unless the Axis alliance too could be broken up, and Japan lured away from the Fascist states, it would be unrealistic to entertain any thought of re-establishing peace, even a temporary one, in the Asian-Pacific region on the basis of Japanese–American agreement. In other words, the United States would have to be prepared to redefine its total strategy, at least for the region, and substitute a new framework for the ABCD alliance if any satisfactory agreement were to be reached with Japan to avoid war. In short, there could be no such thing as a temporary expedient to avoid war; only a major transformation of American policy, which also implied a parallel move in Japan, would do.

The time was not propitious for undertaking such a task. For one thing, the partners in the ABCD *entente* would not support the United States. The Chinese leadership in Chungking remained nervous about any chance of a Japanese–American *rapprochement* and kept in close touch with British diplomats so that the latter would help prevent a rupture in the ranks of the *entente* partners. In the autumn of 1941, in fact, there developed something akin to a little *entente* between China and Britain, for both wanted the United States to remain firm towards Japan. The 'display of firmness', declared Foreign Secretary Anthony Eden, 'is more likely to deter Japan from war than to provoke her to it', and clearly one way of demonstrating firmness was to reinforce the strategic and moral ties with China. Prime Minister Winston Churchill was considering the dispatch of volunteer Commonwealth and British planes and pilots to China to shore up the latter's air power.[8]

Air power was fast becoming a symbol of the ABCD determination to contain Japan. The United States was sending a fleet of B-17 bombers to the Philippines. Together with the Flying Tigers, now in place in China, and whatever Britain could afford to put into the area, those bombers would contribute to the deterrence of Japan. If, despite the deterrence, war should come, they would be effective in combating Japanese forces. It is true that even as late as November 1941 the ABCD partners had not developed a well-defined joint strategy in the event of war. But this was primarily because American leadership in the war was taken for granted. Britain and the Dutch East Indies would follow the American lead, and as for China, it would also view its own strategy as part of the combined effort. (Chiang Kai-shek was to declare soon after Pearl Harbor, 'a general strategy embracing the fullest co-ordination of manpower and material resources is the necessary prelude to victory'.[9] Such an idea had been taken as axiomatic by Chinese leaders for some time. Although no such comprehensive strategy was ever worked out by the ABCD powers, it does not negate the fact that psychologically, at least, they acted as if one existed.)

The Soviet Union, for its part, needed no reminder that a Japanese attack on its territory would be a terrible blow. It was best to keep Japan focused on China and South-East Asia. From the Soviet viewpoint, a crisis in Japanese relations with the ABCD nations was welcome, as it would prevent the Japanese from contemplating an assault on Siberia. Although there was as yet no discussion with the United States for the use of Russian territory as bases for American ships and aircraft, and although the Soviet Union scrupulously adhered to the neutrality treaty with Japan, Comintern agents – most notably Richard Sorge in Tokyo – were redoubling their efforts to discourage any diplomatic settlement of the Japanese war in China or of Japanese–American differences. Ironically, just as such efforts were bearing fruit, Sorge and his Japanese contacts were coming under increased police surveillance, leading to their arrest shortly after Pearl Harbor.

Given such developments, the relationship between Japan and the United States was reaching an impasse. Only a comprehensive understanding would prevent their total rupture, but no comprehensive understanding could be worked out in the short span of time that Tokyo and Washington had available to make the effort. This became painfully evident in the second half of November, when negotiators in Washington made one last attempt to see if Japan's Plan B could be salvaged. That plan, in contrast to Plan A, proposed to set aside the China issue and aimed at restoring the status quo of June 1941, but for that very reason it had little chance of success. American officials, nevertheless, were willing to consider a temporary arrangement so as to postpone a showdown. Aware, through 'Magic' intercepts, that the Japanese would strike unless an agreement had been reached by 1 December, and desirous of putting off a war for at least several months, they drafted a counter-proposal, the so-called *modus vivendi*. A product of high-level deliberations in Washington, the proposal would call for Japanese withdrawal of troops from southern Indo-China, keeping a limited number (25,000) in northern Indo-China, in return for resumption of American shipments of oil to Japan. That was to be a three-month experiment, far from the comprehensive settlement that was needed. Even so, had the British, Chinese, and Dutch governments endorsed the plan, it would have been presented to the Japanese negotiators in Washington, now headed by Kurusu Saburō, special envoy hastily dispatched from Tokyo. Quite predictably, however, the Chinese took strong exception, and from London Churchill cabled his support of the Chinese stance. After all, the maintenance of the ABCD *entente* was at stake, and the United States could not unilaterally deal with Japan. The decision not to submit the *modus vivendi* proposal, then, was added evidence that the ABCD *entente* could not be broken up to placate Japan, even for three months.

If the ABCD *entente* could not be broken up, there was little point in negotiations between Japan and the United States. Kurusu and Nomura recognized this, and so could not have been surprised that their talks with Hull got nowhere. In the short span of time that they had available – from the middle to the end of November – it was impossible either for Japan or the United States to reorient its position. Hull's 26 November note, in which he reiterated the basic principles on which America had insisted, confirmed this state of affairs. Japanese officials in Washington and Tokyo took the Hull note as an indication of the wide cleavage between the two countries, and they were of course right. However, they were off the mark when they viewed the note as an ultimatum. It merely restated the position that the United States would stand with China, Britain, and the Dutch, and would invite Japan to join them in re-establishing order in the Asian-Pacific region. If Japan refused to do so, then no compromise could be achieved.

From that point onward, what was left to the United States was not to negotiate further with Japan but to strengthen the ABCD partnership. On 1 December, President Roosevelt assured Lord Halifax, the British ambassador, that in the event of a Japanese attack on British or Dutch possessions in Asia, 'we should obviously all be together'. In other words, the United States would come to their assistance, so that there would be war between Japan and the ABCD powers together. Japan would get what it had been planning for. In the subsequent days, Roosevelt reiterated the commitment, explicitly stating that America's support meant 'armed support', and that the ABD powers should act together in issuing parallel warnings to Japan not to attack Thailand, Malaya, or the Indies. China, in the meantime, would continue to receive full American support. The ABCD alliance had now come into being in all but name.[10]

PEARL HARBOR

The Hull note was received in Tokyo on 27 November. A meeting of the liaison conference was held immediately the same afternoon, and all agreed that the note was virtually an ultimatum, containing terms which Japan could never accept. The negotiations in Washington, therefore, must be judged to have failed. In accordance with the decisions of 5 November, the nation must undertake preparations for war in the immediate future. The cabinet agreed with these views when it met on the following day. Then on 29 November, the key cabinet ministers and *jūshin* (former prime ministers) repaired to the Imperial Palace to explain the situation to the emperor. Here, too, all agreed that war with the ABD powers had become unavoidable. The emperor appears to have retained some doubt about that judgement and about the prudence of going to war against the United States and its partners. He summoned the naval leaders on 30 November to ascertain whether the navy was really set on war, and if it intended to fight a long war. Admiral Nagano told the emperor that Japan's attacking task force was already at 1,800 nautical miles west of Pearl Harbor, and Navy Minister Shimada Shigetarō expressed his faith that all was ready; even if Germany should pull out of the war, he told the emperor confidently, Japan would be able to continue the war, which must be won no matter what the cost. The emperor then finally endorsed the war decision, which was formalized at a meeting of the top leaders on 1 December.[11]

Crucial decisions concerning Japan's strategy against the ABD powers had been made earlier in November. On 5 November, Nagano had issued a command to Admiral Yamamoto Isoroku, ordering him to prepare the combined fleet for war against the ABD powers by early December. The initial strategy was to concentrate on the destruction of the United States fleet so as to weaken the American will to fight and its capacity to obstruct Japan's southern strategy. Much, thus, depended on the effectiveness of the initial blow. Japan's only hope lay in its devastating impact on America and, by implication, on Britain. Admiral Yamamoto and his staff officers had been working on this strategy for several months, and now they were told to go ahead to implement it. Beginning with 11 November, ships and aircraft comprising Japan's combined fleet were placed at pre-arranged locations, ready to start their advances. Ten days later, the fleet was ordered to prepare for war action, and on the 26th, the attacking task force left for its long journey half-way across the Pacific. On 1 December, the emperor's order for war was received. All was in readiness, but the naval supreme command chose Sunday 7 December as the day of the Pearl Harbor attack, since the American fleet was more likely to be there on a Sunday.

The eleven days between 26 November and 7 December were essentially a prelude to the war. The Japanese were convinced that only a surprise attack would bring an initial success, and thus they did not want to give any inkling about terminating the Washington negotiations until the very last moment. The idea was to hand a declaration of war to the American government at 3 a.m. on 8 December, Tokyo time, or thirty minutes before the Pearl Harbor attack was to take place. That would be 1 p.m. on 7 December in Washington. A long note to accompany the declaration of war was cabled to the Japanese embassy in Washington in fourteen instalments. It took twenty-one hours to complete the cable transmission, the last instalment being wired at 3.30 p.m. on 7 December (1.30 a.m. in Washington). As deciphering and retyping of the message took time, it was not till 2.20 p.m. that the notification of war was handed to Secretary of State Hull, some fifty minutes after the attack had taken place.

The American government, however, had already decoded the Japanese telegram and expected war at any moment. Actually, since 'Magic' intercepts had deciphered the crucial messages between Tokyo and Washington, American officials knew that after 26 November there was little sense in continuing negotiations. Warnings were issued to the American commanders in Hawaii, the Philippines, and elsewhere that a break in relations with Japan was imminent, and that war must be expected. President Roosevelt, however, wanted to try one last time to postpone a showdown by sending a personal message to the emperor. The message, sent on 6 December, asked for a withdrawal of Japanese troops from Indo-China so as to maintain peace in the region. But the president knew this was a futile gesture, as he received the intercepted messages and realized the Japanese were on the point of starting the war. Neither Roosevelt nor any of his aides, however, anticipated the type of massive aerial attack on the fleet that the Japanese carried out. The sense of surprise, disbelief, and disgust at the 'sneak attack' was genuine.

There have been many theories about America's seeming un-preparedness for the Pearl Harbor attack. It does seem strange that despite all the intercepted intelligence about Japanese policy, American leaders should not have been able to foresee what was coming. The key issue is precisely what information they had on the eve of Pearl Harbor. President Roosevelt and his top aides expected a Japanese attack almost any moment, while in Hawaii naval officers had discussed the possibility of Japan's aerial bombardment of Oahu. Nevertheless, none of them had expected an attack on the fleet at Pearl Harbor taking place on 7 December.[12] In part this was because officials in Washington did not know the ships were still at Pearl Harbor rather than at sea, while those in Oahu did not receive a 'command message' from Washington warning them of an impending attack. With more and more officials becoming involved in planning for war with Japan, it was not easy to delineate a clear chain through which information would pass.

Whether or not this was a case of wilful neglect has been debated for years. It could be argued that if Washington had forwarded to Honolulu all the information it had collected on Japanese ship movements and intelligence activities, the naval commanders and army leaders in Hawaii could have better prepared for the defence of the fleet and the islands. Such suspicion could be expanded into a conspiracy theory to the effect that the officials in Hawaii were intentionally kept ignorant of some crucial information so as to let the Japanese fire the first shot, which then would result in a formal declaration of war and mobilize the American nation for a global conflict. A warning to Hawaii might have saved the fleet and many lives in Oahu, but it still would not have prevented a Japanese attack. Moreover, on the dawn of 7 December in Hawaii, an American destroyer spotted and sank a Japanese submarine, a few hours before the actual Japanese attack. The incident indicated that the authorities in Hawaii had some information which could have led them to draw important inferences. It would therefore be wrong to attribute all the blame to Washington. In any event, it remains true that while the sense of shock was genuine, both in Hawaii and Washington, at the way the initial blow was struck, there was little surprise that war had come. It had been expected at least for several months, if not several years, by American officials as well as by Japanese. The sense of confrontation and crisis across the Pacific had grown steadily since the late 1930s so that by late 1941 war had come to appear as the only possibility, unless one side – Japan – made drastic concessions.

Since war was seen as inevitable, some were already thinking of its consequences, of the future of Japanese–American relations after the war. Asakawa Kan'ichi, who taught history at Yale University, was one of them. He believed Japan would lose the war and therefore sought to prepare both nations for a more co-operative relationship afterwards. As he tried to express himself in somewhat exaggerated prose in a draft letter which he hoped President Roosevelt would send to the emperor, there was hope that 'Japan would again of her free will recoil to her noble self, and again spring forward with quick and sure leaps into the broad common life ... of the liberal world whose horizon is bound to widen immensely as soon as the present war is cleared'. The United States and other countries, on their part, would 'co-operate with ... Japan in her work of rehabilitation. And, in years to come, one and all would welcome and rejoice in her growing prosperity and her increasing contributions to the progress of the common civilization of mankind, achievements of which she by nature and talent is eminently capable'. Such hopes were shared by a small number of Americans and would eventually provide a basis for postwar American policy towards Japan. In the context of such thinking, war in the Pacific was a product of Japan's going astray from the course that the nation had followed, the course of co-operation with the United States and other civilized nations. War would be an unfortunate interlude but should not be permitted to obscure the essential continuity and mutuality in Japanese–American relations.[13]

That was quite true, as far as the basic thrust of those relations was concerned. Postwar history was to show that the two nations shared much in common and could co-operate for their mutual benefit. That framework of mutuality and co-operation had been the pattern through most of modern history, and reached a peak during the 1920s. Somehow, however, the framework – the Washington Conference system – had been eroded and a sense of rivalry and conflict had replaced that of friendly coexistence. In the long history of Japanese-American relations, however, the crisis and war of the late 1930s and the 1940s were but a brief interlude.

The story, however, must be put in the larger context of international relations, for Japanese-American relations were never purely bilateral ones. In the 1920s, they were the main proponents, together with Britain, of the Washington system, and during the first half of the 1930s there was little actual crisis across the Pacific as Japan managed to act forcefully in China without incurring the combined opposition of other nations. From the mid-1930s, however, there grew progressively a realignment of powers so that China no longer had to fight alone against Japanese aggression. One after another outside powers' help was obtained, and by the end of the decade there had emerged a loose coalition of the United States, Britain, the Netherlands, France, and the Soviet Union, all desirous of checking Japanese advance. In a sense this was a modified Washington system, shorn of Japan but with the addition of Russia. To counter the trend, Japan tried to detach the Soviet Union from the *entente* and enter into a solid alliance with Germany and Italy. The hope was to form an alternative alignment, consisting of Japan, Germany, Italy, and the Soviet Union to oppose the first. The attempt failed, and the result was that Japan found itself more than ever isolated, 'encircled' as it was said. In the end it was an encircled Japan pitting itself against a fortified coalition. That enhanced the feeling of insecurity and crisis on the part of the Japanese. The only way out of isolation would have been to go back to the Washington Conference system, but this appeared difficult now that China and the Soviet Union were more closely involved in that system. Seeing no way out of the dilemma except through a gamble for an alternative system of Asian-Pacific affairs, Japan struck. It was, as the government declared, a struggle for a new order and for national survival. The two aims were closely linked. But the war was to demonstrate that survival within the old framework would have been just as plausible.

REFERENCES AND NOTES

1.   'Tōjō naikaku kumitsu kiroku' (Secret records of the Tōjō cabinet), NHK (Japanese Broadcasting Corporation) (unpublished 1985), 1: 39, 48–9.
2.   Defence Agency, War History Division (ed.), *Daihonei rikugunbu* (The army supreme command; Tokyo 1968), 2: 526–7.
3.   Ibid., 2: 532.

4. Ibid., 2: 537.
5. Ibid., 2: 555–6.
6. Ibid., 2: 560–2.
7. Ibid., 2: 587.
8. Christopher Thorne, *Allies of a Kind: The United States, Britain and the War against Japan, 1941–1945* (London and New York 1978), pp. 69–70.
9. F14128/13469/10, Foreign Office Archives.
10. Defence Agency, War History Division (ed.), *Daihonei kaigunbu* (The naval supreme command; Tokyo 1975), 2: 61.
11. Ibid., 2: 20.
12. Gordon W. Prange, *At Dawn We Slept: The Untold Story of Pearl Harbor* (New York 1981), pp. 186, 486.
13. Abe Yoshio, *Saigo no 'Nihonjin': Asakawa Kan'ichi no shōgai* (The last 'Japanese': the life of Asakawa Kan'ichi; Tokyo 1983), pp. 337–8. One American counterpart to Asakawa was Sidney Gulick, a former missionary in Japan. Their ideas were virtually identical. See Sandra Taylor, *Advocate of Understanding* (Kent, Ohio 1985).

Bibliographical Essay

The literature on the origins of the Second World War in Asia and the Pacific is enormous. In this brief essay I shall cite only those works, mostly of recent publication, that have been particularly useful in writing this book. For more detailed discussions of the literature, the reader may wish to refer to my other essays: 'Contemporary history as history', in *Pacific Historical Review* (May 1984); 'The Asian factor', in Gordon Martel (ed.) *The Origins of the Second World War Reconsidered* (London 1986); and 'The Americanization of East Asia', in Warren Cohen (ed.) *New Frontiers in American–East Asian Relations* (New York 1983). Useful bibliographical guides can also be found in Ernest R. May and James C. Thomson (eds) *American–East Asian Relations: A Survey* (Cambridge, Mass. 1972), in the just cited Cohen volume, and in Sadao Asada (ed.) *Japanese Research in International History* (New York 1987).

Perhaps the most explored aspect of the road to war is the American–Japanese dimension. Ever since the publication of three authoritative accounts soon after the war – Herbert Feis, *The Road to Pearl Harbor* (Princeton 1950); William L. Langer and S. Everette Gleason, *The Challenge to Isolation* (New York 1952); and the same authors' *The Undeclared War* (New York 1953) – historians have been filling gaps and discovering missing links. On the Japanese side, the best studies are contained in the eight-volume *Taiheiyō sensō e no michi* (The road to the Pacific War; Tokyo 1962–63), which has been partially translated and published in English: James W. Morley (ed.) *The Fateful Choice* (New York 1980), *Deterrent Diplomacy* (New York 1976), *The China Quagmire* (New York 1983), and *Japan Erupts* (New York 1984). The translation project is reflective of the close scholarly collaboration between Japanese and American historians that has characterized the study of the origins of the Pacific war. A particularly notable example of this collaboration has been the binational work: Hosoya Chihiro *et al.* (eds) *Nichi-Bei kankeishi* (History of Japanese–American relations; 3 vols, Tokyo 1971), published in English as Dorothy Borg and Shumpei Okamoto (eds) *Pearl Harbor as History* (New York 1973).

Indispensable for the study of Japanese diplomacy are numerous official and semi-official biographies of decision-makers. Particularly pertinent for this book have been Yabe Teiji, *Konoe Fumimaro* (Tokyo 1952); *Matsuoka Yōsuke* (Tokyo 1974); Kurihara Ken (ed.) *Satō Naotake no menboku* (The real worth of Satō Naotake; Tokyo 1981); and Hagihara Nobutoshi, *Tōgō Shigenori* (Biography of Tōgō Shigenori; Tokyo 1985). Among biographies of non-officials who played indirect roles in American–Japanese relations, especially notable are Matsumoto Shigeharu, *Shanghai jidai* (Shanghai years; 3 vols, Tokyo 1975); and Abe Yoshio, *Saigo no 'Nihonjin': Asakawa Kanichi no shōgai* (The last 'Japanese': the life of Asakawa Kan'ichi; Tokyo 1983). In addition, there are extremely valuable 'official' war histories compiled by the war history section of the Self-Defence Agency, of which the most relevant for the 1931–41 period are the several volumes under the titles of *Daihonei rikugunbu* (The army in the supreme headquarters) and *Daihonei kaigunbu* (The navy in the supreme headquarters). Thousands of primary documents have been published in *Nihon gaikō bonsho* (Japanese diplomatic documents); *Nihon gaikō nenpyō narabi shuyō bunsho* (Chronology of Japanese diplomacy, with key documents); and *Gendaishi shiryō* (Documents on contemporary history). Among private letters, diaries, and memoranda that have been published, particularly useful for the writing of this volume have been *Ugaki Kazushige nikki* (Ugaki Kazushige diary; 2 vols, Tokyo 1970); Ishikawa Junkichi (ed.) *Kokka sōdōin-shi* (History of national mobilization; Tokyo 1975 and ongoing); and Tanemura Sakō, *Daihonei kimitsu nisshi* (A secret diary of the supreme headquarters; Tokyo 1952).

Among English-language studies of American–Japanese relations prior to the outbreak of hostilities, the most important are: Justus Doenecke, *When the Wicked Rise* (Lewisburg 1984); Gary Ostrower, *Collective Insecurity* (Lewisburg 1979); Dorothy Borg, *The United States and the Far Eastern Crisis* (Cambridge, Mass. 1964); Stephen Pelz, *The Race to Pearl Harbor* (Cambridge, Mass. 1974); Waldo Heinrichs, *American Ambassador* (Boston 1966); Jonathan Utley, *Going to War with Japan, 1937–1941* (Knoxville 1984); Irvine H. Anderson, *The Standard-Vacuum Oil Company and United States East Asian Policy 1933–41* (Princeton 1975); and John Stephan, *Hawaii under the Rising Sun* (Honolulu 1984). Two recent books that focus on the Pacific war have chapters dealing with its origins: Christopher Thorne, *Allies of a Kind* (London and New York 1978); and Akira Iriye, *Power and Culture* (Cambridge, Mass. 1981). On the crucial weeks leading up to the Pearl Harbor attack, see Robert J. C. Butow, *John Doe Associates* (Stanford 1974); Gordon Prange, *At Dawn We Slept* (New York 1981); and the same author's *Pearl Harbor: The Verdict of History* (New York 1985). Significant insights are contained in Sandra Taylor, *Advocate of Understanding* (Kent, Ohio 1985), a study of one American who struggled to the end to prevent a rupture across the Pacific.

On United States policy towards China, see Warren Cohen, *The Chinese Connection* (New York 1973); Michael Schaller, *The U.S.*

Crusade in China (New York 1979); and Tang Tsou, *America's Failure in China, 1941–50* (Chicago 1963). Monographs that deal comprehensively with American foreign policy and strategy in the late 1930s and the early 1940s offer valuable data on American–Asian relations. See, in particular, Robert Dallek, *Franklin D. Roosevelt and American Foreign Policy, 1932–1945* (New York 1979); James R. Leutze, *Bargaining for Supremacy* (Chapel Hill 1977); and David Reynolds, *The Creation of an Anglo-American Alliance, 1937–41* (Chapel Hill 1981). See also Arnold A. Offner, *American Appeasement* (Cambridge, Mass. 1969); and Wayne S. Cole, *Roosevelt and the Isolationists, 1932–45* (Lincoln, Neb. 1983).

There are fewer good studies of Chinese–Japanese relations in the 1930s. Apart from the essays in *Taiheiyō sensō e no michi*, the following stand out: Usui Katsumi, *Manshū jihen* (The Manchurian incident; Tokyo 1974); Mark Peattie, *Ishiwara Kanji* (Princeton 1975); Peattie and Ramon Myers (eds) *The Japanese Colonial Empire* (Princeton 1984); and John Hunter Boyle, *China and Japan at War, 1937–1945* (Stanford 1972). I have tried a survey of Chinese foreign affairs in 'Japanese aggression and China's international position', in a forthcoming volume of the *Cambridge History of Modern China*. In preparing for this book, I have found invaluable the recently published and ongoing documentary volumes: *Chung-hua Min-kuo chung-yao shih-liao ch'u-pien* (Important documents of the Republic of China; Taipei 1982–).

A number of authors have examined British–Japanese relations prior to the war. Christopher Thorne, *The Limits of Foreign Policy* (London 1972), is still the best study of the international context of the Manchurian crisis; British economic diplomacy is chronicled in Ann Trotter, *Britain and East Asia* (Cambridge 1975), and Stephen L. Endicott, *Diplomacy and Enterprise* (Vancouver 1975); and British policy towards Japan during and after the outbreak of the Sino-Japanese war is well presented in Bradford Lee, *Britain and the Sino-Japanese War* (Stanford 1973), and Peter Lowe, *Great Britain and the Origins of the Pacific War* (Oxford 1977). See also Roger Louis, *British Strategy in the Far East* (Oxford 1971), and Aron Shai, *Origins of the War in the East* (London 1976). Interesting essays by British and Japanese historians are contained in Ian Nish (ed.) *Anglo-Japanese Alienation* (Cambridge 1982).

On Germany, the best monograph is John P. Fox, *Germany and the Far Eastern Crisis, 1931–1938* (Oxford 1982). Other excellent studies include Gerhard L. Weinberg, *The Foreign Policy of Hitler's Germany* (2 vols, Chicago 1970, 1980); William Kirby, *Germany and Republican China* (Stanford 1984); and Saul Friedlander, *Prelude to Downfall* (New York 1967). Very little exists on Soviet policy in Asia in the 1930s. I have relied heavily on an official Japanese documentary history: *Nis-So kōshō-shi* (History of Japanese–Soviet negotiation; Tokyo 1942). Also useful has been Hayashi Saburō, *Kantōgun to Kyokutō Sorengun* (The Kwantung Army and the Soviet Far Eastern Army; Tokyo 1974). On

Soviet–Chinese relations, see Jonathan Haslam, 'Soviet aid to China and Japan's place in Moscow's foreign policy, 1937–1939, in Ian Nish (ed.) *Some Aspects of Soviet–Japanese Relations in the 1930s* (London 1982).

The tragic road to the war needs to be put in a global and comparative perspective. What were the forces, inside each country and in the world at large, that made for so much violence, conflict, and war in the 1930s? Were the Japanese better 'prepared' militarily, economically, and culturally to undertake an aggressive and imperialistic war than other countries? What enabled others to come together in the end to oppose and punish Japan? What distinguished the wars of the decade from earlier ones? Was peace ever a possibility; if so, what kind of peace would it have been? In this book I have looked at these questions primarily in a 'systemic' framework, to trace changing definitions and patterns of international affairs in the Asian-Pacific region. That is only one approach, however, and I have tried to suggest other themes in an essay, 'War as peace, peace as war', in Nobutoshi Hagihara *et al.* (eds) *Experiencing the Twentieth Century* (Tokyo 1985). Penetrating insights in a comparative perspective are offered by two outstanding books: William McNeill, *The Pursuit of Power* (Chicago 1981), and Alan Milward, *War, Economy, and Society* (Berkeley 1979). The former puts the wars of the 1930s in the context of a modern global population crisis, and the latter compares the economic and political costs of war and war preparedness among the major powers. Such broader approaches are desperately needed today when historians tend either to focus on excessively narrow topics or to depart from narrative and embrace metahistory. If international history means anything, it denotes a commitment both to empirical data based on multiarchival research and to cross-national, cross-cultural perspectives. That, in the end, would seem to be the only sensible way to understand the origins of modern wars.

Maps

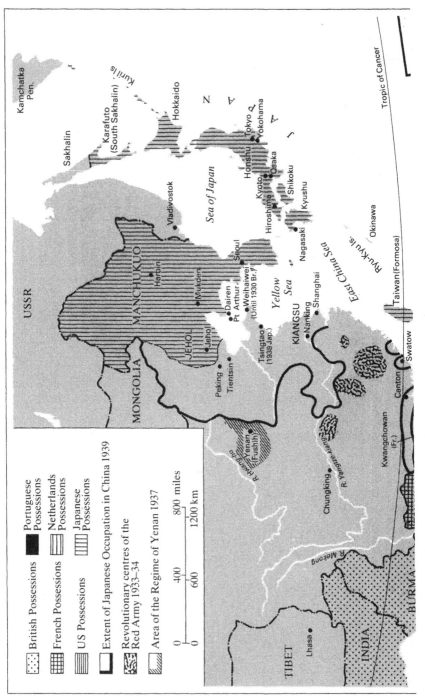

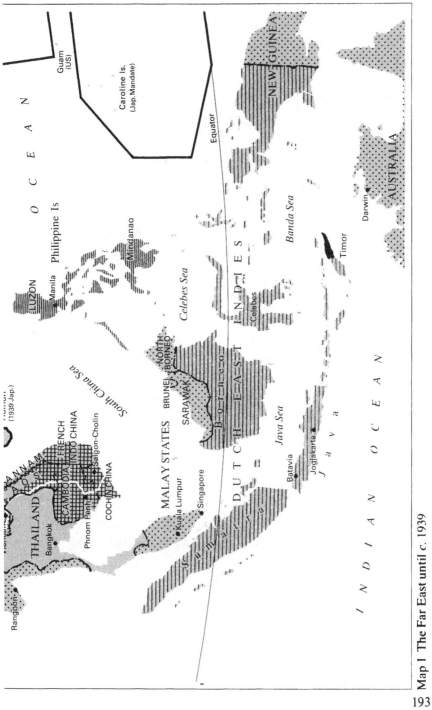

Map 1 The Far East until c. 1939

Map 2 The Pacific *c.* 1939

ALASKA

CANADA

TTU

KISKA Aleutians Dutch Harbor

USA

San Francisco ●

Midway *Hawaii*

Tropic of Cancer

Honolulu

Pearl Harbour HAWAII

larshalls P A C I F I C O C E A N

Gilberts Equator

'*ESIA*

Marquesas

Samoa

ebrides

Fiji Tonga TAHITI Tuamotu Archipelago

Tropic of Capricorn

0		2000		4000 miles

NEW ZEALAND

0	2000	4000 km

INDEX

Made in United States
North Haven, CT
11 September 2023

41427463R00117